Rethinking Political Violence

Series Editor
Roger Mac Ginty⊙, School of Government and International Affairs,
Durham University, Durham, UK

This series provides a new space in which to interrogate and challenge much of the conventional wisdom of political violence. International and multidisciplinary in scope, this series explores the causes, types and effects of contemporary violence connecting key debates on terrorism, insurgency, civil war and peace-making. The timely Rethinking Political Violence offers a sustained and refreshing analysis reappraising some of the fundamental questions facing societies in conflict today and understanding attempts to ameliorate the effects of political violence.

This series is indexed by Scopus.

Brett J. Kyle · Tricia D. Olsen ·
Andrew G. Reiter

State Violence
and Democracy
in Latin America

Inequality, the Rule of Law, and Public Order
Violence

palgrave
macmillan

Brett J. Kyle ⓘ
Department of Political Science
University of Nebraska at Omaha
Omaha, NE, USA

Andrew G. Reiter ⓘ
Department of Politics
Mount Holyoke College
South Hadley, MA, USA

Tricia D. Olsen ⓘ
Humphrey School of Public Affairs
and the Department of Political
Science
University of Minnesota
Minneapolis, MN, USA

ISSN 2752-8588   ISSN 2752-8596   (electronic)
Rethinking Political Violence
ISBN 978-3-032-06411-0   ISBN 978-3-032-06412-7   (eBook)
https://doi.org/10.1007/978-3-032-06412-7

Cover credit: tirc83

This Palgrave Macmillan imprint is published by the registered company Springer Nature
Switzerland AG
The registered company address is: Gewerbestrasse 11, 6330 Cham, Switzerland

If disposing of this product, please recycle the paper.

Acknowledgments

We would like to thank our home institutions—the University of Nebraska at Omaha, the University of Minnesota, and Mount Holyoke College—for the sabbaticals and research funds made available to us to complete the project. We are also indebted to a team of talented research assistants, including Giulia Bova, Ariah Holliman, Mujeeb Jan Talpur, Noori Fatema Mim, Seyma Tufan, and Kianna Vrtiska. Special thanks go to Rebecca Sandoval for taking the lead on the data collection for the new State Security Forces in Latin America dataset and to Beate Kuhns for her work on the tables for Chapters 2 and 3.

CONTENTS

About the Authors

Brett J. Kyle is Associate Professor of Political Science at the University of Nebraska at Omaha and a faculty member in the Office of Latino/Latin American Studies and the Goldstein Center for Human Rights. He is the author of *Recycling Dictators in Latin American Elections: Legacies of Military Rule* (Lynne Rienner, 2016) and co-author (w. Andrew G. Reiter) of *Military Courts, Civil-Military Relations, and the Legal Battle for Democracy: The Politics of Military Justice* (Routledge, 2021).

Tricia D. Olsen is Professor and Harold E. Stassen Chair of World Peace at the University of Minnesota's Humphrey School of Public Affairs and Department of Political Science. Dr. Olsen is the author of *Seeking Justice: Access to Remedy for Corporate Human Rights Abuse* (Cambridge University Press, 2023) and co-author (w. Leigh A. Payne and Andrew G. Reiter) of *Transitional Justice in Balance: Comparing Processes. Weighing Efficacy* (United States Institute of Peace, 2010). Additional published work can be found in *World Development, Organization Studies, Journal of Business Ethics,* and *Business Ethics Quarterly,* among others.

Andrew G. Reiter is Professor of Politics and International Relations at Mount Holyoke College. He is the author of *Fighting Over Peace: Spoilers, Peace Agreements, and the Strategic Use of Violence* (Palgrave, 2016), co-author (w. Brett J. Kyle) of *Military Courts, Civil-Military*

Relations, and the Legal Battle for Democracy: The Politics of Military Justice (Routledge, 2021), and co-author (w. Tricia D. Olsen and Leigh A. Payne) of *Transitional Justice in Balance: Comparing Processes. Weighing Efficacy* (United States Institute of Peace, 2010).

LIST OF TABLES

CHAPTER 1

Public Order Violence in Latin America: Understanding Contemporary Trends

INTRODUCTION

On February 27, 2024, Brazilian State Military Police carried out raids against organized crime groups in the favelas of Alemão, Maré, Penha, and Cidade de Deus in Rio de Janeiro. Nine people were killed, and many others were wounded. In the state of São Paulo, similar police operations resulted in the deaths of 38 people in the first two months of 2024. Governments throughout Latin America justify the use of extreme violence in such "crackdowns" on the basis of fighting crime. Indeed, the Rio State Secretary of Security, Victor Santos, considered the February 27 operation a success because forces killed criminal suspects and brought "peace of mind" to the residents of the favelas (Camargo 2024; Latin American Weekly Report 2024).

State violence across the region is frequently tied to fighting criminal gangs and drug trafficking organizations. In early 2024, for example, Ecuador saw a proliferation of violence from such organizations as they competed for control over shipping routes and simultaneously fought back against the government's arrest of judges, police officers, and prison officials believed to be in league with them (Correal 2024). Prominent drug trafficking organizations were responsible for prison uprisings, assassinations of public officials, a brazen on-air invasion of a television studio, and numerous attacks on the police and ordinary citizens. The newly elected president, Daniel Noboa, designated 22 criminal groups "terrorist organizations" and declared Ecuador to be in a state of "armed internal conflict" (LatinNews Daily 2024). The subsequent suspension of the regular constitutional order and militarization of the state response led to torture, beatings, and at least one extrajudicial execution (Human Rights Watch 2024).

In addition to the abuses associated with day-to-day policing, militarized border enforcement has led to extreme violence and human rights abuses. For example, in February 2023, Mexican soldiers on patrol in Nuevo Laredo, on the border with the United States, fired 117 rounds at a group of men in a pickup truck returning from a celebration, killing five of them and wounding one more. The army unit tried to justify its actions by accusing the victims of having an unmarked vehicle and firing on the patrol, but it was the soldiers who removed the truck's license plates after the shooting, and an investigation by Mexico's National Human Rights Commission showed there were no firearms found in the vehicle and no evidence the soldiers had come under fire (Abi-Habib and Palafox 2023; Associated Press 2023).[1]

Economic interests also motivate state violence in the region. In the name of economic growth, state forces violently repress public protest, forcibly displace people from their land, and target union leaders. While large mining projects, such as Conga in Cajamarca or Tía Maria in Arequipa, have drawn widespread attention for Peru's violent response to protestors, data from the Peruvian Ombudsman's Office illustrate that social conflict occurs across the country (Defensoría del Pueblo 2025). In July 2024, for example, police responded violently to social protest near the Las Bambas mine in Cotabambas; eleven people were reported injured by Peruvian national police with whom the company has contracted to protect its operations (BNamericas 2024). While the company stated the clashes were between illegal miners and the police, multiple outlets reported the clashes occurred with community members after they voiced concerns about water use and pollution (Infobae 2024; Servindi 2024). The Peruvian government subsequently issued a state of emergency (BNamericas 2024).

Alarmingly, these recent events are not out of the ordinary in Latin America. Examples abound and cross-national data indicate a notable increase in violence over the last decade.[2] Across the region, state security forces inflict high levels of violence against civilians at the behest of governments attempting to solve intransigent political, economic, and social problems.

This development is not only alarming but also unexpected. Following the high levels of violence that characterized the Cold War, the region engaged in an unprecedented project to deter state violence as state actors sought to strengthen and consolidate their relatively young democracies. Countries have carried out routine free and fair elections over many cycles, passing the baton from one political party to another, all while weathering sometimes severe economic and political crises. Moreover, as explained later in this chapter, governments accomplished impressive reforms in an effort to prevent future human rights abuses. These included holding past perpetrators to account, organizing truth commissions, reforming constitutions and judicial systems, and establishing human rights ombuds offices. These efforts were meant to deter state violence by illustrating that those who engage in such behavior would be punished for doing so. States also empowered citizens by designing multiple avenues for civilians to bring forward abuses by state agents when they do occur. When domestic options faltered, the Inter-American Commission for Human Rights and the Inter-American Court of Human Rights became active venues to pressure states to fulfill their human rights obligations.

Given the clear efforts to strengthen democracy and respect human rights in Latin America, state violence should be restrained, yet this is in direct contrast to the conditions on the ground today. In this book, we explore this paradox: following an era of democratic state building that aimed to reduce human rights abuses, instead we observe an alarming level of state-led violence toward citizens as well as the proliferation of repressive state institutions. We are not the first to recognize this paradox, as others have written about the shortcomings of Latin America's democracies, calling them violent democracies (Arias and Goldstein 2010), or democracies that operate in states that are anomic (Waldmann 2006), ambivalent (Auyero and Sobering 2019), absent (Nivette 2016), or coopted (Corrales and Freeman 2024). Our objective, however, is to explore how political leaders approach governing through a threat lens, which leads state actors to respond violently to a multitude of issues, from crime to protest to migration. Collectively, whether related to everyday policing, border protection, or economic growth, we argue that *public order violence* characterizes state use of force in the region today.

In this chapter, we begin by defining state violence and detailing the parameters of our study. Next, we briefly trace the history of state violence in the region and the democratization process that followed. We then discuss the political and legal reforms undertaken in the contemporary democratic era intended to deter future state violence: transitional justice initiatives, new and amended constitutions, and judicial and other institutional reforms across the region. In the next section, we discuss the relationship between state violence and democracy, with attention to the problems of uneven state capacity, weak rule of law, and socioeconomic inequalities—what we term "legacy conditions"—that we argue explain the resurgence of state violence in Latin America. We conclude the chapter by outlining the remainder of the book.

DEFINING STATE VIOLENCE

State violence is the use of physical force by agents of the state in their capacity as state actors within their domestic jurisdiction. This definition separates state violence from related but distinct concepts such as state terror, state repression, and political violence. Scholarly attention to historical state terror in Latin America has led to well-developed ideas about this behavior in which the state seeks to instill fear in the public (e.g., Blakeley 2016, 95; Mitchell et al. 1986, 9). The related concept of state repression describes a state acting to impede political activity (Ritter 2014). In both instances, state conduct may or may not involve physical force. The state may be violent and repressive when it openly kills opponents to suppress dissent (e.g., Green 2015) or non-violent and repressive when it targets media outlets through burdensome regulations (e.g., de la Torre 2013). Political violence can be an expansive term involving virtually every form of mass conflict with an intent to obtain or maintain power, and it may be carried out against or by the state (Darby 2016, 46–49). Even if limiting the scope to acts by the state, political violence carries with it a partisan or ideological mission. State violence, however, may bring harm regardless of the political content or intent of the act. In the democratic era, elected administrations of varied ideologies have used state violence (Kyle and Reiter 2019, 21–23), and at times, the harm inflicted by state forces is unintentional, as in the case of those wounded or killed by stray bullets (e.g., Correal and Glatsky 2024).

We are focused on state violence as action rather than structure. Our study aligns with what Johan Galtung (1969) defined as intended or unintended manifest, personal, physical violence (169–172). The underlying societal systems that create and impose economic and social inequalities constitute structural violence against a population, even without a specific actor carrying out direct acts of violence (Galtung 1969, 170). The state may be part of this form of violence and contribute to these inequalities, but our focus is on violence as the actual use of physical force (Imbusch 2003, 15). In Max Weber's well-known formulation, the state "lays claim to the *monopoly of legitimate physical violence* within a particular territory" (2004 [1919], 33).[3] The order provided by this monopoly on violence is most efficiently exercised through the expectation of coercion in the event of transgressing the law, rather than the constant application of physical violence. The state amounts to the "bridling of violence," including from the state itself (Imbusch 2003, 17).

Far from the Weberian model of holding a monopoly on violence in their territories, state sovereignty is contested in Latin America. The power vacuum in "vast ungoverned spaces" allows other violent actors to operate by their own rules and to prey on populations unprotected by the state (Marcella et al. 2022, 2). Rather than having a monopoly on violence, the state is but one actor that competes, colludes, and negotiates control with other violent actors such as paramilitaries, criminal gangs, and drug trafficking organizations (Cruz 2016). These practices reflect a state that is not categorically strong or weak but rather "ambivalent" toward its duty to provide security for the public (Auyero and Sobering 2019, 11). Frequent overlap between state violence and criminal violence—as when criminal organizations infiltrate security services or when members of the security services also work as private security, paramilitaries, or death squads (Cruz 2011, 2016)—also demonstrates the myriad forms of state-sponsored or state-aligned violence that take place in the region. Ultimately, however, we are concerned with understanding state violence as conduct by state security forces in their role as representatives of public institutions. As Charles Tilly (2003) observes, "the boundary between legitimate and illegitimate uses of coercive means" is always contested (27–28), and what is lawful in one jurisdiction may not be in another, thereby eroding clear differences between what can be considered legitimate (legal) and illegitimate (illegal) violence (Imbusch 2003, 31). Even so, in the democratic era, the public should expect to be as free as possible from state violence while the state should curtail all violence through its duty to protect human rights.

Ironically, state failures to inhibit violence among non-state actors, to provide institutional channels to resolve anti-state dissent peacefully, and to restrain its own violence have created a troubling self-reinforcing state practice in which "these new violent challengers...have offered the state a new form of legitimation: internal 'wars' with violent youth, drugs traffickers, and the remaining insurgent forces in the region" (Pearce 2010, 298–299). Non-state violence grows due to the lack of state monopoly on power, which the state then uses to justify its own violent behavior against those perceived threats. States then contribute to violent conditions by employing violence of their own. Violence from the police, the military, intelligence agencies, prison services, and other security forces is significant enough that states play a notable part in overall homicide rates in the region (Cruz 2016, 383).

THE TRANSFORMATION OF STATE VIOLENCE IN LATIN AMERICA

State violence in Latin America has taken different forms over time. We display the eras and characteristics of violence in Table 1.1. Mobilization for wars of independence in the early 1800s created the "first generation of military *caudillos*," local leaders who used their armed followers to assert their position against rivals (Loveman 1999, 32). This practice of armed conflict among proto-state actors continued until the 1870s, with the routine use of violence in local power struggles as well as to lend (or withdraw) support from nominal national rulers (Rouquié 1982, 49–54). Beginning in the 1870s, processes of national consolidation began to create more centralized states under the leadership of oligarchs (Loveman and Davies 1997, 26–27; Wiarda 1981, 46). State violence in this era was characterized by "the private appropriation of public power" to maintain the socioeconomic hierarchies of highly unequal societies, where "violence against the underprivileged masses was a routine affair" (Kruijt and Koonings 1999, 7). State consolidation was often very violent as new national militaries fought caudillos and crushed local rebellions (e.g., Middlebrook 1995, 23–24; Rock 1987, 129–131). As we discuss at length in Chapter 2, this was also the beginning of the era of professionalization of national militaries through foreign missions. In the 1930s–40s, with the turn toward new political forms—notably populism and corporatism—the state grew in size and relevance in mediating relationships between social groups, which increased the use of violence to secure or maintain access to state power, including the presence of newly assertive national militaries, willing and able to use violence to overthrow governments by force (Kruijt and Koonings 1999, 8–10; Malloy 1977).

Military coups in the region became widespread beginning in the early 1930s (Loveman 1999, 101), often justified as the means to economic modernization (Malloy 1977, 16). With the beginning of the Cold War in the 1940s, revolutionary-counterrevolutionary politics led to the establishment of reactionary military regimes dedicated to the use of ideologically motivated state violence against the public (Kruijt and Koonings 1999, 8–10). Militaries embraced National Security Doctrine in their anti-communist mission, turning national defense into a fight against internal enemies, especially leftist and popular movements (Lopez 1986). Coercion was essential to the economic development project of the bureaucratic-authoritarian state, which sought to deactivate and exclude labor, students, intellectuals, and the urban poor from politics (O'Donnell 1979, 96–99). Governments engaged in campaigns of "social cleansing" to physically eliminate people who were deemed undesirable (Arias 2008; Clemencia Ramírez 2010). The United States contributed to this violence by helping to establish many of the Latin American intelligence organizations involved as well as by providing long-term training and financing to repressive forces in the region (Gill 2004; Huggins 1998).

Table 1.1 The transformation of state violence in Latin America

Dates	Political era	Characteristics of state violence
1820s–70s	Post-independence	Caudillo Rivalry and Proto-State Conflict
1870s–1930s	Oligarchy	National Centralization and Consolidation
1930s–40s	Corporatism and populism	Modernization and Economic Development
1940s–80s	Cold War authoritarian rule	National Security Doctrine and Anti-Communism
1990s–2010s	Post-Cold War democratic stabilization	Security Sector Reform and a Reduction of Violence
2010s–present	Punitive populism	Public Order Violence in Response to Governing Challenges

As the region transitioned to democracy in the 1980s–90s, violence in the region transformed. There was a proliferation of violence from "a multitude of actors in pursuit of all kind of goals" (Kruijt and Koonings 1999, 11). As measured by rates of intentional homicide, Latin America is consistently the most violent region in the world (Rivera 2016; United Nations Office on Drug and Crime 2024). While violence from non-state actors proliferated in the 1990s, state violence declined significantly from its Cold War-era high. Beginning in the 2010s, however, there has been a resurgence of state violence in an era of Punitive Populism (Bonner 2019) in which democratically elected leaders view many governing challenges through a threat lens and respond violently in pursuit of public order.[4]

DEMOCRATIZATION AND EFFORTS TO END STATE VIOLENCE

From the late 1970s to the early 1990s, Latin American countries transitioned away from authoritarianism as part of a global trend termed the Third Wave of democratization (Huntington 1991).[5] Militaries in the region transferred power to elected civilian leaders and civil wars came to an end.

While political transitions moved countries in Latin America away from authoritarianism, as Linz and Stepan (1996) argue, democratic consolidation occurs when democracy is "the only game in town" (15). All major actors at the elite and mass levels must commit to the system, even in moments of crisis, and become "habituated to the resolution of conflict within…the new democratic process" (Linz and Stepan 1996, 16). Since this period of democratic transitions, many Latin American countries have successfully weathered economic and political crises without abandoning democracy. Severe financial crisis in Argentina at the end of the 1990s saw the rapid departure of multiple presidents, but democracy held (Levitsky 2005). Military agitation in Argentina and Ecuador in the late 1980s failed to undo their democracies (Isaacs 1991; Norden 1996). Conflict between executive and legislative branches at times mean that "elected *governments* continue to fall, but in contrast to previous decades, democratic *regimes* do not break down" (Pérez-Liñán 2007, 3).[6] Partisan conflict similarly stabilized. Parties that won transitional elections stepped down at the end of their terms, passing the two-turnover test of consolidation (Huntington 1991, 267).

With democratic consolidation came reduced state violence. Democracies generally experience less violence than non-democracies (Fox and Hoelscher 2012), because political actors expect to compete again in future elections, giving them "fewer incentives to resort to disorder and violence" to gain or maintain power (Huntington 1989, 23). Through the twin pillars of elections and constitutional guarantees on power, democracy empowers and restrains political actors to compete and govern within recognizable boundaries (Schmitter and Karl 1991, 82–83). In short, "democracy is a system in which parties lose elections" (Przeworski 1991, 10). Moreover, countries benefit from a domestic democratic peace brought about by constraints on power and the promise of legal and electoral consequences for leaders who employ state repression (Davenport 2007, 11). Latin America thus entered an era where there were alternatives to state violence as a means of pursuing political goals.

Given the record of widespread disappearances, torture, and politically motivated killings under the previous authoritarian regimes, preventing state violence was one of the foremost objectives of democratic reformers. The region's new democracies implemented a range of policies intended to directly monitor and punish state violence, in turn deterring it from recurring. As described here, these included reforms to the security sector, transitional justice initiatives, and constitutional reforms. Moreover, states created National Human Rights Institutions and Ombuds Offices, and reformed the judiciary, whose work was bolstered by the Inter-American Court of Human Rights, which played an important regional role, as well.

Security Sector Reform

Upon transitioning to democracy, newly elected leaders often needed to cope with politically powerful militaries, with institutional protections that could ensure their continued influence in the new era. Reducing the political power of militaries thus became a high priority. While it took time, and was often contentious, civilian governments largely succeeded in reducing or eliminating many of these military prerogatives. For example, in Brazil, President José Sarney halved the number of seats in the cabinet that the military had secured for itself in the transition (Hunter 1997, 63). In Chile, the military-written 1980 constitution originally gave the military the power to name members of the senate and designated former presidents as senators-for-life, which guaranteed Augusto Pinochet a lifetime seat. Constitutional reforms in 2005 ended these reserve domains (Fuentes 2015). Civilian governments also successfully reduced the size and budgets of militaries. El Salvador, for example, demobilized at the end of its civil war, cutting personnel numbers by more than half (Córdova Macías 2001, 27). In Paraguay, as in many other countries, military expenditures as a share of the national budget declined significantly in post-transition years—in this case—from nearly 35 percent prior to the transition to just over 6 percent a decade later.[7]

Countries in the region also reformed the missions of militaries and other security services to reduce state violence. Reforms to the military sought to orient them toward external defense rather than internal deployment (Martínez 2013, 68). Other security services were moved out from the control of ministries of defense and placed in civilian ministries (Dammert 2007). Governments reorganized police to demilitarize their ranking systems (Sozzo 2016). Police services also embraced community-oriented policing and new training around respect for human rights (Arias and Ungar 2009; Bobea 2012). We discuss the transformation in the architecture of state violence extensively in Chapter 3. The goal of these efforts was to ensure that state security forces were fully subordinated to civilian authorities and operated transparently under clearly defined mandates.

Transitional Justice Initiatives

The high levels of state violence in the authoritarian era also represented an immediate challenge for the nascent democracies. In many countries, the extent of the violence was then unknown; much of the violence was committed clandestinely with further efforts by the regimes to eliminate witnesses and destroy records. Yet many human rights activists discovered archives documenting the previous regimes' abuses, while victims and their families came forward to tell their stories. Survivors of the repression called on their new governments to recognize abuses by the previous regimes, assist them in rebuilding their lives, and investigate past events to provide them with some measure of closure and guarantees of nonrecurrence. Moreover, they demanded that the perpetrators, many of whom still held positions of privilege in military and police forces, face accountability for their wrongdoing. Debates over transitional justice, broadly defined as the "judicial and nonjudicial processes designed to reckon with past human rights violations following periods of political turmoil, state repression, and armed conflict" (Dancy et al. 2019, 99), dominated the political landscape of the new democracies.

Latin America became a global leader in the field, often setting the norms that the rest of the world followed.[8] Argentina's prosecution of the military juntas in 1984–85, for example, was the most prominent human rights trial since the Nuremberg trials held by the Allies after World War II (Sikkink and Booth Walling 2006). The goal of trials is two-fold: to punish and prevent the perpetrator from committing crimes again and to deter other state agents from committing similar crimes in the future. While justice was delayed in some cases, across the region democratic governments prosecuted former authoritarian actors vigorously, including high-profile trials of former heads of state: Chile's Augusto Pinochet, Uruguay's Juan María Bordaberry, Bolivia's Luis García Meza, Peru's Alberto Fujimori, and Guatemala's Efraín Ríos Montt. Courts across the region have also convicted hundreds of lower level perpetrators.

At the same time, new democratic leaders needed to ensure that their pursuit of prosecutions would not risk the success of the country's democratic transition. This required a delicate balance between trials and amnesty laws designed specifically to limit trials (Dancy et al. 2019). This meant accepting some self-amnesties that were enacted before authoritarian regimes left power, such as in Chile (1978) and Brazil (1979), while issuing other amnesties under democracy, such as in Uruguay (1986).[9] Amnesties in El Salvador (1992) and Guatemala (1996) were also key components of the peace processes that helped to end their long-running civil wars. When the initial wave of prosecutions in Argentina prompted backlash by the military, the government there too implemented a series of amnesties and pardons (Nino 1991). Yet these laws were later circumvented and struck down by courts, leading to a new wave of prosecutions when the political climate was more conducive and the risks were lower (Engstrom and Pereira 2012).

Moreover, even where trials were not immediately possible, governments aimed to at least punish perpetrators in the eyes of public opinion, thereby damaging these individuals' reputations, eroding their influence, and limiting their ability to commit violence again. To do so, many countries pursued truth commissions—temporary bodies officially sanctioned by the state to investigate past human rights abuses—often at the time of transition (Hayner 2010). In Argentina, the National Commission on the Disappearance of Persons' work led to the publication of a final report—*Nunca Más* (Never Again)—in 1984 that documented over 8,000 enforced disappearances by the former military regime, further catalyzing the demand for prosecutions. Uruguay's Investigative Commission on the Situation of Disappeared People and Its Causes (1985), Chile's National Commission for Truth and Reconciliation (1990–91), the Commission on the Truth for El Salvador (1992–93), Guatemala's Commission for Historical Clarification (1997–99), Panama's Truth Commission (2001–2002), Peru's Truth and Reconciliation Commission (2001–2003), and Paraguay's Truth and Justice Commission (2004–2008) all served to expose the crimes of the past. These efforts helped to debunk the lies of the previous regimes that state violence did not happen or was exaggerated by their opponents. They also challenged the narratives of the authoritarian regimes that any use of force was necessary because they were fighting wars against subversives who threatened the state.

The region's efforts to expose prior human rights violations and punish those responsible were impressive—and there is strong evidence that they were worth it. Many studies have demonstrated that the use of trials (Kim and Sikkink 2010; Sikkink 2011) and amnesties (Snyder and Vinjamuri 2003) has led to improvements in human rights and democracy, including in Latin America specifically. Additionally, the positive effects of transitional justice are enhanced when governments pursue a mix of trials and amnesties (Dancy et al. 2019; Olsen et al. 2010), just as the democracies in the region did. Scholarship on truth commissions, which were extensive across the region, has likewise found that they lead to notable improvements in physical integrity rights (Dancy and Thoms 2022). In particular, they have been linked to lower homicide rates in post-authoritarian Latin America by deterring "state specialists in violence from becoming major actors in the production of criminal violence" (Trejo et al. 2018, 800). Latin America's democratization and related reduction in state violence likely owes part of its success to the transitional justice approach taken by the region's activists and new democratic leaders.

Constitutional Reform

While the authoritarian regimes of the Cold War era went to great lengths to hide the nature and extent of their violence, they also made a concerted effort to justify their seizures of power and attacks against their adversaries. The Uruguayan military issued eight Institutional Acts that provided a legal framework with which to govern in place of the constitution (Barahona de Brito 1997, 41–42). Many of the authoritarian governments used powers embedded in the existing democratic institutions to declare martial law and various states of war, siege, and emergency. These "regimes of exception" allowed them to rule by decree and suspend constitutional guarantees (Loveman 1993). They also granted militaries expanded legal powers, including the right to apprehend citizens preemptively to prevent crimes, imprison them on military bases, and try them in military courts (Kyle and Reiter 2021). These practices have a long history in Latin America but were particularly severe during the Cold War.

Many of the new democratic regimes thus worked to revise constitutional frameworks to impose stronger constraints on executive and military power. The new 1992 constitution in Paraguay, for example, allows for the executive to declare a state of exception, but the powers vested in them after doing so are extremely limited. The executive may only detain people for acts specified in the declaration, and habeas corpus remains in effect.[10] The 1991 constitution in Colombia replaced the previous state of siege with the far more restrictive "state of internal commotion" that authorized the new Constitutional Court to automatically review all decrees passed during this constitutional emergency measure through a fast-track process.[11] New democratic leaders prohibited the trial of civilians in military courts in newly written constitutions in Honduras (1982) and Guatemala (1985), the reinstated 1967 constitution in Uruguay, and in a 1992 amendment to the constitution in El Salvador.[12]

Such constitutional reforms were also bolstered by the broad expansion of human rights protections around the world. Activists, now able to influence democratic politicians, lobbied for the inclusion of expanded rights in their countries' constitutions. Simultaneously, they often encouraged new governments to join prominent international treaties. Bolivia (1982), Argentina (1986), Brazil (1992), Guatemala (1992), and Paraguay (1992) joined the rest of the region as parties to the International Covenant on Civil and Political Rights.[13] While torture by authoritarian regimes had been the norm in the region, by 1996 all Latin American countries were party to the Convention against Torture and Other Cruel, Inhuman or Degrading Treatment or Punishment.[14] The rights protected in these treaties became law of the land in the region.

Overall, the changes in the region were sweeping. In the wake of democratic transitions, constitutions, with significantly expanded rights and protections, were reinstated or newly created in Ecuador (1978), Honduras (1982), Guatemala (1985), Uruguay (1985), Brazil (1988), Colombia (1991), Paraguay (1992), Argentina (1994), and the Dominican Republic (1994). Other democratic leaders significantly reformed existing constitutions, including in Panama (1993–94), Bolivia (1994), and Nicaragua (1994–95).[15] Moreover, the negotiated peace agreements that ended Central America's long-running civil wars, with input from the United Nations, included extensive protections for human rights (Burgerman 2000) and led to major constitutional changes in El Salvador (1991–92).

Scholars have demonstrated that constitutional reform is best when the process is broadly participatory. Those constitutions last longer (Elkins et al. 2009), lead to improvements in democratic institutions (Blount et al. 2012; Carey 2009; Eisenstadt et al. 2015), reduce violence (Widner 2005), and result in more human rights protections and stronger account-ability mechanisms for them (Samuels 2006). Latin America epitomized this approach. Almost all of the major constitutional rewrites "occurred through highly participatory processes, that is, through constituent assemblies composed of elected delegates, rather than by negotiations among a restricted circle of elites" (Corrales 2013, 13). In Brazil in 1985, for example, the entire 559-member Congress took on the task of writing a new constitution. Each of its 24 subcommittees was required to hear from representatives of different sectors of Brazilian society, leading to 21,000 speeches and 61,142 proposed amendments (Rosenn 1990, 777). In Colombia, a diverse group of civil society actors organized the Second National Forum for Human Rights in 1981 and a subsequent national commission in 1987. The movement grew and urged Colombians to cast an extralegal ballot in favor of a National Constituent Assembly in the 1990 elections. With over five million Colombians voting in favor, the government was forced to act. The subsequent assembly, which included representatives from indigenous groups and guerrilla movements, began operating in February 1991 and produced a new constitution in July (Fox et al. 2010).[16] Citizen involvement in constitutional change was the norm across the region (Negretto 2018, 17–18). There is no doubt that following the end of authoritarian rule there was broad agreement on protecting human rights and limiting state power across Latin America.

Ombuds Offices and National Human Rights Institutions

While the increased protections for human rights were applauded, questions remained about who would monitor the behavior of state agents going forward. After years of authoritarian rule, there was a deep distrust of state institutions, and new avenues were needed to report abuses by state agents. To that end, almost all countries established ombuds offices or similar national human rights institutions intended to promote and protect human rights.[17] These institutions are permanent bodies designed to be independent from the government and serve as a venue for citizens to safely bring complaints against state agents. They publicize their work and often name individuals and government agencies that have not complied with their recommendations (Uggla 2011). They also participate in the legislative process by providing legal analysis of draft legislation to ensure compliance with human rights standards (Reif 2004). When working well, they can serve as a type of "fourth estate" that checks government power (Moreno 2016b). The proliferation of such institutions following the wave of democratic transitions is striking, with new institutions established in Guatemala (1985), Mexico (1990), Colombia (1992), Paraguay (1992), El Salvador (1992), Costa Rica (1993), Peru (1993), Brazil (1993, 1994), Argentina (1994, 2003), Honduras (1995), Nicaragua (1995), Ecuador (1996), Bolivia (1997), Panama (1997), Venezuela (1999), the Dominican Republic (2001), Chile (2005), and Uruguay (2008).[18]

National human rights institutions have a strong track record of leading to improvements in physical integrity rights (Cole and Ramirez 2013) and democracy (Reif 2004). This has particularly been the case in Latin America (Moreno and Witmer 2016) where they have "played a significant role in this consolidation of democracy" (González Volio 2003, 219) by reducing human rights violations (Moreno and Witmer 2016) and corruption (Moreno 2016b). Those in Honduras, Peru, and Bolivia, in particular, became influential actors in domestic politics in the 1990s (Uggla 2004).

Judicial Reform

The increase in human rights protections and monitoring of state agents were expected to reduce state violence in the region. To limit the occurrence of abuses, and to prevent a return to unrestrained state violence, an effective deterrent was needed, as well. This required a strong and independent judiciary, where citizens felt comfortable bringing cases forward and judges were willing to rule against the government.[19] In many countries, constructing such a system was a monumental task. Because of "frequent political interference, and consequent internal disorder, the region's judiciaries were widely regarded as incapable of performing their basic functions in a fair and competent manner" (Hammergren 2007, 3). Moreover, in many countries, the judiciary had worked closely with the authoritarian regimes in carrying out state violence (Pereira 2005); building citizen trust in this branch of government would therefore be difficult.

To reform the judiciary, governments worked to enact new procedural codes and offices of public defense and prosecution. Increased legal training was required throughout judiciaries, leading to more professionalized staff overseen by stronger monitoring and evaluation processes. They also invested in new infrastructure and technology and provided greater security for judges (Hammergren 2007, 8–21). To accomplish all of this, judicial budgets increased considerably across the region (Vargas Vivancos 2009). Processes for selecting judges were also improved to increase transparency and reduce political influence. Since 1994 in Argentina, the appointment of Supreme Court justices requires public hearings and consent by two-thirds of the senate (Brinks 2005, 606). The 2016 Law on the Judicial Career in Guatemala allows civil society actors to object to candidates during the confirmation process.[20] In Bolivia, since the 2009 constitution, judges for the Supreme Court of Justice, the Plurinational Constitutional Court, the Agro-Environmental Court, and the Judicial Council are directly elected by popular vote; the requirement that the candidates reflect the pluri-nationality of the country has led to a high percentage of indigenous and female judges.[21] Many countries also implemented new requirements of legal education and experience to shift the focus from political appointments of judges to selecting judges based on merit (Hammergren 2002).

Beyond improving existing judicial bodies, many governments created new ones. More lower level courts increased citizen access to the system and provided a non-violent means of dispute resolution. Brazil's establishment of small claims courts (Rodycz 2001) and Peru's creation of justice of the peace courts (Cerron 2008) were two of the most successful initiatives in the region. Moreover, to protect the extensive human rights now enshrined in constitutions, many countries created new constitutional courts, such as in Costa Rica (1989), Colombia (1991), Ecuador (1996), and Bolivia (1999). Peru also created a constitutional court in 1979, and its powers were significantly expanded through a 1993 constitutional amendment. These courts have become important in restraining state violence in the region. Costa Rica's court, in particular, quickly became "one of the most influential and activist courts in Latin America" (Wilson 2005, 47). In the decade after its creation, the Colombian Constitutional Court grew more assertive, solidifying its role as a check on state power and increasing the protection of human rights through multiple landmark rulings (Kyle and Reiter 2021, 109–110; Ríos-Figueroa 2016, 46–81). Overall, in the last two decades of the twentieth century, constitutional courts dramatically expanded their independence from other branches of government and their power to influence politics (Ríos-Figueroa 2011). This came about because of better appointment and removal procedures of judges, increased term limits, and an expansion of instruments for constitutional review. In many countries, citizens have used the *writ of amparo* or *acción de tutela* extensively to bring cases before the court to win injunctions against state action (Brewer-Carías 2009; Zamudio 1979).[22]

While there is notable variation across countries (Brinks and Blass 2018), in the decades since democratization, judicial independence has grown throughout the region and courts are able to make decisions without pressure from other branches of the government or the military (Couso 2005). Courts in Latin America have become powerful political actors (González-Ocantos 2019; Helmke 2002; Hilbink 2007), especially in the area of human rights (González-Ocantos 2016; Helmke and Ríos-Figueroa 2011), because activists and democratic reformers strategically turned to courts to pursue their agendas (Carothers 2001). High courts, for example, have been successful in moving trials for human rights violations committed by members of the military to civilian, rather than military, courts in Bolivia, the Dominican Republic, Mexico, and Peru.[23] Newly empowered courts also struck down or circumvented the amnesty laws that had been negotiated as part of peace agreements or passed as prerequisites for leaving power, including in Argentina (Engstrom and Pereira 2012) and Uruguay (Soltman 2013). These efforts opened the way for prosecutions of past perpetrators of abuses.

The Inter-American Court of Human Rights

Domestic reform efforts have been strengthened by the Inter-American Court of Human Rights, established by the Organization of American States to oversee compliance with the American Convention on Human Rights. Most of the countries in the region ratified the Convention prior to it coming into force in 1978 or shortly thereafter, but those that had not ratified it quickly did so following their transitions to democracy: Argentina (1984), Brazil (1992), Chile (1990), Paraguay (1989), Uruguay (1985).[24] The ratification brought them under the jurisdiction of the court.

The influence of the Court on restraining state violence has been significant. Since its first contentious judgment in 1988 against Honduras, the Court has been assertive in protecting human rights and gradually expanded the scope of issues upon which it rules.[25] It has developed a unique practice of ordering specific remedies, aiming to push states to modify their laws and practices to come into compliance with the Convention (Huneeus 2017, 303–305). Through a series of cases in the mid-1990s against Peru and Chile, the Court established that amnesty laws aiming to protect state agents who committed human rights violations contravened the Convention.[26] It ruled against states in high-profile cases of massacres, including Guatemala and Colombia.[27] Its jurisdiction on enforced disappearances is extensive, with rulings against almost every state party.[28] In addition, it has been influential in reforming military justice systems in Argentina, Chile, Colombia, and Mexico.[29] Moreover, the Inter-American Commission on Human Rights processes hundreds of cases a year; most end in friendly settlements rather than going to trial. In short, the Inter-American human rights system has provided an important external check on the behavior of state agents in the region and helped bolster domestic-level democratic reforms.

EXPLAINING STATE VIOLENCE IN MODERN LATIN AMERICA

Despite the impressive democratization processes and concerted efforts to contain state violence described above, it is nonetheless on the rise again in Latin America. While militaries have largely stayed out of politics and many security forces were disbanded, police forces have been resistant to reform (González 2020) and have often "remained tied to their authoritarian traditions and structures" (Malone et al. 2023, 2). Additionally, as we show in Chapter 3, state security forces have proliferated, creating ever more "specialized" agencies. While transitional justice efforts and new or reformed constitutions are impactful on many levels, they have not had the long-term deterrent effect that many anticipated. Chapter 7 illustrates, instead, that executives and legislatures are seeking ways to provide pardons and amnesties to violent state security forces while also frequently employing states of exception that suspend many of the new rights that constitutions sought to protect.

Similarly, the creation of national human rights institutions has been a positive development. Yet their effectiveness is dependent on the degree of independence from the government (Uggla 2004, 450), and there are instances of state actors manipulating the appointment process for national human rights institutions in Mexico (Finkel 2012) and El Salvador (Dodson and Jackson 2004) to weaken them. Politicians retaliated against the national human rights institution in Honduras to undermine its activities (Dodson 2006). In other cases, governments have defunded institutions that challenged their actions, as happened in Nicaragua in 2000 when the government cut the ombudsman's budget by 40 percent (Uggla 2004, 427).

Likewise, high courts have made important rulings across the region, but judicial performance overall is poor, and impunity persists (Le Clerq et al. 2016; Staats et al. 2005), especially when it comes to holding security forces accountable (Brinks 2008; Muñoz and Pappier 2020). Judiciaries do not enjoy the public's confidence and governments turn to security forces to show they are "tough on crime." [30] Even the work of the Inter-American Court of Human Rights has been limited. There is a growing resistance to the court in Latin America (Contesse 2019), and some countries have openly defied its rulings. Brazil, for example, ignored a 2010 ruling that declared the military's 1979 self-amnesty incompatible with the American Convention on Human Rights.[31] Venezuela has refused to reform its military justice system, which the government uses to shield its forces from accountability and to prosecute civilians, despite multiple court rulings ordering it to make changes (Driscoll and Nelson 2012).[32]

Cycle of Violence

We argue that the combination of uneven state capacity, weak rule of law, and socioeconomic inequalities—what we term "legacy conditions"—are part of a vicious cycle of public order violence in democracy, as depicted in Fig. 1.1. First, violent state institutions such as militarized police and the armed forces are highly developed. Meanwhile, those state institutions that are necessary to assert non-violent authority—such as criminal investigators, prosecutors, courts, immigration services, border control, and economic regulators—are ineffective or overwhelmed. Second, weak rule of law permits insecurity, to which the state responds with force, unrestrained by the deterrent effect of probable accountability. Third, social inequalities activate electoral incentives to direct state violence against otherized out-groups (e.g., urban and rural poor, non-citizens, indigenous groups). In turn, state actors' public order violence exacerbates these problems and reinforces illiberal democratic systems that undercut the efforts to contain state violence discussed above. In sum, the state has few tools—other than violence—with which to respond to the perceived and real threats posed by crime, population flows, and economic shortfalls. Violent responses are prominent options for decision-makers, yet violent responses do not help address the underlying legacy conditions. Instead, they feed into the cycle of violence and fail to build institutional capacity or legitimacy that could help reduce state and non-state actors' use of violence.

Governance based on the rule of law requires "compliance with the law, when the law is general, public, prospective, clear, consistent, performable, and stable" (Sánchez-Cuenca 2003, 69). People must be treated equally before the law, and government actors must be subject to it (O'Donnell 2004). Yet, disjunctive democratization in the region

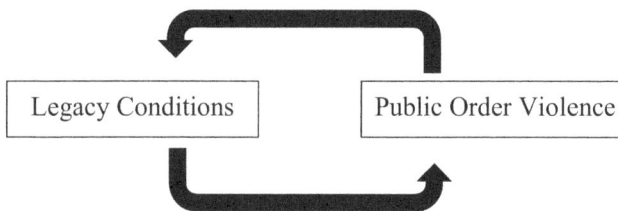

| Legacy Conditions | Public Order Violence |

Fig. 1.1 The cycle of violence in Latin America

has meant progress in establishing the rules of political competition along-side regression in other areas, including violence in society and from the state (Caldeira and Holston 1999). The proliferation of violence and shortcomings in the rule of law have proven to be stubborn problems that undermine the quality of democracy itself (Arias and Goldstein 2010).

Overwhelmingly, Latin American political systems today can be described as electoral democracies: they meet procedural requirements of democracy such as holding routine free and fair multiparty elections (Nord et al. 2024, 15). They do not, however, rise to the standard of being liberal democracies in which executive power is restrained, civil liberties are guaranteed, and people are equal before the law. Others are in the "grey zone" between democracy and autocracy (Nord et al. 2024, 12). This problem is consistent with the finding that hybrid regimes, or those that are neither fully democratic nor fully authoritarian, experience the most violence (Fein 1995; Fox and Hoelscher 2012). Failures in the rule of law threaten the notion of whether such systems should be labeled democracies at all (Balderacchi 2022; O'Donnell 2007). Shortcomings in the rule of law mean that governments are failing to protect their populations from violence, including violence committed by the state.

Long-standing socioeconomic inequalities also undermine the political equality based on citizenship, or shared belonging to the political community, which is necessary for democracy to function. Democratic citizenship ties people to each other and to government with shared rights and obligations (Tilly 2003, 42). Instead of democratic citizenship, however, as O'Donnell argues, Latin American transitions produced democracies of "low-intensity citizenship" (1993, 1361). The crisis of citizenship undermines public confidence in democracy and threatens its survival in the region (Hagopian 2007). Lack of social inclusion, combined with compromised rule of law, leave regimes descriptively closer to Tilly's "fragmented tyranny" in which violent non-state actors "and other polit-ical predators typically work their ways in collusion with or in defiance of nominal rulers" (42).

In the electoral democracies of today, the political rights necessary to hold elections (e.g., the right to vote) are largely assured (Nord et al. 2024), but inclusion in the benefits of citizenship is denied. The combination of competitive regimes with low-capacity states results in "patronage democracies" (Mazzuca and Munck 2020, 6), in which the provision of basic public goods such as electricity, water, or security against arbitrary violence is dependent on political connections rather than guaranteed by the state. This state of affairs reinforces conditions of "informal citizenship" that erode the social cohesion necessary for democracy to thrive (Kruijt et al. 2002). Full citizenship for all is essential to achieve the political equality that underpins democracy (Dahl 2015, 37). Put simply, democratization in the 1980s–90s did not solve the problems of economic, social, and political inequality characteristic of the region. Moreover, with the political transition to democracy, governments in the region also made an economic transition toward neoliberalism, which rolled back social programs and resulted in increases in poverty and inequality (Castillo Fernandez 2022).

Public Order Violence

Where citizenship rights are threatened, democratic legitimacy is weakened, and people are put at risk of state violence. Democratic legitimacy is predicated on the notion that "those affected by [a government decision] have been included in the decision-making process and have had the opportunity to influence the outcomes" (Young 2000, 5–6). Failure to uphold citizenship rights makes people vulnerable to state violence and further undermines the social connections and practices, such as political organizing, necessary to deepen citizenship (González 2017). Social inequalities expressed in marginalized race and class identities are reproduced in the uneven exercise of state power in day-to-day policing (Bonner 2021; Iturralde 2010). Under such conditions, people are excluded from moral consideration; they are not extended the same rights and protections as others in government decisions to use violence in policing and military operations (Succi Junior 2022). The same is true in the areas of migration and economic development, where state violence targets excluded populations such as non-citizens, indigenous people, and the rural poor (Taylor and Bonner 2017; Weber 2013).

Finally, under conditions of weak rule of law and extreme inequality, democracy itself creates a paradox in which politicians are incentivized to use state violence and voters are incentivized to support them doing so. Rather than democracy being an outlet for equal expression of interests, "where there are structural inequalities of wealth and power, formally democratic procedures are likely to reinforce them, because privileged people are able to marginalize the voices and issues of those less privileged" (Young 2000, 34). State responses to demands for protection follow these social hierarchies (González 2017, 501–503). General insecurity has produced well-known fears among the public of being the victim of violent crime (e.g., Dammert 2012).[33] In the democratic era, expansion of news and entertainment media, and their embrace of sensational violence, has fueled citizens' fears of violent crime (Fortete and Cesano 2009; Martín-Barbero 2002). These fears are socially constructed in a manner that reinforces social divisions of class, race, and geography (Duce and Pérez Perdomo 2003, 81–82). Democracy provides the political incentives for elected leaders and candidates for office to emphasize violent crime in their campaigns, heightening the personal stakes of an election through appeals to voters' individual safety (Chevigny 2003). Candidates, media, and voters in a violent democracy are thus in a mutually reinforcing cycle of promoting hardline responses that meet criminal violence with state violence.

At the same time, governments have securitized many issues such as drugs and migration, conflating them with crime, as well as criminalizing protest. Treating all of these as *threats* opens the door to state violence motivated by a promise of *public order*—providing those voters frustrated by poor government performance with a quick and tangible response (Malone 2023, 19–24), such as *mano dura* ("iron fist") policies involving "(i) longer and/or expedited sentences, (ii) extralegal detention, (iii) absence or limits of due process rights, and (iv) the militarization of domestic security" (Cutrona and Rosen 2023, 5). Despite their general ineffectiveness (Rodrigues and Rodríguez-Pinzón 2020), hardline responses are so electorally useful they have given rise to a new political form known as punitive populism. This political strategy enables a leader to unify disparate constituencies through "tough-on-crime" rhetoric that promises a reward (security) for those of the "citizen" in-group, and punishment (harsh treatment, prison time) for those of the "criminal" out-group (Bonner 2019, 9–10), corresponding to instrumentalized notions of who belongs and who does not. Thus, while electoral competition provides a vehicle for anti-crime rhetoric, the ever-present inequalities that pervade state-society relations provide incentives for ongoing state violence.

PLAN OF THE BOOK

The aim of the book is to explore how political leaders approach the challenges of governance through a threat lens and thus engage in public order violence that exacerbates underlying legacy conditions while weakening the prospects of democracy. Chapters 2 and 3 explore the institutional attributes of this process by explaining how violence has been redistributed within the state. In Chapter 2, we begin by providing a comprehensive overview of the evolution of state security forces in Latin America from independence until the Third Wave of democratization. We demonstrate how weak states gradually expanded and professionalized their security forces, often with foreign influence. During the Cold War, state security forces grew in size and became increasingly specialized, leading to an era of heightened repression, driven by US-influenced National Security Doctrine. We follow this in Chapter 3 by providing a comprehensive assessment of the structure and mission scope of Latin American state security forces, drawing from a newly created dataset with information on 286 active forces across 18 countries. We describe at length the actors involved in state violence across the region. Too often the focus is on the military's involvement in politics or police violence in the context of fighting crime. We show, however, that the military and police are but two actors in a complex architecture of violence that includes various quasi-police and quasi-military units, gendarmerie and border guards, and intelligence services, among many others.

The next four chapters, then, uncover why violence occurs in various facets of life, drawing on case studies from across Latin America, to explore political (Chapters 4 and 5), economic (Chapter 6), and legal (Chapter 7) justifications for public order violence. In Chapter 4, we examine policing as a source of state violence, with a focus on Brazil. The extreme violence associated with policing as well as special military deployments have persisted in the democratic era. Moreover, police violence in the favelas ("informal settlements") illustrate the consequences of socioeconomic and geographic inequalities, where the state has often ceded control to criminal gangs, only to exercise their own power through episodic violence. We find that (re-)militarization, the electoral appeal of harsh tactics, and impunity contribute to the resurgence of police violence in the region.

In Chapter 5, we investigate state violence on international borders in Latin America. Governments have increasingly militarized their borders in response to organized crime and illicit drug trafficking. Contemporary populist governments have securitized the issue of international migration, often treating population flows as a threat to be met with violence. We detail the case of Mexico, given its significance in migration in the Americas, and the militarization of the US-Mexico border in recent decades. Confirming the overall pattern of resurgent state violence in recent years, we find that countries across the region are responding to a multitude of transnational issues with physical barriers and military force.

In Chapter 6, we explore how violence proliferates in the name of economic growth by investigating extractive industries in Peru. Governments—through direct and indirect participation—commit human rights abuses against their citizens to protect economic actors' investments. The chapter shows how state actors engage in violence through the criminalization of protest, use force in collaboration with private security actors on behalf of companies, and directly participate as state-owned enterprises perpetuating violence. The chapter draws from the Peruvian case while illustrating how these patterns are present across Latin America.

We conclude the book (Chapter 7) by examining the legal foundations of state violence today. We demonstrate three major legal strategies that governments use. First, they invoke constitutional regimes of exception to suspend civil liberties and empower security forces. Second, they enact new legislation and regulations that transform the security sector in ways that make it easier to mete out violence. Third, they create systems of impunity to prevent accountability for abuses committed by their forces. We also highlight three avenues for change. Democratic electoral politics, civic action, and judicial rulings have all proven to be effective at limiting or rolling back initiatives that increase state violence.

Notes

1. Comisión Nacional de los Derechos Humanos (CNDH Mexico), Recomendación No. 95 VG/2023, https://www.cndh.org.mx/sites/default/files/documentos/2023-03/RecVG_95.pdf. Copies of all primary documents cited in the book are available at www.andyreiter.com.
2. Since our study is focused on state violence in democratic systems, we exclude Cuba from our analysis since it has never been democratic in the post-Cold War period. We thus examine

18 countries: Argentina, Bolivia, Brazil, Chile, Colombia, Costa Rica, the Dominican Republic, Ecuador, El Salvador, Guatemala, Honduras, Mexico, Nicaragua, Panama, Paraguay, Peru, Uruguay, and Venezuela. The Political Terror Scale, for example, indicates a clear increase in violence, with the average score for the region increasing notably since it reached its lowest level (2.31) in 2015 to 2.68 in 2023 (Gibney et al. 2024).

3. Emphasis in the original.

4. The V-Dem "Physical violence index" marks substantial improvement in the Latin America and the Caribbean regional average every year of the 1980s, rising from 0.39, on a scale of 0 to 1, in 1980 to 0.69 by 1990. The region saw continued improvement to reach its height of 0.8 in the 2000s (Coppedge et al. 2025).

5. Three countries in the region—Costa Rica, Colombia, and Venezuela—democratized prior to the Third Wave.

6. Emphasis in the original.

7. World Bank Indicators, Paraguay: Military expenditure (% of general government expenditure), 1989–99, https://databank. worldbank.org/source/world-development-indicators#.

8. For a global dataset of transitional justice mechanisms, see the Transitional Justice Research Collaborate: https://transitionaljus ticedata.org/en/.

9. Despite efforts by civil society actors in Uruguay to overturn the 1986 Expiry Law, the public voted twice in national referendums (1989 and 2009) to retain it. The law is "Funcionarios Militares y Policiales Se Reconoce Que Ha Caducado El Ejercicio De La Pretension Punitiva del Estado Respecto de Los Delitos Cometidos Hasta El 1 de Marzo de 1985," Ley N34 15.848 de 22 diciembre de 1986.

10. Article 288, Paraguay's Constitution of 1992 with Amendments through 2011, https://www.constituteproject.org/constitution/ Paraguay_2011.

11. Article 214, Colombia's Constitution of 1991 with Amendments through 2014, https://www.constituteproject.org/constitution/ Colombia_2015.

12. Articles 90 and 91, Honduras's Constitution of 1982 with Amendments through 2013, https://www.constituteproject.org/consti tution/Honduras_2013; Article 219, Guatemala's Constitution of

1985 with Amendments through 1993, https://www.constitutepr
oject.org/constitution/Guatemala_1993; Article 253, Uruguay's
Constitution of 1966, Reinstated in 1985, with Amendments
through 2004, https://www.constituteproject.org/constitution/
Uruguay_2004; Mexico Agreement, April 27, 1991, https://pea
cemaker.un.org/en/node/9286. The constitutional amendment
was officially made in El Salvador with Article 7 of Decree No.
152 of January 30, 1992; see Article 216, El Salvador's Constitution of 1983 with Amendments through 2014, https://www.con
stituteproject.org/constitution/El_Salvador_2014.
13. International Covenant on Civil and Political Rights, December
16, 1966, 999 U.N.T.S. 14668, https://treaties.un.org/doc/Tre
aties/1976/03/19760323%2006-17%20AM/Ch_IV_04.pdf. For
a full list of signing, accession, and ratification dates, see: https://
treaties.un.org/Pages/ViewDetails.aspx?src=TREATY&mtdsg_
no=IV-4&chapter=4&clang=_en.
14. Convention against Torture and Other Cruel, Inhuman or
Degrading Treatment or Punishment, December 10, 1984, 1465
U.N.T.S. 24841, https://treaties.un.org/doc/Treaties/1987/
06/19870626%2002-38%20AM/Ch_IV_9p.pdf. For a full list of
signing, accession, and ratification dates, see: https://treaties.un.
org/pages/ViewDetails.aspx?src=TREATY&mtdsg_no=IV-9&cha
pter=4&clang=_en.
15. For data on all constitutions and amendments in the region see the
Comparative Constitutions Project· https://comparativeconstituti
onsproject.org/.
16. Constitución Política de República de Colombia 1991, http://
pdba.georgetown.edu/Constitutions/Colombia/colombia91.pdf.
17. While there are important distinctions between national human
rights institutions and ombuds offices, the line between them is
often blurred (Office of the United Nations High Commission for
Human Rights 2010).
18. The date listed is the year of the legislation or constitution that
created the institution. These are only national institutions; many
more exist at the sub-national level throughout the region. A full
list of the current national institutions can be found at the website
of the La Federación Iberoamericana del Ombudsman: http://
www.portalfio.org/miembros_regiones/nacionales/.

19. Some of this pressure also came from international actors who wanted to improve the legal systems of the region to make it a more conducive environment for the implementation of free market economic reforms.
20. Ley de Carrera Judicial, Decree No. 32-2016 de 29 de junio de 2016.
21. Bolivia's Constitution of 2009, https://www.constituteproject. org/constitution/Bolivia_2009.
22. The *writ of amparo* is an "extraordinary judicial remedy specifically conceived for the protection of constitutional rights against harms or threats inflicted by authorities or individuals" (Brewer-Carías 2009, 1).
23. Sentencia Constitucional 0663/2004-R, Sucre May 5, 2004, Expediente 2004-08468-17-RAC, https://jurisprudenciaconstit ucional.com/resolucion/57-sentencia-constitucional-0663-2004- r; Sentencia Constitucional 0664/2004-R, Sucre May 6, 2004, Expediente 2004-08469-17-RAC, https://jurisprudenciaconstit ucional.com/resolucion/25238-sentencia-constitucional-0664- 2004-r; Sentencia del 26 de Diciembre del 2001, No. 4, https:// transparencia.poderjudicial.gob.do/documentos/PDF/boletines/ 2001/Diciembre.pdf; Amparo Review No. 133/2012 (Sup. Ct. Mex. [SCJN] 21 de agosto de 2012), https://www2.scjn.gob. mx/AsuntosRelevantes/pagina/SeguimientoAsuntosRelevante sPub.aspx?Id=131182&SeguimientoId=478d; *Marcelino Tineo Silva y Más de 5,000 Ciudadanos*, Tribunal Constitucional, EXP. N.° 010-2002-AIITC, 3 de enero de 2003, https://tc.gob.pe/jur isprudencia/2003/00010-2002-AI.pdf.
24. American Convention on Human Rights: "Pact of San José, Costa Rica," August 22, 1969, 1144 U.N.T.S. 17955, https:// treaties.un.org/doc/publication/unts/volume%201144/volume- 1144-i-17955-english.pdf. For a full list of signing, accession, and ratification dates, see: https://treaties.un.org/pages/showdetails. aspx?objid=08000002800f10e1.
25. *Velásquez-Rodríguez v. Honduras*, Judgment, Inter-Am. Ct. H.R. (ser. C) No. 04 (July 29, 1988), https://www.corteidh.or.cr/ docs/casos/articulos/seriec_04_ing.pdf.
26. *Barrios Altos v. Peru*, Reparations and Costs, Inter-Am. Ct. H.R. (ser. C) No. 87 (November 30, 2001), http://www.cor teidh.or.cr/docs/casos/articulos/Seriec_87_esp.pdf; *La Cantuta*

v. *Peru*, Merits, Reparations and Costs, Inter-Am. Ct. H.R. (ser. C) No. 162 (November 29, 2006), http://www.corteidh.or. cr/docs/casos/articulos/seriec_162_esp.pdf; *Almonacid-Arellano et al.* v. *Chile*, Preliminary Objections, Merits, Reparations and Costs, Inter-Am. Ct. H.R. (ser. C) No 154 (September 26, 2006), https://www.corteidh.or.cr/docs/casos/articulos/seriec_ 154_ing.pdf.

27. *Plan de Sánchez Massacre* v. *Guatemala*, Judgment, Inter-Am. Ct. H.R. (ser. C) No. 105 (April 29, 2004), https://www.cor teidh.or.cr/docs/casos/articulos/seriec_105_ing.pdf; *"Mapiripán Massacre"* v. *Colombia*, Judgment, Inter-Am. Ct. H.R. (ser. C) No. 134 (September 15, 2005), https://www.corteidh.or.cr/docs/ casos/articulos/seriec_134_ing.pdf.

28. For example: *Bámaca Velásquez* v. *Guatemala*, Judgment, Inter-Am. Ct. H.R. (ser. C) No. 70 (November 25, 2000), https:// www.corteidh.or.cr/docs/casos/articulos/seriec_70_ing.pdf; *Gómez Palomino* v. *Peru*, Merits, Reparations and Costs, Inter-Am. Ct. H.R. (ser. C) No. 136 (November 22, 2005), https://www. corteidh.or.cr/docs/casos/articulos/seriec_136_ing.pdf; *Ticona Estrada et al.* v. *Bolivia*, Merits, Reparations and Costs, Inter-Am. Ct. H.R. (ser. C) No. 191 (November 27, 2008), https://www. corteidh.or.cr/docs/casos/articulos/seriec_191_ing.pdf; *Gelman* v. *Uruguay*, Merits and Reparations, Inter-Am. Ct. H.R. (ser. C) No. 221 (February 24, 2011), https://www.corteidh.or.cr/ docs/casos/articulos/seriec_221_ing.pdf; *Torres Millacura et al.* v. *Argentina*, Merits, Reparations and Costs, Inter-Am. Ct. H.R. (ser. C) No. 229 (August 26, 2011), https://www.corteidh. or.cr/docs/casos/articulos/seriec_229_ing.pdf; *Contreras et al.* v. *El Salvador*, Merits, Reparations and Costs, Inter-Am. Ct. H.R. (ser. C) No. 232 (August 31, 2011), https://www.cor teidh.or.cr/docs/casos/articulos/seriec_232_ing.pdf; *Gonzalez Medina and family* v. *Dominican Republic*, Preliminary Objec-tions, Merits, Reparations and Costs, Inter-Am. Ct. H.R. (ser. C) No. 240 (February 27, 2012), https://www.corteidh.or.cr/docs/ casos/articulos/seriec_240_ing1.pdf; *Rodríguez Vera et al. (The Disappeared from the Palace of Justice)* v. *Colombia*, Preliminary Objections, Merits, Reparations and Costs, Inter-Am. Ct. H.R. (ser. C) No. 287 (November 14, 2014), https://www.corteidh. or.cr/docs/casos/articulos/seriec_287_ing.pdf; *Vásquez Durand*

et al. v. *Ecuador*, Preliminary Objections, Merits, Reparations and Costs, Inter-Am. Ct. H.R. (ser. C) No. 332 (February 15, 2017), https://www.corteidh.or.cr/docs/casos/articulos/seriec_332_esp.pdf; *Alvarado Espinoza et al.* v. *Mexico*, Merits, Reparations and Costs, Inter-Am. Ct. H.R. (ser. C) No. 370 (November 28, 2018), https://www.corteidh.or.cr/docs/casos/articulos/seriec_370_ing.pdf; *Heliodoro Portugal* v. *Panama*, Preliminary Objections, Merits, Reparations, and Costs, Inter-Am. Ct. H.R. (ser. C) No. 186 (August 12, 2008), https://www.corteidh.or.cr/docs/casos/articulos/seriec_186_ing.pdf.

29. Report No. 15/10, Petition 11.758, Rodolfo Correa Belisle, https://cidh.oas.org/annualrep/2010eng/ARSA11758 EN.DOC; *Palamara Iribarne* v. *Chile*, Inter-Am. Ct. H.R. (ser. C). 135, (November 22, 2005), http://www.corteidh.or.cr/docs/casos/articulos/seriec_135_esp.pdf; *Caballero Delgado and Santana* v. *Colombia*, Merits, Inter-Am. Ct. H.R. (ser. C) No. 22 (December 8, 1995), https://www.corteidh.or.cr/docs/casos/articulos/seriec_22_ing.pdf; *Radilla Pacheco* v. *Mexico*, Preliminary Exceptions, Merits, Reparations and Costs, Inter-Am. Ct. H.R. (ser. C) No. 209 (November 23, 2009), http://www.corteidh.or.cr/docs/casos/articulos/seriec_209_esp.pdf.

30. The regional average from the 2023 Latinobarómetro survey shows large percentages of respondents have "Little" (35.7%) or "No trust" (33.0%) in their national judiciaries. Data available at: https://www.latinobarometro.org/latOnline.jsp.

31. *Gomes Lund et al. ("Guerrilha do Araguaia")* v. *Brazil*, Preliminary Objections, Merits, Reparations, and Costs, Inter-Am. Ct. H.R. (ser. C) No. 219 (November 24, 2010), http://www.corteidh.or.cr/docs/casos/articulos/seriec_219_ing.pdf.

32. *El Amparo* v. *Venezuela*, Reparations and Costs, Inter-Am. Ct. H.R. (ser. C) No. 28 (September 14, 1996), http://www.corteidh.or.cr/docs/casos/articulos/seriec_28_ing.pdf; *Montero-Aranguren et al. (Detention Center of Catia)* v. *Venezuela*, Preliminary Objection, Merits, Reparations and Costs, Inter-Am. Ct. H.R. (ser. C) No. 150 (July 5, 2006), http://www.corteidh.or.cr/docs/casos/articulos/seriec_150_ing.pdf; *Usón Ramírez* v. *Venezuela*, Preliminary Objections, Merits, Reparations, and Costs, Inter-Am. Ct. H.R. (ser. C) No. 207 (November 20, 2008), http://www.corteidh.or.cr/docs/casos/articulos/seriec_207_ing.pdf.

33. The Latinobarómetro survey, for example, asks: "How often, if at all, do you worry about becoming a victim of violent crime?" Regional results from the 2023 survey are as follows: "All the time" (30.6%), "Some of the time" (28.6%), "Just occasionally" (17.3%), and "Never" (22.6%). Data available at: https://www.lat inobarometro.org/latOnline.jsp.

REFERENCES

Abi-Habib, Maria, and Galia García Palafox. 2023. Deadly Attack Exposes Growing Threat in Mexico: The Military. *New York Times*. April 7. https://www.nytimes.com/2023/04/07/world/americas/mexico-military-killings-nuevo-laredo.html.

Amnesty International. 1979. *Political Imprisonment in Uruguay*. London: Amnesty International.

Arias, Arturo. 2008. And the Storm Raged On: The Daily Experience of Terror during the Central American Civil Wars, 1966–1996. In *Daily Lives of Civilians in Wartime Latin America: From the Wars of Independence to the Central American Civil Wars*, ed. Pedro Santoni, 263–288. Westport, CT: Greenwood.

Arias, Enrique Desmond, and Daniel M. Goldstein. 2010. Violent Pluralism: Understanding the New Democracies of Latin America. In *Violent Democracies in Latin America*, eds. Enrique Desmond Arias and Daniel M. Goldstein, 2–34. Durham: Duke University Press.

Arias, Enrique Desmond, and Mark Ungar. 2009. Community Policing and Latin America's Citizen Security Crisis. *Comparative Politics* 41 (4): 409–429.

Associated Press. 2023. Mexico Rights Agency: 4 Soldiers Killed Unarmed Men. March 22. https://apnews.com/article/mexico-soldiers-killings-una rmed-men-nuevo-laredo-a94ec57da1c7861979b6e4f56d66a4a4.

Auyero, Javier, and Katherine Sobering. 2019. *The Ambivalent State: Police-Criminal Collusion at the Urban Margins*. Oxford: Oxford University Press.

Balderacchi, Claudio. 2022. Overlooked Forms of Non-Democracy? Insights from Hybrid Regimes. *Third World Quarterly* 43 (6): 1441–1459.

Barahona de Brito, Alexandra. 1997. *Human Rights and Democratization in Latin America: Uruguay and Chile*. Oxford: Oxford University Press.

Blakeley, Ruth. 2016. State Violence as State Terrorism. In *The Ashgate Research Companion to Political Violence*, ed. Marie Breen-Smyth, 95–112. London: Routledge.

Blount, Justin, Zachary Elkins, and Tom Ginsburg. 2012. Does the Process of Constitution-Making Matter? In *Comparative Constitutional Design*, ed. Tom Ginsburg, 31–65. New York: Cambridge University Press.

BNamericas. 2024. New Wave of Conflict Threatens to Delay Las Bambas Expansion Works. July 16. https://www.bnamericas.com/en/news/new-wave-of-conflict-threatens-to-delay-las-bambas-expansion-works.

Bobea, Lilian. 2012. The Emergence of the Democratic Citizen Security Policy in the Dominican Republic. *Policing and Society* 22 (1): 57–75.

Bonner, Michelle D. 2019. *Tough on Crime: The Rise of Punitive Populism in Latin America*. Pittsburgh: University of Pittsburgh Press.

Bonner, Michelle D. 2021. Reclaiming Citizenship from Police Violence. *Citizenship Studies* 25 (3): 317–332.

Brewer-Carías, Allan R. 2009. *Constitutional Protection of Human Rights in Latin America. A Comparative Study of Amparo Proceedings*. New York: Cambridge University Press.

Brinks, Daniel M. 2005. Judicial Reform and Independence in Brazil and Argentina: The Beginning of a New Millennium? *Texas International Law Journal* 40 (3): 595–622.

Brinks, Daniel M. 2008. *The Judicial Response to Police Killings in Latin America: Inequality and the Rule of Law*. New York: Cambridge University Press.

Brinks, Daniel M., and Abby Blass. 2018. *The DNA of Constitutional Justice in Latin America*. New York: Cambridge University Press.

Burgerman, Susan D. 2000. Building the Peace by Mandating Reform: United Nations—Mediated Human Rights Agreements in El Salvador and Guatemala. *Latin American Perspectives* 27 (3): 63–87.

Caldeira, Teresa P. R., and James Holston. 1999. Democracy and Violence in Brazil. *Comparative Studies in Society and History* 41 (4): 691–729.

Camargo, Cristina. 2024. Megaoperação da PM em favelas do Rio deixa 9 mortos. *Folha de São Paulo*. February 27. https://www1.folha.uol.com.br/cotidiano/2024/02/policia-militar-faz-megaoperacao-em-favelas-do-rio-e-encontra-barreiras.shtml.

Carey, John M. 2009. Does It Matter How a Constitution is Created? In *Is Democracy Exportable?*, eds. Zoltan Barany and Robert G. Moser, 155–177. New York: Cambridge University Press.

Carothers, Thomas. 2001. The Many Agendas of Rule of Law Reform in Latin America. In *Rule of Law in Latin America: The International Promotion of Judicial Reform*, eds. Pilar Domingo and Rachel Sieder, 4–15. London: University of London Press.

Castillo Fernandez, Dídimo. 2022. Development Model, Labour Precariousness and New Social Inequalities in Latin America. *CEPAL Review* 136: 45–61.

Cerron, Maria Elana Guerra. 2008. Justice of the Peace in Peru: An Efficient Justice Service. *Florida Journal of International Law* 20 (4): 65–92.

Chevigny, Paul. 2003. The Populism of Fear: Politics of Crime in the Americas. *Punishment and Society* 5 (1): 77–96.

Clemencia Ramírez, María. 2010. Maintaining Democracy in Colombia through Political Exclusion, States of Exception, Counterinsurgency, and Dirty War. In *Violent Democracies in Latin America*, eds. Enrique Desmond Arias and Daniel M. Goldstein, 84–107. Durham: Duke University Press.

Cole, Wade, and Francisco Ramirez. 2013. Conditional Decoupling Assessing the Impact of National Human Rights Institutions, 1981 to 2004. *American Sociological Review* 78 (4): 702–725.

Comisión de la Verdad. 2022. *Hay futuro si hay verdad: Informe final de la Comisión para el Esclarecimiento de la Verdad, la Convivencia y la No Repetición*. Bogotá: Comisión de la Verdad.

Contesse, Jorge. 2019. Resisting the Inter-American Human Rights System. *Yale Journal of International Law* 44 (2): 179–238.

Coppedge, Michael, John Gerring, Carl Henrik Knutsen, Staffan I. Lindberg, Jan Teorell, David Altman, Fabio Angiolillo, Michael Bernhard, Agnes Cornell, M. Steven Fish, Linnea Fox, Lisa Gastaldi, Haakon Gjerløw, Adam Glynn, Ana Good God, Sandra Grahn, Allen Hicken, Katrin Kinzelbach, Kyle L. Marquardt, Kelly McMann, Valeriya Mechkova, Anja Neundorf, Pamela Paxton, Daniel Pemstein, Johannes von Römer, Brigitte Seim, Rachel Sigman, Svend-Erik Skaaning, Jeffrey Staton, Aksel Sundström, Marcus Tannenberg, Eitan Tzelgov, Yi-ting Wang, Felix Wiebrecht, Tore Wig, and Daniel Ziblatt. 2025. "V-Dem Codebook v15" Varieties of Democracy (V-Dem) Project.

Córdova Macías, Ricardo. 2001. Demilitarizing and Democratizing Salvadoran Politics. In *El Salvador: Implementation of the Peace Accords*, ed. Margarita S. Studemeister. Washington, DC: United States Institute of Peace.

Corkill, David. 1985. Democratic Politics in Ecuador, 1979–1984. *Bulletin of Latin American Research* 4 (2): 63–74.

Corrales, Javier. 2013. Constitutional Rewrites in Latin America, 1987–2009. In *Constructing Democratic Governance in Latin America*, eds. Jorge I. Domínguez and Michael Shifter, 4th ed., 13–47. Baltimore: Johns Hopkins University Press.

Corrales, Javier, and Will Freeman. 2024. How Organized Crime Threatens Latin America. *Journal of Democracy* 35 (4): 149–161.

Correal, Annie. 2024. Ecuador's Attorney General Took on Drug Gangs. Then Chaos Broke Out. *New York Times*. January 13. https://www.nytimes.com/2024/01/13/world/americas/ecuador-drug-gangs-unrest.html.

Correal, Annie, and Genevieve Glatsky. 2024. Ecuadoreans Split on President's Drastic New Measure to Combat Drug Gangs. *New York Times*.

January 10. https://www.nytimes.com/2024/01/10/world/americas/ecu ador-violence-gangs-prison.html.

Couso, Javier. 2005. The Judicialization of Chilean Politics: The Rights Revolution that Never Was. In *The Judicialization of Politics in Latin America*, eds. Rachel Sieder, Line Schjolden, and Alan Angell, 105–129. New York: Palgrave Macmillan.

Cruz, José Miguel. 2011. Criminal Violence and Democratization in Central America: The Survival of the Violent State. *Latin American Politics and Society* 53 (4): 1–33.

Cruz, José Miguel. 2016. State and Criminal Violence in Latin America. *Crime, Law and Social Change* 66 (4): 375–396.

Cutrona, Sebastián A., and Jonathan D. Rosen. 2023. Introduction. In Mano Dura *Policies in Latin America*, eds. Jonathan D. Rosen and Sebastián A. Cutrona, 1–14. New York: Routledge.

Dahl, Robert. 2015. *On Democracy*, 2nd ed. New Haven: Yale University Press.

Dammert, Lucía. 2007. *Report on the Security Sector in Latin America and the Caribbean*. Santiago: Facultad Latinoamericana de Ciencias Sociales (FLACSO-Chile).

Dammert, Lucía. 2012. *Fear and Crime in Latin America: Redefining State-Society Relations*. New York: Routledge.

Dancy, Geoff, and Oskar Timo Thoms. 2022. Do Truth Commissions Really Improve Democracy? *Comparative Political Studies* 55 (4): 555–587.

Dancy, Geoff, Bridget E. Marchesi, Tricia D. Olsen, Leigh A. Payne, Andrew G. Reiter, and Kathryn Sikkink. 2019. Behind Bars and Bargains: New Findings on Transitional Justice in Emerging Democracies. *International Studies Quarterly* 63 (1): 99–110.

Darby, John. 2016. Political Violence: An Overview. In *The Ashgate Research Companion to Political Violence*, ed. Marie Breen-Smyth, 42–59. London: Routledge.

Davenport, Christian. 2007. *State Repression and the Domestic Democratic Peace*. Cambridge: Cambridge University Press.

Defensoría del Pueblo. 2025. Reporte de conflictos sociales, N. 255. May. https://www.defensoria.gob.pe/wp-content/uploads/2025/06/Reporte-de-conflictos-sociales-n.%C2%BA-255-%E2%80%93-mayo-2025.pdf.

De la Torre, Carlos. 2013. Technocratic Populism in Ecuador. *Journal of Democracy* 24 (3): 33–46.

Dodson, Michael. 2006. The Human Rights Ombudsman in Central America: Honduras and El Salvador Case Studies. *Essex Human Rights Review* 3 (1): 29–45.

Dodson, Michael, and Donald Jackson. 2004. Horizontal Accountability in Transitional Democracies: The Human Rights Ombudsman in El Salvador and Guatemala. *Latin American Politics and Society* 46 (4): 1–27.

Driscoll, Amanda, and Michael J. Nelson. 2012. The 2011 Judicial Elections in Bolivia. *Electoral Studies* 31 (3): 628–632.

Duce, Mauricio, and Rogelio Pérez Perdomo. 2003. Citizen Security and Reform of the Criminal Justice System in Latin America. In *Crime and Violence in Latin America: Citizen Security, Democracy, and the State*, eds. Hugo Frühling, Joseph S. Tulchin, and Heather A. Golding, 69–91. Washington, DC: Wilson Center.

Eisentstadt, Todd A., A. Carl LeVan, and Tofigh Maboudi. 2015. When Talk Trumps Text: The Democratizing Effects of Deliberation during Constitution-Making, 1974–2011. *American Political Science Review* 109 (3): 592–612.

Eisentstadt, Todd A., A. Carl LeVan, and Tofigh Maboudi. 2017. *Constituents before Assembly: Participation, Deliberation, and Representation in the Crafting of New Constitutions*. New York: Cambridge University Press.

Elkins, Zachary, Tom Ginsburg, and James Melton. 2009. *The Endurance of National Constitutions*. New York: Cambridge University Press.

Engstrom, Par, and Gabriel Pereira. 2012. From Amnesty to Accountability: The Ebb and Flow in the Search for Justice in Argentina. In *Amnesty in the Age of Human Rights Accountability: Comparative and International Perspectives*, eds. Francesca Lessa and Leigh A. Payne, 97–122. New York: Cambridge University Press.

Fein, Helen. 1995. More Murder in the Middle: Life-Integrity Violations and Democracy in the World, 1987. *Human Rights Quarterly* 17 (1): 170–191.

Finkel, Jodi. 2012. Explaining the Failure of Mexico's National Commission of Human Rights (Ombudsman's Office) After Democratization: Elections, Incentives, and Unaccountability in the Mexican Senate. *Human Rights Review* 13 (4): 473–495.

Fortete, Cesar, and Jose Daniel Cesano. 2009. Punitive Attitudes in Latin America. *European Journal on Criminal Policy and Research* 15 (1–2): 121–136.

Fox, Donald T., Gustavo Gallón-Giraldo, and Anne Stetson. 2010. Lessons of the Colombian Constitutional Reform of 1991: Toward the Securing of Peace and Reconciliation? In *Framing the State in Times of Transition: Case Studies in Constitution Making*, ed. Laurel E. Miller, 467–482. Washington, DC: United States Institute of Peace.

Fox, Sean, and Kristian Hoelscher. 2012. Political Order, Development and Social Violence. *Journal of Peace Research* 49 (3): 431–444.

Fuentes, Claudio. 2015. Shifting the Status Quo: Constitutional Reforms in Chile. *Latin American Politics and Society* 57 (1): 99–122.

Galtung, Johan. 1969. Violence, Peace, and Peace Research. *Journal of Peace Research* 6 (3): 167–191.

Gibney, Mark, Peter Haschke, Daniel Arnon, Attilio Pisanò, Gray Barrett, Baekkwan Park, and Jennifer Barnes. 2024. The Political Terror Scale 1976–2023. https://www.politicalterrorscale.org/.

Gill, Lesley. 2004. *The School of the Americas: Military Training and Political Violence in the Americas*. Durham: Duke University Press.

González-Ocantos, Ezequiel. 2016. *Shifting Legal Visions. Judicial Change and Human Rights Trials in Latin America*. New York: Cambridge University Press.

González-Ocantos, Ezequiel. 2019. Courts in Latin American Politics. In *The Oxford Encyclopedia of Latin American Politics*, eds. Harry E. Vanden and Gary Prevost. Oxford: Oxford University Press. https://oxfordre.com/pol itics/display/10.1093/acrefore/9780190228637.001.0001/acrefore-978 0190228637-e-1680.

González Volio, Lorena. 2003. The Institution of the Ombudsman. The Latin American experience. *Revista Institute Interamericano de Derechos Humanos* 37: 219–248.

González, Yanilda María. 2017. 'What Citizens Can See of the State': Police and the Construction of Democratic Citizenship in Latin America. *Theoretical Criminology* 21 (4): 494–511.

González, Yanilda María. 2020. *Authoritarian Police in Democracy: Contested Security in Latin America*. Cambridge: Cambridge University Press.

Green, W. John. 2015. *A History of Political Murder in Latin America: Killing the Messengers of Change*. Albany: State University of New York Press.

Grupo de Memoria Histórica. 2016. *Basta Ya! Colombia: Memories of War and Dignity*. Bogotá: National Center for Historical Memory.

Hafner-Burton, Emilie M. 2008. Sticks and Stones: Naming and Shaming the Human Rights Enforcement Problem. *International Organization* 62 (4): 689–716.

Hagopian, Frances. 2007. Latin American Citizenship and Democratic Theory. In *Citizenship in Latin America*, eds. Joseph S. Tulchin and Meg Ruthenburg, 11–56. Boulder: Lynne Rienner Publishers.

Hammergren, Linn. 2002. Do Judicial Councils Further Judicial Reform? Lessons from Latin America. Carnegie Endowment for International Peace, Working Paper. https://carnegieendowment.org/research/2002/06/do-jud icial-councils-further-judicial-reform-lessons-from-latin-america?lang=en.

Hammergren, Linn. 2007. *Envisioning Reform: Conceptual and Practical Obstacles to Improving Judicial Performance in Latin America*. University Park: Pennsylvania State University Press.

Hayner, Priscilla B. 2010. *Unspeakable Truths: Transitional Justice and the Challenge of Truth Commissions*, 2nd ed. New York: Routledge.

Helmke, Gretchen. 2002. The Logic of Strategic Defection: Court-Executive Relations in Argentina under Dictatorship and Democracy. *American Political Science Review* 96 (2): 291–303.

Helmke, Gretchen, and Julio Ríos-Figueroa, eds. 2011. *Courts in Latin America*. New York: Cambridge University Press.

Hilbink, Lisa. 2007. *Judges Beyond Politics in Democracy and Dictatorship: Lessons from Chile*. Cambridge: Cambridge University Press.

Hudson, Rex, and Dennis Hanratty, eds. 1991. *Bolivia: A Country Study*. Washington, DC: Library of Congress.

Huggins, Martha K. 1998. *Political Policing: The United States and Latin America*. Durham: Duke University Press.

Human Rights Watch. 2024. Letter to President Noboa on 'Internal Armed Conflict' and Human Rights Violations in Ecuador. May 22. https://www.hrw.org/news/2024/05/22/letter-president-noboa-internal-armed-conflict-and-human-rights-violations-ecuador.

Huneeus, Alexandra. 2017. The Institutional Limits of Inter-American Constitutionalism. In *Comparative Constitutional Law in Latin America*, eds. Rosalind Dixon and Tom Ginsburg, 300–324. Northampton, MA: Edward Elgar.

Hunter, Wendy. 1997. *Eroding Military Influence in Brazil: Politicians Against Soldiers*. Chapel Hill: University of North Carolina Press.

Huntington, Samuel P. 1989. The Modest Meaning of Democracy. In *Democracy in the Americas: Stopping the Pendulum*, ed. Robert A. Pastor, 11–28. New York: Holmes and Meier.

Huntington, Samuel P. 1991. *The Third Wave: Democratization in the Late Twentieth Century*. Norman: University of Oklahoma Press.

Imbusch, Peter. 2003. The Concept of Violence. In *International Handbook of Violence Research*, eds. Wilhelm Heitmeyer and John Hagan, 13–40. Dordrecht, Netherlands: Kluwer Academic Publishers.

Infobae. 2024. Represión policial deja varios heridos en las comunidades Huancuire y Pumamarca por conflicto de tierra y agua. June 1. https://www.infobae.com/peru/2024/06/01/represion-policial-deja-varios-heridos-en-las-comunidades-huancuire-y-pumamarca-por-conflicto-de-tierra-y-agua/.

Isaacs, Anita. 1991. Problems of Democratic Consolidation in Ecuador. *Bulletin of Latin American Research* 10 (2): 221–238.

Iturralde, Manuel. 2010. Democracies without Citizenship: Crime and Punishment in Latin America. *New Criminal Law Review* 13 (2): 309–332.

Kim, Hun Joon, and Kathryn Sikkink. 2010. Explaining the Deterrence Effect of Human Rights Prosecutions. *International Studies Quarterly* 54 (4): 939–963.

Kruijt, Dirk, and Kees Koonings. 1999. Introduction: Violence and Fear in Latin America. In *Societies of Fear: The Legacy of Civil War, Violence and Terror in*

Latin America, eds. Kees Koonings and Dirk Kruijt, 1–30. New York: St. Martin's.

Kruijt, Dirk, Carlos Sojo, and Rebeca Grynspan. 2002. *Informal Citizens: Poverty, Informality and Social Exclusion in Latin America*. Amsterdam, Netherlands: Rozenberg Publishers.

Kyle, Brett J., and Andrew G. Reiter. 2019. A New Dawn for Latin America's Militaries. *NACLA Report on the Americas* 51 (1): 18–28.

Kyle, Brett J., and Andrew G. Reiter. 2021. *Military Courts, Civil-Military Relations, and the Legal Battle for Democracy: The Politics of Military Justice*. New York: Routledge.

Latin American Security & Strategic Review. 2023. Venezuela: Tensions Rise Between Authorities and Illegal Miners. October.

Latin American Security & Strategic Review. 2024. Venezuela: Disaster Renews Focus on Illegal Mining. April.

Latin American Weekly Report. 2024. Brazil: Rio Police Launch More Raids in Favelas. February 29.

LatinNews Daily. 2024. Ecuador: 'Internal Armed Conflict' Declared Amid Security Meltdown. January 10.

Le Clerq, Juan Antonio, Azucena Cháidez, Gerardo Rodríguez. 2016. Midiendo la impunidad en América Latina: retos conceptuales y metodológicos. *Iconos: Revista de Ciencias Sociales* 20 (55): 69–91.

Levitsky, Steven. 2005. Argentina: Democratic Survival amidst Economic Failure. In *The Third Wave of Democratization in Latin America*, eds. Frances Hagopian and Scott P. Mainwaring, 63–89. Cambridge: Cambridge University Press.

Linz, Juan J., and Alfred Stepan. 1996. Toward Consolidated Democracies. *Journal of Democracy* 7 (2): 14–33.

Lopez, George A. 1986. National Security Ideology as an Impetus to State Violence and State Terror. In *Government Violence and Repression: An Agenda for Research*, eds. Michael Stohl and George A. Lopez, 73–95. New York: Greenwood.

Loveman, Brian. 1993. *The Constitution of Tyranny: Regimes of Exception in Spanish America*. Pittsburgh: University of Pittsburgh Press.

Loveman, Brian. 1999. *For la Patria: Politics and the Armed Forces in Latin America*. Wilmington, DE: Scholarly Resources.

Loveman, Brian, and Thomas M. Davies, Jr. 1997. The Politics of Antipolitics. In *The Politics of Antipolitics: The Military in Latin America*, eds. Brian Loveman and Thomas M. Davies, Jr, 3–28. Wilmington, DE: Scholarly Resources Inc.

Mackenbach, Werner, and Günther Maihold, eds. 2015. *La Transformación de la Violencia en América Latina*. Colonia, Guatemala: F&G Editores.

Malloy, James M. 1977. Authoritarianism and Corporatism in Latin America: The Modal Pattern. In *Authoritarianism and Corporatism in Latin America*, ed. James M. Malloy, 3–19. Pittsburgh: University of Pittsburgh Press.

Malone, Mary Fran T. 2023. Raising an Iron Fist: The Militarization of Public Security Policies in Latin America. In Mano Dura *Policies in Latin America*, eds. Jonathan D. Rosen and Sebastián A. Cutrona, 15–28. New York: Routledge.

Malone, Mary Fran T., Lucía Dammert, and Orlando J. Pérez. 2023. *Making Police Reform Matter in Latin America*. Boulder: Lynne Rienner.

Marcella, Gabriel, Orlando J. Pérez, and Brian Fonseca. 2022. Introduction. In *Democracy and Security in Latin America: State Capacity and Governance under Stress*, eds. Gabriel Marcella, Orlando J. Pérez, and Brian Fonseca, 1–5. New York: Routledge.

Martín-Barbero, Jesús. 2002. The City: Between Fear and the Media. In *Citizens of Fear: Urban Violence in Latin America*, ed. Susana Rotker, 7–22. New Brunswick, NJ: Rutgers University Press.

Martínez, Rafael. 2013. Objectives for Democratic Consolidation in the Armed Forces. In *Debating Civil-Military Relations in Latin America*, eds. Rafael Martínez and David R. Mares, 43–95. Liverpool, United Kingdom: Liverpool University Press.

Mazzuca, Sebastián L., and Gerardo L. Munck. 2020. *A Middle-Quality Institutional Trap: Democracy and State Capacity in Latin America*. Cambridge: Cambridge University Press.

McSherry, J. Patrice. 2010. 'Industrial Repression' and Operation Condor in Latin America. In *State Violence and Genocide in Latin America: The Cold War Years*, eds. Marcia Esparza, Henry R. Huttenbach, and Daniel Feierstein, 107–123. New York: Routledge.

Middlebrook, Kevin J. 1995. *The Paradox of Revolution: Labor, the State, and Authoritarianism in Mexico*. Baltimore: The Johns Hopkins University Press.

Mitchell, Christopher, Michael Stohl, David Carleton, and George A. Lopez. 1986. State Terrorism: Issues of Concept and Measurement. In *Government Violence and Repression: An Agenda for Research*, eds. Michael Stohl and George A. Lopez, 1–25. New York: Greenwood.

Moreno, Erika. 2016a. The Contributions of the Ombudsman to Human Rights in Latin America, 1982–2011. *Latin American Politics and Society* 58 (1): 98–120.

Moreno, Erika. 2016b. Improving the Democratic Brand Through Institution Building: Ombudsmen and Corruption in Latin America, 2000–2011. *Latin American Policy* 7 (1): 126–146.

Moreno, Erika, and Richard Witmer. 2016. The Power of the Pen: Human Rights Ombudsmen and Personal Integrity Violations in Latin America, 1982–2006. *Human Rights Review* 17 (2): 143–164.

Müller, Markus-Michael. 2018. Governing Crime and Violence in Latin America. *Global Crime* 19 (3–4): 171–191.

Muñoz, César, and Juan Pappier, 2020. Human Rights Watch: Latin America, It's Time to End Police Abuse. November 18. https://www.hrw.org/news/2020/11/18/latin-america-its-time-end-police-abuse.

Negretto, Gabriel. 2018. Constitution-Building Processes in Latin America. International IDEA Discussion Paper 3/2018. https://www.idea.int/sites/default/files/publications/constitution-building-processes-in-latin-america.pdf.

Nino, Carlos S. 1991. The Duty to Punish Past Abuses of Human Rights Put into Context. *Yale Law Journal* 100 (8): 2619–2640.

Nivette, Amy E. 2016. Institutional Ineffectiveness, Illegitimacy, and Public Support for Vigilantism in Latin America. *Criminology* 54 (1): 142–175.

Nord, Marina, Martin Lundstedt, David Altman, Fabio Angiolillo, Cecilia Borella, Tiago Fernandes, Lisa Gastaldi, Ana Good God, Natalia Natsika, and Steffan I. Lindberg. 2024. *Democracy Report 2024: Democracy Winning and Losing at the Ballot.* Gothenburg, Sweden: University of Gothenburg, V-Dem Institute.

Norden, Deborah L. 1996. *Military Rebellion in Argentina: Between Coups and Consolidation.* Lincoln: University of Nebraska Press.

O'Donnell, Guillermo. 1979. *Modernization and Bureaucratic-Authoritarianism.* Berkeley: University of California Press.

O'Donnell, Guillermo. 1993. On the State, Democratization and Some Conceptual Problems: A Latin American View with Glances at Some Postcommunist Countries. *World Development* 21 (8): 1355–1369.

O'Donnell, Guillermo. 2004. Why the Rule of Law Matters. *Journal of Democracy* 15 (4): 32–46.

O'Donnell, Guillermo. 2007. *Dissonances: Democratic Critiques of Democracy.* South Bend, IN: University of Notre Dame Press.

Office of the United Nations High Commissioner for Human Rights. 2010. National Human Rights Institutions: History, Principles, Roles and Responsibilities. http://www.ohchr.org/Documents/Publications/PTS-4Rev1-NHRI_en.pdf.

Olsen, Tricia D., Leigh A. Payne, and Andrew G. Reiter. 2010. *Transitional Justice in Balance: Comparing Processes, Weighing Efficacy.* Washington, DC: United States Institute of Peace.

Pearce, Jenny. 2010. Perverse State Formation and Securitized Democracy in Latin America. *Democratization* 17 (2): 286–306.

Pensado, Jaime M. 2013. *Rebel Mexico: Student Unrest and Authoritarian Political Culture During the Long Sixties.* Stanford: Stanford University Press.

Pereira, Anthony W. 2005. *Political (In)Justice: Authoritarianism and the Rule of Law in Brazil, Chile, and Argentina*. Pittsburgh: University of Pittsburgh Press.

Pérez-Liñán, Aníbal. 2007. *Presidential Impeachment and the New Political Instability in Latin America*. Cambridge: Cambridge University Press.

Przeworski, Adam. 1991. *Democracy and the Market: Political and Economic Reforms in Eastern Europe and Latin America*. Cambridge: Cambridge University Press.

Reif, Linda C. 2004. *The Ombudsman, Good Governance and the International Human Rights System*. Leiden, The Netherlands: Springer Dordrecht.

Ríos-Figueroa, Julio. 2011. Institutions for Constitutional Justice in Latin America. In *Courts in Latin America*, eds. Gretchen Helmke and Julio Ríos-Figueroa, 27–54. New York: Cambridge University Press.

Ríos-Figueroa, Julio. 2016. *Constitutional Courts as Mediators: Armed Conflict, Civil-Military Relations, and the Rule of Law in Latin America*. Cambridge: Cambridge University Press.

Ritter, Emily. 2014. Policy Disputes, Political Survival, and the Onset and Severity of Repression. *Journal of Conflict Resolution* 58 (1): 143–168.

Rivera, Mauricio. 2016. The Sources of Social Violence in Latin America: An Empirical Analysis of Homicide Rates, 1980–2010. *Journal of Peace Research* 53 (1): 84–99.

Rock, David. 1987. *Argentina 1516–1987: From Spanish Colonization to Alfonsín*. Berkeley: University of California Press.

Rodrigues, Thiago, and Erika Rodríguez-Pinzón. 2020. 'Mano Dura' y Democracia en América Latina: Seguridad Pública, Violencia y Estado de Derecho. *América Latina Hoy* 84: 89–113.

Rodycz, Wilson Carlos. 2001. El juzgado especial y de pequeñas causas en la solución del problema del acceso a la justicia en el Brasil. Paper prepared for World Bank Conference, 'New Approaches to Meeting the Demand for Justice,' Mexico City, May 11, https://biblioteca.cejamericas.org/bitstream/handle/2015/1067/rodycz-juzgado-especial.pdf.

Rosenn, Keith S. 1990. Brazil's New Constitution: An Exercise in Transient Constitutionalism for a Transitional Society. *American Journal of Comparative Law* 38 (4): 773–802.

Rouquié, Alain. 1982. *The Military and the State in Latin America* [Translated by Paul E. Sigmund]. Berkeley: University of California Press.

Samuels, Kirsti. 2006. Post-Conflict Peace-Building and Constitution-Making. *Chicago Journal of International Law* 6 (2): 663–682.

Sánchez-Cuenca, Ignacio. 2003. Power, Rules, and Compliance. In *Democracy and the Rule of Law*, eds. José María Maravall and Adam Przeworski, 62–92. New York: Cambridge University Press.

Sandoval, Javier Pérez, and Daniel Barker Flores. 2023. The Persistence of Latin America's Violent Democracies: Reviewing the Research Agenda on Policing, Militarization, and Security Across the Region. *Alternatives: Global, Local, Political* 48 (3): 1–9.

Schmitter, Philippe C., and Terry Lynn Karl. 1991. What Democracy Is...and Is Not. *Journal of Democracy* 2 (3): 75–88.

Seligson, Mitchell, and Vincent McElhinny. 1996. Low-Intensity Warfare, High-Intensity Death: The Demographic Impact of the Wars in El Salvador and Nicaragua. *Canadian Journal of Latin American and Caribbean Studies* 21 (42): 211–241.

SERVINDI. 2024. Represión a conflictos en Las Bambas deja heridos. May 31. https://www.servindi.org/actualidad-noticias/31/05/2024/repres ion-conflictos-en-las-bambas-deja-heridos.

Sikkink, Kathryn. 2011. *The Justice Cascade: How Human Rights Prosecutions Are Changing World Politics.* New York: W.W. Norton.

Sikkink, Kathryn, and Carrie Booth Walling. 2006. Argentina's Contribution to Global Trends in Transitional Justice. In *Transitional Justice in the Twenty-First Century: Beyond Truth and Justice*, eds. Naomi Roht-Arriaza and Javier Mariezcurrena, 301–324. New York: Cambridge University Press.

Skladowska, Joanna. 2016. The Institution of Ombudsman in Latin America as a Guarantee for Propagation of Culture of Peace and Respect for Cultural Diversity, as Exemplified by Selected Countries. *Ad Americam: Journal of American Studies* 17: 61–78.

Snyder, Jack, and Leslie Vinjamuri. 2003. Trials and Errors: Principle and Pragmatism in Strategies of International Justice. *International Security* 28 (3): 5–44.

Soltman, Daniel. 2013. Applauding Uruguay's Quest for Justice: Dictatorship, Amnesty, and Repeal of Uruguay Law No. 15.848. *Washington University Global Studies Law Review* 12 (4): 829–848.

Sozzo, Máximo. 2016. Policing after Dictatorship in South America. In *The Sage Handbook of Global Policing*, eds. Ben Bradford, Beatrice Jauregui, Ian Loader, and Jonny Steinberg. London: Sage. https://doi.org/10.4135/978 1473957923.n20.

Staats, Joseph L., Shaun Bowler, and Jonathan T. Hiskey. 2005. Measuring Judicial Performance in Latin America. *Latin American Politics and Society* 47 (4): 77–106.

Succi Junior, David P. 2022. Violence and Moral Exclusion: Legitimizing Domestic Military Operations in Brazil. *Armed Forces and Society* 48 (3): 634–656.

Taylor, Ariel, and Michelle D. Bonner. 2017. Policing Economic Growth. *Latin American Research Review* 52 (1): 3–17.

Tilly, Charles. 2003. *The Politics of Collective Violence*. Cambridge: Cambridge University Press.

Trejo, Guillermo, Juan Albarracín, and Lucía Tiscornia. 2018. Breaking State Impunity in Post-Authoritarian Regimes: Why Transitional Justice Processes Deter Criminal Violence in New Democracies. *Journal of Peace Research* 55 (6): 787–809.

Uggla, Fredrik. 2004. The Ombudsman in Latin America. *Journal of Latin American Studies* 36 (3): 423–450.

Uggla, Fredrik. 2011. Through Pressure or Persuasion? Explaining Compliance with the Resolutions of the Bolivian Defensor del Pueblo. In *Human Rights, State Compliance, and Social Change: Assessing National Human Rights Institutions*, eds. Ryan Goodman and Thomas Pegram, 270–294. New York: Cambridge University Press.

United Nations Office on Drugs and Crime. 2024. United Nations Crime Trends Survey. https://dataunodc.un.org/dp-intentional-homicide-victims-est.

Vargas Vivancos, Juan Enrique. 2009. Las cortes supremas y la reforma judicial en Latinoamérica. *Reforma Judicial: Revista Mexicana de Justicia* 13: 271–300.

Waldmann, Peter. 2006. *El Estado Anómico: Derecho, Seguridad Pública y Vida Cotidiana en América Latina*. Madrid: Iberoamericana Vervuert.

Weber, Max. 2004 [1919]. Politics as a Vocation. In *The Vocation Lectures*, eds. David Owen and Tracy B. Strong, 32–94. Indianapolis: Hackett.

Weber, Leanne. 2013. *Policing Non-Citizens*. London: Routledge.

Wiarda, Howard J. 1981. *Corporatism and National Development in Latin America*. Boulder: Westview Press.

Widner, Jennifer. 2005. Constitution Writing and Conflict Resolution. United Nations University, World Institute for Development Economics Research, Research Paper No. 2005.51. https://www.wider.unu.edu/sites/default/files/rp2005-51.pdf.

Wilson, Bruce M. 2005. Changing Dynamics: The Political Impact of Costa Rica's Constitutional Court. In *The Judicialization of Politics in Latin America*, eds. Rachel Sieder, Line Schjolden, and Alan Angell, 47–65. New York: Palgrave Macmillan.

Young, Iris Marion. 2000. *Inclusion and Democracy*. New York: Oxford University Press.

Zamudio, Hector Fix. 1979. A Brief Introduction to the Mexican Writ of Amparo. *California Western International Law Journal* 9 (2): 306–348.

CHAPTER 2

The Evolution of State Security Forces in Latin America: From Caudillos to Cold Warriors

INTRODUCTION

State violence, in general, and state violence in Latin America, in particular, is not new. For over 200 years state actors and others associated with the state have perpetrated violence against civilians. Yet which actors engage in violence and the type of violence they perpetrate have changed considerably over time. In this chapter, we provide a comprehensive overview of the evolution of state security forces in the region, from independence until the end of the Cold War.[1] In doing so, we show the dramatic evolution of these forces from informal militia with little training to a vast network of professional agencies with defined spheres of responsibility. We also highlight the role that the United States has played in shaping national security institutions and their doctrines. We begin this chapter by examining the state security forces that developed in the decades following independence in a period dominated by caudillo politics. We then discuss the gradual professionalization that took place in the late 1800s and early 1900s as part of a broader process of national consolidation and centralization. External wars and rivalries drove the evolution of state security forces during this period. The United States then played an integral role in shaping state security forces beginning in the early 1900s in Central America and the Caribbean and then after World War II in the rest of the region. During the Cold War, most countries in the

© The Author(s), under exclusive license to Springer Nature Switzerland AG 2025
B. J. Kyle et al., *State Violence and Democracy in Latin America*, Rethinking Political Violence, https://doi.org/10.1007/978-3-032-06412-7_2

45

region were under authoritarian rule, and the United States facilitated the expansion of their state security forces, spurred the creation of specialized agencies, and shifted the overall focus of state violence toward combatting domestic threats.

INDEPENDENCE AND STATE FORMATION: STARTING FROM SCRATCH (1820S–70S)

As Latin America emerged from colonial rule, leaders faced the challenge of creating new state institutions, including those necessary to maintain internal and external security. The armies that secured independence were small and mostly disbanded shortly after accomplishing their goal. The short-lived Gran Colombia and Federal Republic of Central America collapsed in part because the central governments were unable to develop effective federal agencies, including security forces. Newly sovereign states in the region gradually established formal land armies, which were the only security forces operating domestically at the time.[2] Table 2.1 shows the year in which each country established a functional, standing army, based on our analysis of primary and secondary sources. Many armies make claim to earlier founding dates, but they often were not operational. In Honduras, for example, the military in the mid-to-late 1800s mainly existed on paper, as "militia lists compiled in each department from which names could theoretically be drawn in times of emergency" (Ropp 1974, 506).

Once established, the national armies were functional, but miniscule. Immediately after independence in 1821, for example, the Costa Rican military numbered just 135 professional soldiers (Booth 2022). Colombia's first constitution in 1832 limited the military to 2,300 men, and the many wars during the next 50 years were fought by "amateur officer-politicians" from the opposing Conservative and Liberal parties who assembled their own militias (Osterling 1989, 47; Ruhl 1980, 18).[3] Until the 1901 constitution, the federal government in Venezuela was prohibited from maintaining a standing army; state militias controlled by local leaders provided security (Krzywicka 2012, 250). In Brazil, state-level militias were the most significant armed forces, which governors used for internal security and to assert their power at the national level (Keith 1976, 58–59).[4] Meanwhile, the National Guard was an informal militia whose ranks elected their own officers until 1850 (Skidmore 1999, 56).

Table 2.1 Founding dates of national armies

Country	Army and Founding Date
Argentina	Argentine Army (1810)
Bolivia	Bolivian Army (1825)
Brazil	Imperial Brazilian Army (1822)
Chile	National Army of Chile (1818)
Colombia	Army of New Grenada (1832)
Costa Rica	Public Force (1826)
Dominican Republic	Army of the Dominican Republic (1844)
Ecuador	Ecuadorian Army (1830)
El Salvador	Salvadoran Army (1841)
Guatemala	Guatemalan Army (1851)
Honduras	Army of Honduras (1838)
Mexico	Mexican Imperial Army (1821)
Nicaragua	National Army (1895)
Panama	National Army (1903)
Paraguay	Paraguayan Army (1811)
Peru	Peruvian Guard Legion (1821)
Uruguay	National Army (1828)
Venezuela	National Army (1901)

Politicians and landowners raised temporary militias to respond to crises in the region during this era, which was dominated by caudillos—local or regional leaders who mobilized armed followers through "personalism and charisma" (Loveman and Davies 1997, 18). In the Dominican Republic, various caudillos raised armies in its wars of independence from Haiti (1844–56) and Spain (1863–65) as well as in its civil wars after independence. They were unorganized, temporary forces and their "ranks were mutinous, desertions were high, and social class distinctions were evident" (Peguero 2004, 18). There were still "up to a thousand local leaders calling themselves 'generals' in 1880" (Roorda 1998, 12). In Argentina, it was not until 1869 that the government began to create a professional army to replace the "improvised gaucho militias of provincial caudillos" that had fought each other continuously since independence (Goldwert 1968, 190).

The urban–rural divide was also stark. Caudillo presidents "still thought in regional terms, often seeking to dominate only the capital city" (Loveman and Davies 1997, 18). For example, in Guatemala in the 1840s–60s, José Rafael Carrera mainly controlled the capital while his appointed military chieftains controlled the countryside (Woodward 1993, 253). Similarly, the military in Uruguay only controlled the capital until the 1870s, with local caudillos and their peasant armies governing the rest of the country (Altman and Jenne 2020).

The development of state security forces was also hindered by frequent changes in rulers. While El Salvador created a national army in 1841, the presidency changed hands 42 times between 1841 and 1861, as rival patronage networks fought for control. The army was highly politicized with presidents rewarding their supporters with military commands (Holden 2004, 58). Between 1821 and 1845, Peru endured 53 governments, as different factions of creole elites vied for power. It was not until Ramón Castilla came to power in 1845 that a centralized state apparatus was created, including an effective national army (Kurtz 2013, 74). Bolivia was the most extreme case, experiencing 179 coups from independence in 1825 until the national revolution in 1952 (Corbett 1972, 400). It was more of a case of "the judiciary and legislature lending ephemeral...legitimacy to the passage of victors" (Dunkerly 1981, 15).

Nicaragua best epitomizes the instability of security forces in the region during this period. It was in a constant state of internal conflict from the time it broke away from Spain until the 1860s, with a central government that barely functioned and no centralized security forces. So weak was the government that American mercenary William Walker was able to create an alliance with three local caudillos and their men to capture the state in 1856 (Holden 2004, 80–81).

With the exceptions of Chile and Paraguay, which created more professional, permanent security forces of modest size much earlier, most of the region's forces did not even have limited control over the entire country; there was little professionalization.[5] Jobs in the security sector were typically doled out as a form of patronage and few people made it a career. Training was almost nonexistent. It took decades, or a century in some cases, for the new states to establish professional security forces. Those that did exist owed their allegiance primarily to individual elites for whom they would fight in violent intra-elite conflict over control of the state.

Expansion, Centralization, and Professionalization (1870s–1930s)

Starting in the late 1800s, Latin America went through a period of state consolidation. National governments became stronger and more stable in many countries, and they gradually reduced the influence of regional elites in the domain of security.[6] This often meant replacing many local caudillos with one that was more centralized, and thus there was little change in political culture and practices. The effect on state security forces, however, was profound.

In the Dominican Republic, Ulises Heureaux, who became president in 1882, established a centralized state with a centralized security apparatus, with the aid of the French and Spanish (Betances 1995, 20). The process started in El Salvador, with help from Chile, under General Tomás Regalado who assumed the presidency in 1899. Over the next two decades, the military became the best trained and equipped in Central America (Holden 2004, 60–61). In Venezuela, General Cipriano Castro, who ruled from 1899 to 1908, created a new constitution in 1901 that removed the restriction on the federal government's ability to maintain a standing army.[7] He took away the power of state militias and made the national government the exclusive authority on military issues (Krzywicka 2012, 250–251).

At times, the modernization of security forces was driven by external security threats.[8] In South America, the War of the Triple Alliance (1865–70) and the War of the Pacific (1879–83) were fought by "rag-tag militia forces, haphazardly assembled in wartime" which, not surprisingly, performed poorly on the battlefield. This prompted states to engage in a large-scale military "emulation" process to modernize their forces along European lines (Resende-Santos 1996, 225). They contracted with France or Germany to help in the process, particularly in training professional officer corps (Nunn 1983).[9]

In Argentina, the modernization process started under the rule of Julio Argentino Roca (1880–86, 1898–1904). Aided by Germany, he created the first military academy in 1900. In 1901, military service became obligatory. By 1910, promotions were no longer doled out by the president based on favoritism, but instead the military controlled them and they were based on merit (Goldwert 1968, 190–191). Bolivia (Corbett 1972,

402) and Uruguay (Altman and Jenne 2020) followed similar trajectories. Chile became so effectively "Prussian-ized" that it began exporting its expertise to others in the region (Resende-Santos 1996, 214). Elsewhere, the Costa Rican military grew in strength following the 1857 Filibuster War when its forces led an alliance of Central American armies to defeat the forces led by American mercenary William Walker in Nicaragua. Leading up to the war, the government had increased the army's "size to 9,000 troops, acquired weapons, and modernized the institution by establishing a military academy headed by Polish and Prussian veteran instructors" (Booth 2022). Costa Rica's victory in the war cemented the military as a political force and it further grew to 15,000 troops by 1874 and was modernized with new weapons and additional foreign training (Booth 2022).

In addition, as Table 2.2 shows, those states that did not already have a national police force created one during this period, and there was increased training and professionalization of these forces across the region as well.[10] While militaries frequently played an active role in internal security, they were no longer the sole state security force.

Table 2.2 Founding dates of national police forces

Country	National Police Force and Founding Date
Argentina	Police of the Capital (1880)
Bolivia	National Police (1886)
Brazil	Federal Department of Public Safety (1944)
Chile	Carabineros (1927)
Colombia	Colombian National Police (1891)
Costa Rica	Order and Security Police (1892)
Dominican Republic	National Police (1936)
Ecuador	National Police (1884)
El Salvador	National Police (1867)
Guatemala	National Police (1881)
Honduras	National Police (1882)
Mexico	Rural Police (1861)
Nicaragua	Sandinista Police (1925)
Panama	Military Police Corps (1904)
Paraguay	Asunción Police Department (1843)
Peru	National Gendarmerie of Peru (1852)
Uruguay	National Police (1829)
Venezuela	National Police Guard (1841)

US Intervention in Central America
and the Caribbean (1890s–1930s)

While most of the states discussed above were heavily influenced by Europeans, at their request, the experience of much of Central America and the Caribbean was dominated by the United States, often without their consent.[11] As we discuss later in this chapter, during the Cold War, US influence led to the growth and strengthening of Latin American security forces. In the first half of the twentieth century, however, it had the opposite effect in many cases. The United States deliberately prevented the emergence of any domestic forces that could potentially challenge its influence.

US President James Monroe famously articulated the Monroe Doctrine in 1823, proclaiming to European powers that the Americas was its own sphere of influence.[12] At the time, however, this was more boastful than practical. This changed following the end of the Spanish-American War in 1898 when the United States gained Cuba and Puerto Rico, among other territories, and emerged as a global power. In 1904, President Theodore Roosevelt expanded the role of the United States toward Latin America in what became known as the Roosevelt Corollary to the Monroe Doctrine. Following efforts by the British, Germans, and Italians to blockade Venezuela's ports due to it defaulting on foreign loans, Roosevelt made clear that the United States would intervene in the *domestic* affairs of Latin American countries if necessary to keep European powers out and maintain internal order and security (Maass 2009). US foreign policy thus became one of the most important factors influencing state violence in Central America and the Caribbean.

The US approach toward Latin America is best illustrated in the case of Panama. During the construction of the Panamanian Railroad in the 1850s, a private force, called the Isthmus Guard, maintained security. Led by former Texas Ranger Randolph Runnels, it was "composed of Americans and supplemented by Mexicans, Chileans, and Peruvians, but not Panamanians" and it "used a variety of terror tactics to impose order" (Harding 2006, 20). With US assistance, Panama gained independence from Colombia in 1903. Shortly after, the United States pressured the government to disband the newly formed national army that had just fought to achieve independence, setting up the Police Force in its stead. It was small, fewer than 1,200 men, and the United States eventually confiscated its rifles to remove any threat to its control (Conniff 2012, 74;

Harding 2006, 38). Until the 1940s, the National Police was primarily "a source of employment for political supporters who could be counted on to apply goon squad tactics at the polling booths when necessary" (Ropp 1972, 48). Once the Panama Canal was built, the United States maintained its own police presence in the Canal Zone, and the 1904 Panamanian constitution gave the United States the right to intervene in the country to restore order whenever it felt it necessary.[13]

The United States also sought to keep the rest of Central America under its control in pursuit of its economic interests. It intervened militarily, for example, multiple times in Honduras in the early 1900s to protect the interests of the United Fruit Company and the Standard Fruit Company, orchestrating regime changes when necessary. In 1923, the General Treaty of Peace and Amity, signed by the Central American countries at the behest of the United States, limited Honduras' military to just 2,500 men. The same treaty restricted Guatemala's to 5,000, El Salvador's to 4,200, and Costa Rica's to 2,000 (Finch 1923). The United States had become the de facto guarantor of Costa Rica's security, intervening several times to protect it, making the maintenance of a large standing army less important. By the late 1940s it had shrunk in size to only about 1,000 troops and shifted its primary focus to suppressing internal dissent (Høivik and Aas 1981, 340–342).

In other cases, the United States supported the growth of state security forces, but it organized, trained, and professionalized them according to its standards, ensuring long-term political influence among its members. The United States began helping the Dominican Republic police its border with Haiti in the early 1900s (Tillman 2021) and occupied the country directly from 1916 to 1924. During this time, it replaced the previous armed forces with the Dominican Constabulary Guard, which was led by US Marines until Dominican officers were sufficiently trained (Betances 1995, 83). The United States also opened the first military academy (Haina Military Academy) and increased training of the National Police (Roorda 1998, 19). Rafael Trujillo was a member of the first class of officers trained by the United States and was promoted to the commander of the National Police when the US left. He later ruled as a dictator from 1930 to 1961, providing the United States with significant influence.

The same pattern played out in Nicaragua. The United States intervened militarily in 1909 and again in 1912, at which point it based a detachment of US Marines there until 1925, helping to establish a

National Guard. When the new force faltered in the 1925–33 civil war, the United States intervened again and reestablished the National Guard. When US troops left in 1933, the National Guard was much stronger, modeled off of the US Marine Corps, and the only legal armed force, combining police and military functions (Grossman 2004). The United States pressured the new government to appoint Anastasio Somoza García as the director of the National Guard. He soon purged the forces of any members who were not loyal to him, took over the country in a coup in 1936, and ruled until his death in 1956, after which his sons ruled the country until 1979, ensuring a strong US ally in the region for four decades.

Overall, the early twentieth century for most of Latin America was a period of growing state capacity and in turn the modernization and professionalization of state security forces. Armies and national police forces were now capable of exerting greater control over their populations. At the same time, this process had drawbacks. Newly professionalized forces adopted a self-conception as defenders of *la patria* ("fatherland") that put them above civilian governments (Fitch 1998). In a period that saw the decline of oligarchic politics and the rise of populism and corporatism in the 1930s–40s (Malloy 1977), military coups became widespread (Loveman 1999, 101). Thus, when the Cold War began after World War II, the region was filled with militaries accustomed to seizing power and dictators already using violence to suppress internal dissent.[14] The geopolitical tensions of the Cold War, combined with heavy US influence across the entire region, led to an era of authoritarian states that suppressed civilian populations with high levels of violence. Moreover, the security forces committing this violence proliferated with the advent of national intelligence agencies, secret police, and specialized counter-insurgency units.

The Cold War: Growth, Specialization, and Institutionalization of State Violence (1950s–80s)

The advent of the Cold War fundamentally changed the nature of state security forces in Latin America. There were three important developments. First, the rise of authoritarian regimes, many of which were controlled directly by the military, led to a significant growth in the size and lethality of state security forces. Second, security forces' proclivity to protect the state from internal threats became more engrained and their commitment to maintaining order deepened. Third, security forces underwent a dramatic process of specialization, with new units and agencies dedicated to defined tasks. The United States played an important role in all three of these developments.

The spread of authoritarian regimes across the region set the stage for the expansion of state security forces. With the exceptions of Colombia, Costa Rica, Mexico, and Venezuela, dictators and military juntas seized and held power throughout Latin America for most of the Cold War, as shown in Table 2.3.[15]

The stronger and more professionalized militaries that developed over the first half of the twentieth century viewed their role as defenders of the nation and seized power when they disagreed with the politics of civilian politicians. The United States was heavily involved in this regional shift. It launched a covert operation to overthrow President Jacobo Árbenz in Guatemala in 1954 and supported coups in Brazil (1964), Bolivia (1971), and Chile (1973).

As militaries rose to political prominence, they increased their budgets, grew in size, gained more advanced weaponry, including airborne and

Table 2.3
Authoritarian rule in Latin America during the Cold War

Country	Years of authoritarian rule
Argentina	1945–56, 1966–72, 1976–82
Bolivia	1936–51, 1964–81
Brazil	1964–84
Chile	1973–88
Colombia	1948–56
Dominican Republic	1844–1977
Ecuador	1945–1947, 1963–66, 1970–78
El Salvador	1945–1959, 1961–83
Guatemala	1954–65, 1974–85
Honduras	1945–79
Mexico	1945–93
Nicaragua	1945–89
Panama	1945–54, 1968–88
Paraguay	1945–88
Peru	1948–55, 1962, 1968–78
Uruguay	1945–51, 1972–84
Venezuela	1945–57

naval assets not previously held in significant numbers (Institute for Strategic Studies 1970, 72–81; Loveman 1999, 182–183; Stockholm International Peace Research Institute 1969, 56–60). There were now dedicated forces for land, sea, and air with high degrees of independence. They also often absorbed the police, shifting them from the Ministry of Interior, or other civilian agencies, to the Ministry of Defense. In Honduras, for example, the military made the police the fourth branch of the armed forces, called the Public Security Force, in 1975. In the Dominican Republic, Trujillo shifted the national police from the ministry of the interior to the military and it became a paramilitary force (Peguero 2004, 167). During military rule in Guatemala, most of the directors and sub-directors of the police were army officials, and even regular police officers often held positions in the National Police while also working for military intelligence (Glebbeek 2001, 434).

The strengthening of security forces was facilitated by US aid. US intervention in the region increased during World War II. In 1942, the United States established the Emergency Advisory Committee for Political Defense—consisting of representatives from Argentina, Brazil, Chile, Mexico, Uruguay, and Venezuela—to target Axis nationals in the region. It provided funds through the Lend-Lease program to several countries and increased troop deployments to Panama to protect the canal. The United States also developed a close relationship with Guatemala during this time and by mid-1942 there were nearly 2,000 US troops stationed there. They took over multiple airfields and obtained rights to ports and transportation lines. Guatemalan military officers began training in large numbers at numerous US military schools and academic institutions (Holden 2004, 135).

As the Cold War began to intensify, the US Congress passed the Mutual Security Act in 1951, which helped to modernize the region's militaries. Funds were available through bilateral mutual defense assistance agreements, which were signed with more than a dozen countries in Latin America over the next decade.[16] The initial focus was on conventional arms for hemispheric defense, but this shifted after the Cuban Revolution. US President John F. Kennedy launched the Alliance for Progress initiative in 1961, which provided economic aid to Latin America to prevent the spread of communism (Taffet 2007). Yet it had a parallel Military Assistance Program focused on equipping and training the region's military forces for internal security (Lieuwen 1967). At the same time, the Office of Public Safety inside the Agency for International

Development provided funds to equip and train the region's police forces (Huggins 1998). Overall, total US aid to Latin America grew to over $7.5 billion in the early 1960s (in constant 2022 USD).[17] After a gradual decline, it accelerated again following the victory of the Sandinistas in Nicaragua in 1979. Total aid just to Honduras during the 1980s was almost $1.6 billion (Pérez and Pestana 2016, 15).

The larger and more lethal forces adopted versions of a National Security Doctrine that emphasized combatting internal threats (Pion-Berlin 1989).[18] They took a clear anti-communist stance, overthrew socialist leaders, and repressed leftist and popular movements. This was facilitated by US training and doctrine.[19] The most prominent location for training was the US Army School of the Americas in the Panama Canal Zone, where the focus was on anti-communist indoctrination and counter-insurgency training (Gill 2004).[20] Many of the leaders of the authoritarian regimes and high-ranking officers in the security forces were graduates.[21] Yet this was only a small part of US training programs (Klare 1968). The US Army's Command and General Staff College, Infantry and Ranger Schools, and Jungle Operations Training Center also played a prominent role.[22] Other branches participated in training Latin American forces as well, including the US Air Force's Inter-American Air Forces Academy and the US Navy's Small Craft Instruction and Technical Training School. The International Police Academy helped train the region's police forces. This training has been facilitated since 1976 by the International Military and Education Program. Additionally, US Army Special Forces provided training on the ground throughout the region via mobile training teams.

Moreover, the United States supplied expertise in intelligence gathering, encouraging countries to create dedicated intelligence agencies with which it could partner. Prior to this period, the only significant intelligence gathering units in the region were Army Intelligence and Navy Intelligence (often identified as G-2 and N-2, respectively), but they were typically domain specific and externally focused. Their attention turned inward during the Cold War, as governments created complex standalone intelligence gathering units for the first time to monitor domestic populations for communist supporters and threats to government control, as shown in Table 2.4.[23] The United States helped establish the National Intelligence Directorate in Chile, the Technical Department for the Repression of Communism in Paraguay, and the National Information Service in Brazil, for example.[24] The National Security Agency was founded in Costa Rica in 1963 after a visit by President Kennedy

Table 2.4 Creation of national intelligence agencies in Latin America during the Cold War

Country	National intelligence agencies and founding date
Argentina	State Intelligence Coordination (1946)
Brazil	Federal Service of Information and Counter-Intelligence (1946)
Chile	National Intelligence Directorate (1974)
Colombia	Colombian Intelligence Service (1953)
Costa Rica	National Security Agency (1963)
Ecuador	Directorate General for Information (1960)
El Salvador	National Intelligence Agency of El Salvador (1962)
Mexico	Federal Security Directorate (1947)
Peru	National Intelligence Service (1960)
Uruguay	Intelligence and Liaison Service (1947)
Venezuela	National Security Service (1948)

and was effectively operated by the US Central Intelligence Agency (CIA) for the next decade (Hernández-Naranjo et al. 2022, 193–194; Méndez-Coto and Rivera Vélez 2018, 9–10).

Moreover, the intelligence agencies of the authoritarian regimes coordinated with their counterparts across the region. On November 28, 1975, high-ranking intelligence officers from Argentina, Bolivia, Chile, Paraguay, and Uruguay signed an agreement founding Operation Condor, a "covert inter-American program of political repression…designed to prevent and reverse emerging movements in Latin America that were advocating political and structural change" (McSherry 2005, 28). Brazil subsequently joined as well and Ecuador and Peru participated in a more peripheral role. Its operations were supported by the United States, particularly the CIA.[25]

The strengthening of forces, increased US aid, greater intelligence gathering, and new focus on internal security resulted in a dramatic increase in the number and type of units engaged in committing violence against civilians. The result of the US training discussed above led to the proliferation of special forces throughout the region that were focused on counter-insurgency; unsurprisingly, they were modeled on, and organized like, US special forces units (McSherry 2005, 29–30). Police forces also established specialized commando and riot units. Intelligence units within the military and police coordinated with their civilian counterparts to create surveillance networks that closely monitored the

Table 2.5 Major counterinsurgency forces in Latin America during the Cold War

Country	Major counter-insurgency forces
Argentina	Argentine Anticommunist Alliance; Army Intelligence Battalion 601; State Intelligence Secretariat
Bolivia	Special Security Service
Brazil	Department of Information Operations—Center for Internal Defense Operations; Department of Political and Social Order
Chile	Directorate of National Intelligence; National Information Center
Colombia	Mobile Brigades in Counter-Guerilla Battalions
Costa Rica	National Directorate of Counter-insurgency; Atlantic Command; Cobra Battalion
Dominican Republic	Military Intelligence Service; Democratic Anti-Communist and Anti-Terrorist Front; Green Berets; Red Berets; Mountain Hunters; Macheteros
Ecuador	Criminal Investigation Service
El Salvador	Nationalist Democratic Organization; Rapid Deployment Infantry Battalions
Guatemala	Special Operations Brigade; Ambulant Military Police; Sixth Command; Detective Corps; Army High Command's Directorate of Intelligence (G-2); Presidential General Staff's Intelligence Unit
Honduras	National Directorate of Investigations; Battalion 3-16
Mexico	Federal Security Directorate
Nicaragua	National Guard
Panama	Military Intelligence Section (G-2); Department of National Investigations; Doberman and Centurion Riot Police; Special Anti-Terror Service Units
Paraguay	Technical Division for the Repression of Communism
Peru	Sinchis; Antiterrorist Directorate; Civil Defense Units
Uruguay	Anti-Subversive Activities Co-Ordination Organization

civilian population, often complemented by secret police forces and death squads to remove enemies of the state clandestinely.[26] While many forces participated in such operations, Table 2.5 highlights the main counter-insurgency forces in the region during the Cold War.[27]

STATE TERROR IN COLD WAR LATIN AMERICA

The authoritarian regimes during the Cold War closely linked the operations of the military, police, intelligence services, and other government agencies to create a security apparatus that could terrorize the public. Secret police units and death squads in the Southern Cone, such as Army

Intelligence Battalion 601 in Argentina, the Department of Informa-
tion Operations—Center for Internal Defense Operations in Brazil, the
Directorate of National Intelligence in Chile, and the Anti-Subversive
Activities Co-Ordination Organization in Uruguay, became synonymous
with kidnapping, torture, and murder (Heinz and Frühling 1999). The
Technical Division for the Repression of Communism helped Alfredo
Stroessner maintain control over society in Paraguay for the entirety of
his dictatorship (Sondrol 1992, 109–110). The Army High Command's
Directorate of Intelligence (G-2) also played a major role in the repression
carried out by the military in Guatemala.[28]

The violence committed by this new apparatus of state security forces
was staggering. In Argentina, the military juntas of the 1976–83 Process
of National Reorganization used systematic abduction, detention, and
torture against the public. The post-dictatorship truth commission documented the enforced disappearance of 8,960 people with estimates as
high as 30,000 disappeared (McSherry 2010, 107).[29] In Bolivia, violent
suppression of the population, including assassinations of political leaders
and massacres of peasants and miners, characterized nearly 20 years
(1964–82) of military rule (Green 2015, 62; Hudson and Hanratty 1991,
40–44).[30] Brazil's military used torture extensively to suppress political
dissent during the 1964–85 regime.[31] In Chile, the military dictatorship of Augusto Pinochet (1973–90) engaged in a systematic campaign
of torture against political opponents and was responsible for thousands
of disappearances.[32] In Panama, the military regime of Omar Torrijos
(1968–81) tortured supporters of the former president, Arnulfo Arias
Madrid.[33] Stroessner's dictatorship (1954–89) in Paraguay subjected the
public to politically motivated repression, including executions, disappearances, and nearly 19,000 documented cases of torture.[34] In Uruguay,
the 1973–85 military regime conducted a vast campaign of state terror
against its people, including dozens of documented cases of disappearances and the political imprisonment of thousands: an "estimated one in
every 500 citizens" in the country (Amnesty International 1979, 4).[35]
Under the one-party state of the Revolutionary Institutional Party in
Mexico, army and police responded to student activism in the 1950s–
60s with repression, including the 1968 Tlatelolco Massacre in which
hundreds of demonstrators and bystanders were killed and thousands
more were wounded (Pensado 2013, 209).

The civil wars in Central America took a brutal toll on their populations, and state forces were responsible for a sizable share of the deaths

in these conflicts. In El Salvador, the post-war truth commission documented 22,000 acts of violence and attributed 85 percent of those to state forces or paramilitaries and death squads aligned with the state.[36] In Guatemala, the cause of 93 percent of the estimated 200,000 deaths during the conflict was attributed to state agents.[37] In Nicaragua, the fighting associated with the Sandinista revolution in the 1970s cost 50,000 lives. The National Guard of the Somoza dictatorship engaged in "bombing of popular neighborhoods and indiscriminate retaliation" against civilian populations (Seligson and McElhinny 1996, 225). The long-running civil war in Colombia was also devastating for the population. From 1958 to 2012, an estimated 220,000 people were killed, during which time the state carried out "arbitrary detentions, torture, selective assassinations and forced disappearances" (Grupo de Memoria Histórica 2016, 26). During the height of the conflict, from 1985 to 2018, 56,094 of the 450,664 deaths (12%) were attributed to agents of the state (Comisión de la Verdad 2022, 127–128).

The organization, ideology, and tactics of state security forces permeated throughout the region in far-reaching and long-lasting ways. Even though Honduras democratized in 1982, for example, it remained a heavily repressive state, with the secret police (National Office of Investigation) and Battalion 3-16 death squad carrying out Dirty War tactics adopted from Argentina through the decade (Ruhl 1996, 38; Ungar 2021, 282).[38] While Costa Rica was democratic during the entire Cold War and had no military, the Civil Guard grew in size, was organized along military lines, and its members were trained at US military institutions, including the School of the Americas (Høivik and Aas 1981, 347). In 1983, the government created the National Directorate of Counter-Insurgency and established elite forces, such as the Atlantic Command and Cobra Battalion, which were deployed along the border with Nicaragua (Hochmüller and Müller 2023, 373). The Cold War-fueled state violence was felt by civilians in every country in Latin America.

CONCLUSION

As we have shown in this chapter, state security forces in Latin America underwent a dramatic transformation from independence through the Cold War. Informal militias loyal to local caudillos became a vast network of specialized security forces with the ability to control and inflict violence on their populations. Indeed, security forces became well-developed state institutions while those necessary to assert non-violent authority, such as the judiciary, remained comparatively weak. With weak rule of law, these forces were able to perpetrate violence with few restraints. As we show in Chapter 3, reforming these institutions in the post-Cold War democratic era has been exceedingly difficult and one of the reasons that state-led public order violence has resurged today.

NOTES

1. Our study is focused on security forces officially part of the government's apparatus. This excludes paramilitary forces, which are "an organized form of coercive (military) capacity that is modeled upon a military format but does not belong to the official, hence legitimate, domain of the security forces" (Koonings and Kruijt 2004, 27).
2. We focus here on land armies because every state established one and they have played a major role in maintaining security within the state and committing state violence. Some states also established navies designed for external defense during this period. Chile, for example, created a navy in 1818 led by British Captain Lord Thomas Cochrane, which became an effective force in the coming decades.
3. Constitución Política del Estado de Nueva Granada 1 de 1832 (1 de Marzo de 1832), https://www.funcionpublica.gov.co/eva/gestornormativo/norma.php?i=13694. Copies of all primary documents cited in the book are available at www.andyreiter.com.
4. Brazil's state militias became the modern-day Military Police, which we discuss at length in Chapter 4.
5. Chile's comparatively more effective forces helped it succeed in the War of the Peruvian-Bolivian Confederation (1836–39) (Solar et al. 2020, 10). In Paraguay, José Gaspar Rodríguez de Francia ruled as a dictator from 1814 to 1840. He abolished the aristocratic militia system inherited from the Spanish (Williams 1975, 75) and created a standing army of "common men owing their elevation and allegiance to him" (Williams 1973, 141–142).
6. Honduras was a notable exception to this pattern. It was not until the 1930s that a true national army was formed (Mahoney 2013, 213–214). Prior to that, "what was called the Honduran army

was, in reality, an irregular, partisan force composed of the armed followers of whatever caudillo, party, or faction happened to be in power at the time" (Ruhl 1996, 35). Moreover, it had little permanence in peacetime, existing primarily as a militia, scattered throughout the country, that could be raised in times of emergency (Ropp 1974, 506). Police forces were also weak, resulting in little state presence in the security sector domestically.

7. Constitución de los Estados Unidos de Venezuela, de 29 de marzo de 1901.

8. There is considerable debate among scholars about the overall relationship between war and state building in Latin America. Some argue that it had little effect (Sofier 2015), others that the benefits were mostly limited to the victors of wars (Schenoni 2021), and others that it was the presence of interstate rivalries, rather than war, that improved state capacity (Thies 2005). Regardless of the overall effect on state building broadly, external conflicts played a crucial role in increasing the capacity of state security forces.

9. Spain also played a role in Central America, staffing Guatemala's first military academy in 1872 (Holden 2004, 52) and training officers from the Dominican Republic beginning in the 1880s (Betances 1995, 20). When it came to naval forces, the states of South America emulated Britain until the United States stepped into that role in the mid-1900s (Resende-Santos 1996, 227).

10. While most of the region is comprised of unitary states, Argentina, Brazil, Mexico, and Venezuela are federal systems with police forces operating at the state and local levels. The years in the table for these countries are those in which federal forces became operational and obtained some level of oversight over sub-national forces, often through a federal ministry.

11. While Haiti lies outside of our study, it is important to note that the United States also intervened there, occupying the country from 1915 to 1934.

12. Message of President James Monroe at the commencement of the first session of the 18th Congress, February 12, 1823, https://www.archives.gov/milestone-documents/monroe-doctrine.

13. Constitution of the Republic of Panama, Chapter XV, Article 136, https://history.state.gov/historicaldocuments/frus1904/d550.

14. While the military did not intervene directly in politics in Uruguay, its civilianization has been overstated: "Although the military

became politically marginalized and accepted civilian authority during the republican era, political neglect also meant that a moderately politicized officer corps had a considerable degree of autonomy in handling military and defense matters" (Altman and Jenne 2020).

15. The years are taken from Polity5 dataset's polity2 variable (Marshall and Gurr 2018). Mexico was a one-party state governed by the Institutional Revolutionary Party from 1929 until electoral reforms in 1997. Costa Rica is the only country in our study that was democratic for the entire Cold War period.

16. United States Treaties and Other International Agreements (U.S.T.), 1950–84, https://www.loc.gov/collections/united-sta tes-treaties-and-other-international-agreements/articles-and-ess ays/ust/.

17. The number includes all foreign assistance, a portion of which is military assistance. See: U.S. Foreign Assistance to Latin America and the Caribbean: FY2025 Appropriates, Congressional Research Service, Report R48266, https://www.congress.gov/crs-product/R48266.

18. While the French only trained Argentina's military briefly in the 1950s before the United States took on the primary role, French counterrevolutionary doctrine shaped the thinking of the institution during the Cold War (Armony 2005, 312–313).

19. While the United States played the dominant role in training Latin American security forces, when US President Jimmy Carter (1977–81) reduced US support for many regimes on human rights grounds, Argentina provided military training and expertise to El Salvador, Guatemala, and Honduras (Armony 1997; Rostica 2022).

20. The center started as the Latin American Training Center-Ground Division at Fort Amador in 1946, was moved to Fort Gulick and renamed the US Army Caribbean School in 1950. Its name was changed to the US Army School of the Americas in 1963. It relocated to Fort Benning, Georgia in 1984 and it became the Western Hemisphere Institute for Security Cooperation in 2001.

21. School of the Americas Watch, Most Notorious SOA Graduates, https://soaw.org/notorious-soa-graduates.

22. The US Army Jungle Operations Training Center was based at Fort Sherman in the Panama Canal Zone until it closed in 1999.

It reopened in Hawaii in 2014 at the 25th Infantry Division's Lightning Academy, which offers a Jungle Operations Training Course.

23. The Pinochet regime created the National Intelligence Directorate in secret in 1973, followed by its official formation in 1974: https://nsarchive.gwu.edu/document/32158-document-1-chilean-interior-ministry-decreto-ley-521-crea-la-direccion-de.

24. The National Information Service in Brazil was created by the military after it seized power in 1964, replacing the Federal Service of Information and Counter-Intelligence.

25. The region's authoritarian regimes had been cooperating in similar ways before Operation Condor was established, often with US support (McSherry 2002).

26. Categorizing units as secret police or deaths squads is analytically challenging (Choulis et al. 2024). We do not attempt to do that here, but rather list the main forces engaged in domestic repression.

27. The list is not exhaustive. The clandestine and repressive nature of the work led regimes to hide the existence of units, change their names frequently, or close units and open different ones with the same personnel and responsibilities. In Peru, civil defense units (*rondas campesinos*) became part of the Peruvian military's counter-insurgency campaign against the Shining Path beginning in 1982 in Ayacucho (Mauceri 1991, 101). In 1989, the government asserted more direct control over these groups, organizing them as Civil Defense Committees (Mucha 2016, 332), as well as creating the Counter-insurgency Civil Defense in Apurímac in 1984 (Comisión de la Verdad y Reconciliación 2003, 441; Mucha 2016, 332–333).

28. In Guatemala, army intelligence was organized hierarchically as D-2 (Directorate of Intelligence), followed by S-2 (Section Intelligence Chiefs in each military zone), and then G-2 (Group Patrols at the battalion to company levels). G-2, however, is the commonly used term to refer to army intelligence as a whole (Schirmer 1998, 152).

29. National Commission on the Disappeared (1984), https://www.cultura.gob.ar/que-es-la-conadep-9904/; International Commission on Missing Persons: Argentina, https://www.cultura.gob.ar/que-es-la-conadep-9904/.

30. Bolivia's truth commission, the National Commission for Investigation of Forced Disappearances (1982–84), was dissolved before

it was able to finish its work and issue a report, yet it documented 155 cases of disappearances. See: https://www.iranrights.org/lib rary/document/3068.
31. Brazil: No More (1986), https://bnmdigital.mpf.mp.br/pt-br/.
32. National Commission for Truth and Reconciliation (1991), https://www.memoriachilena.gob.cl/602/w3-article-94640. html; National Commission on Political Imprisonment and Torture (2005), https://www.indh.cl/destacados-indh/comision-valech/.
33. Panama Truth Commission (2002), https://www.defensoria.gob. pa/books/informe-de-la-comision-de-la-verdad/.
34. Truth and Justice Commission (2008), https://www.codehupy. org.py/verdadyjusticia/.
35. Commission for Peace (2003), https://sitiosdememoria.uy/rec urso/1274.
36. Commission on the Truth for El Salvador (1993), https://digita llibrary.un.org/record/183599?ln=en&v=pdf.
37. Commission for Historical Clarification (1999), https://www.cen trodememoriahistorica.gov.co/descargas/guatemala-memoria-sil encio/guatemala-memoria-del-silencio.pdf.
38. Battalion 3-16, created in 1979, went by various names over time, including the Special Investigations Division, Group of Ten, and Group of Fourteen (Kruckewitt 2005, 183–184).

References

Altman, David, and Nicole Jenne. 2020. Uruguay: No Country for a Military? *Oxford Research Encyclopedia of Politics*. https://doi.org/10.1093/acrefore/9780190228637.013.1864.
Amnesty International. 1979. *Political Imprisonment in Uruguay*. London: Amnesty International.
Armony, Ariel C. 1997. *Argentina, the United States, and the Anti-Communist Crusade in Central America, 1977–1984*. Athens: Ohio University Center for International Studies.
Armony, Ariel C. 2005. Producing and Exporting State Terror: The Case of Argentina. In *When States Kill: Latin America, the U.S., and Technologies of Terror*, eds. Cecilia Menjívar and Néstor Rodríguez, 305–331. Austin: University of Texas Press.

Betances, Emelio. 1995. *State and Society in the Dominican Republic*. Boulder: Westview.

Booth, John A. 2022. Costa Rica: Demilitarization and Democratization. In *Oxford Encyclopedia of the Military in Politics*, eds. William R. Thompson and Hicham Bou Nassif. New York: Oxford University Press. https://oxfordre.com/politics/display/10.1093/acrefore/9780190228637.001.0001/acrefore-9780190228637-e-1888.

Choulis, Ioannis, Abel Escribà-Folch, and Marius Mehrl. 2024. Preventing Dissent: Secret Police and Protests in Dictatorships. *Journal of Politics* 86 (3): 1104–1109.

Comisión de la Verdad. 2022. *Hay futuro si hay verdad: Informe final de la Comisión para el Esclarecimiento de la Verdad, la Convivencia y la No Repetición*. Bogotá: Comisión de la Verdad.

Comisión de la Verdad y Reconciliación. 2003. *Informe Final*. Lima: CVR.

Comisión para el Esclarecimiento Histórico. 1999. *Guatemala: Memoria del Silencio: Informe de la Comisión para el Esclarecimiento Histórico, Tomos I-V*. Ciudad de Guatemala: La Comisión para el Esclarecimiento Histórico.

Conniff, Michael L. 2012. *Panama and the United States: The End of the Alliance*, 3rd ed. Athens: University of Georgia Press.

Corbett, Charles D. 1972. Military Institutional Development and Sociopolitical Change: The Bolivian Case. *Journal of Interamerican Studies and World Affairs* 14 (4): 399–435.

Dunkerly, James. 1981. Reassessing Caudillismo in Bolivia, 1825–79. *Bulletin of Latin American Research* 1 (1): 13–25.

Finch, George A. 1923. The Central American Conference. *The American Journal of International Law* 17 (2): 313–326.

Fitch, J. Samuel. 1998. *The Armed Forces and Democracy in Latin America*. Baltimore: Johns Hopkins University Press.

Gill, Lesley. 2004. *The School of the Americas: Military Training and Political Violence in the Americas*. Durham: Duke University Press.

Glebbeek, Marie-Louise. 2001. Police Reform and the Peace Process in Guatemala: The Fifth Promotion of the National Civilian Police. *Bulletin of Latin American Research* 20 (4): 431–443.

Goldwert, Marvin. 1968. The Rise of Modern Militarism in Argentina. *Hispanic American Historical Review* 48 (2): 189–207.

Green, W. John. 2015. *A History of Political Murder in Latin America: Killing the Messengers of Change*. Albany: State University of New York Press.

Grossman, Richard. 2004. 'The Blood of the People': The Guardia Nacional's Fifty-year War against the People of Nicaragua, 1927–1979. In *When States Kill: Latin America, the U.S., and Technologies of Terror*, eds. Cecilia Menjívar and Néstor Rodríguez, 59–84. Austin: University of Texas Press.

Grupo de Memoria Histórica. 2016. *Basta Ya! Colombia: Memories of War and Dignity*. Bogotá: National Center for Historical Memory.

Harding, Robert C. 2006. *The History of Panama*. Westport, CT: Greenwood Press.

Heinz, Wolfgang, and Hugo Frühling. 1999. *Human Rights Violations By State and State-Sponsored Actors in Brazil, Uruguay, Chile, and Argentina 1960–1990*. The Hague: Martinus Nijhoff.

Hernández-Naranjo, Gerardo, Marco Vinicio Méndez-Coto, and Carlos Humberto Cascante-Segura. 2022. Costa Rica. In *The Handbook of Latin American and Caribbean Intelligence Cultures*, eds. Florina Cristiana Matei, Carolyn Halladay, and Eduardo E. Estévez, 189–207. Lanham, MD: Rowman & Littlefield.

Hochmüller, Markus, and Markus-Michael. Müller. 2023. The Myth of Demilitarization in Costa Rica. *NACLA Report on the Americas* 55 (4): 370–376.

Høivik, Tord, and Solveig Aas. 1981. Demilitarization in Costa Rica: A Farewell to Arms? *Journal of Peace Research* 18 (4): 333–351.

Holden, Robert H. 2004. *Armies Without Nations: Public Violence and State Formation in Central America, 1821–1960*. New York: Oxford University Press.

Hudson, Rex, and Dennis Hanratty, eds. 1991. *Bolivia: A Country Study*. Washington, DC: Library of Congress.

Huggins, Martha K. 1998. *Political Policing: The United States and Latin America*. Durham, NC: Duke University Press.

Institute for Strategic Studies. 1970. *The Military Balance*. London: Institute for Strategic Studies.

Keith, Henry H. 1976. Armed Federal Interventions in the States During the Old Republic. In *Perspectives on Armed Politics in Brazil*, eds. Henry H. Keith and Robert A. Hayes, 51–77. Tempe: Center for Latin American Studies, Arizona State University.

Klare, Mike. 1968. U.S. Military Operations / Latin America: The Changing Nature of American Military Aid. *NACLA: Report on the Americas* 2 (6): 1–7.

Koonings, Kees, and Dirk Kruijt. 2004. Armed Actors, Organized Violence and State Failure in Latin America: A Survey of Issues and Arguments. In *Armed Actors: Organized Violence and State Failure in Latin America*, eds. Kees Koonings and Dirk Kruijt, 5–32. London: Zed.

Kruckewitt, Joan. 2005. U.S. Militarization of Honduras in the 1980s and the Creation of CIA-backed Death Squads. In *When States Kill: Latin America, the U.S., and Technologies of Terror*, eds. Cecilia Menjívar and Néstor Rodríguez, 170–97. Austin: University of Texas Press.

Krzywicka, Katarzyna. 2012. The Armed Forces in the Process of Transformation of the State—The Case of Venezuela. *Polish Political Science* 41: 247–263.

Kurtz, Marcus J. 2013. *Latin American State Building in Comparative Perspective: Social Foundations of Institutional Order*. Cambridge: Cambridge University Press.

Lieuwen, Edwin. 1967. Survey of the Alliance for Progress: The Latin American Military. A Study Prepared at the Request of the Subcommittee on American Republics Affairs of the Committee on Foreign Relations, United States Senate. Washington, DC: U.S. Government Printing Office.

Loveman, Brian. 1999. *For la Patria: Politics and the Armed Forces in Latin America*. Wilmington, DE: Scholarly Resources.

Loveman, Brian, and Thomas M. Davies, Jr. 1997. Instability, Violence, and the Age of the Caudillos. In *The Politics of Antipolitics: The Military in Latin America*, eds. Brian Loveman and Thomas M. Davies, Jr., 15–31. Wilmington, DE: Scholarly Resources.

Maass, Matthias. 2009. Catalyst for the Roosevelt Corollary: Arbitrating the 1902–1903 Venezuela Crisis and Its Impact on the Development of the Roosevelt Corollary to the Monroe Doctrine. *Diplomacy & Statecraft* 20 (3): 383–402.

Mahoney, James. 2013. Militarization without Bureaucratization in Central America. In *State and Nation Making in Latin America and Spain: Republics of the Possible*, eds. Miguel A. Centeno and Agustín E. Ferraro, 203–224. New York: Cambridge University Press.

Malloy, James M. 1977. Authoritarianism and Corporatism in Latin America: The Modal Pattern. In *Authoritarianism and Corporatism in Latin America*, ed. James M. Malloy, 3–19. Pittsburgh: University of Pittsburgh Press.

Marshall, Monty G., and Ted Robert Gurr. 2018. Polity5 Political Regime Characteristics and Transitions, 1800–2018. https://www.systemicpeace.org/polityproject.html.

Mauceri, Philip. 1991. Military Politics and Counter-Insurgency in Peru. *Journal of Interamerican Studies and World Affairs* 33 (4): 83–109.

McSherry, J. Patrice. 2002. Tracking the Origins of a State Terror Network: Operation Condor. *Latin American Perspectives* 29 (1): 38–60.

McSherry, J. Patrice. 2005. Operation Condor as a Hemispheric 'Counterterror' Organization. In *When States Kill: Latin America, the U.S., and Technologies of Terror*, eds. Cecilia Menjívar and Néstor Rodríguez, 28–56. Austin: University of Texas Press.

McSherry, J. Patrice. 2010. 'Industrial Repression' and Operation Condor in Latin America. In *State Violence and Genocide in Latin America: The Cold War Years*, eds. Marcia Esparza, Henry R. Huttenbach, and Daniel Feierstein, 107–123. New York: Routledge.

Méndez-Coto, Marco Vinicio, and Fredy Rivera Vélez. 2018. The Intelligence Service in Costa Rica: Between the New and the Old Paradigm. *The*

International Journal of Intelligence, Security, and Public Affairs 20 (1): 6–19.

Mucha, Witold. 2016. Securitisation and Militias During Civil War in Peru. *Conflict, Security & Development* 16 (4): 327–346.

Nunn, Frederick M. 1983. *Yesterday's Soldiers: European Military Professionalism in South America, 1890–1940.* Lincoln: University of Nebraska Press.

Osterling, Jorge P. 1989. *Democracy in Colombia: Clientelist Politics and Guerrilla Warfare.* New Brunswick, NJ: Transaction.

Peguero, Valentina. 2004. *The Militarization of Culture in the Dominican Republic from the Captains General to General Trujillo.* Lincoln: University of Nebraska Press.

Pensado, Jaime M. 2013. *Rebel Mexico: Student Unrest and Authoritarian Political Culture During the Long Sixties.* Stanford: Stanford University Press.

Pérez, Orlando J., and Randy Pestana 2016. Honduran Military Culture. Jack Gordon Institute Research Publications. https://gordoninstitute.fiu.edu/res earch/military-culture-series/orlando-j-perez-and-randy-pestana-2016-hon duran-military-culture1.pdf.

Pion-Berlin, David. 1989. Latin American National Security Doctrines: Hard- and Softline Themes. *Armed Forces & Society* 15 (3): 411–429.

Resende-Santos, João. 1996. Anarchy and the Emulation of Military Systems: Military Organization and Technology in South America, 1870–1930. *Security Studies* 5 (3): 193–260.

Roorda, Eric Paul. 1998. *The Dictator Next Door: The Good Neighbor Policy and the Trujillo Regime in the Dominican Republic, 1930–1945.* Durham, NC: Duke University Press.

Ropp, Steve C. 1972. Military Reformism in Panama: New Directions or Old Inclinations. *Caribbean Studies* 12 (3): 45–63.

Ropp, Steve. C. 1974. The Honduran Army in the Sociopolitical Evolution of the Honduran State. *The Americas* 30 (4): 504–528.

Rostica, Julieta Carla. 2022. The Collaboration of the Argentine Military Dictatorship with the Governments of Guatemala and Honduras in their 'Fight against Subversion' (1980–3). *Journal of Latin American Studies* 54 (3): 431–456.

Ruhl, J. Mark. 1980. *Colombia: Armed Forces and Society.* Syracuse: Maxwell School of Citizenship and Public Affairs, Syracuse University Press.

Ruhl, J. Mark. 1996. Redefining Civil-Military Relations in Honduras. *Journal of Interamerican Studies and World Affairs* 38 (1): 33–66.

Schenoni, Luis L. 2021. Bringing War Back In: Victory and State Formation in Latin America. *American Journal of Political Science* 65 (2): 405–421.

Schirmer, Jennifer. 1998. *The Guatemala Military Project: A Violence Called Democracy.* Philadelphia: University of Pennsylvania Press.

Seligson, Mitchell, and Vincent McElhinny. 1996. Low-Intensity Warfare, High-Intensity Death: The Demographic Impact of the Wars in El Salvador and Nicaragua. *Canadian Journal of Latin American and Caribbean Studies* 21 (42): 211–241.

Skidmore, Thomas E. 1999. *Brazil: Five Centuries of Change.* New York: Oxford University Press.

Soifer, Hillel David. 2015. *State Building in Latin America.* New York: Cambridge University Press.

Solar, Carlos, Javier Urbina, and G. Alexander Crowther. 2020. Chilean Military Culture. Florida International University, Steven J. Green School of International & Public Affairs. https://gordoninstitute.fiu.edu/research/military-culture-series/chilean-military-culture-11.pdf.

Sondrol, Paul C. 1992. The Paraguayan Military in Transition and the Evolution of Civil-Military Relations. *Armed Forces & Society* 19 (1): 105–122.

Stockholm International Peace Research Institute. 1969. *SIPRI Yearbook of World Armaments and Disarmament 1968/69.* Stockholm: Almqvist & Wiksell.

Taffet, Jeffrey. 2007. *Foreign Aid as Foreign Policy: The Alliance for Progress in Latin America.* New York: Routledge.

Thies, Cameron G. 2005. War, Rivalry, and State Building in Latin America. *American Journal of Political Science* 49 (3): 451–465.

Tillman, Ellen D. 2021. The Dominican Republic: From Military Rule to Democracy. In *Oxford Encyclopedia of the Military in Politics*, eds. William R. Thompson and Hicham Bou Nassif. Oxford University Press. https://oxfordre.com/politics/display/10.1093/acrefore/9780190228637.001.0001/acrefore-9780190228637-e-1811.

Ungar, Mark. 2021. The Police of Honduras. In *Global Perspectives in Policing and Law Enforcement*, ed. Josepter M. Mbuba, 281–294. Lanham, MD: Lexington.

Williams, John Hoyt. 1973. The 'Conspiracy of 1820', and the Destruction of Paraguayan Aristocracy. *Revista de Historica de América* 75/76.

Williams, John Hoyt. 1975. From the Barrel of a Gun: Some Notes on Dr. Francia and Paraguayan Militarism. *Proceedings of the American Philosophical Society* 119 (1): 73–86.

Woodward, Ralph Lee, Jr. 1993. *Rafael Carrera and the Emergence of the Republic of Guatemala, 1821–1871.* Athens: University of Georgia Press.

CHAPTER 3

The Architecture of State Violence in Latin America: Incomplete Reform and Proliferation of Security Forces

INTRODUCTION

While Chapter 1 illustrated the many ways in which new, democratic leaders sought to reform security forces, this chapter highlights the challenges to this effort. It builds on Chapter 2, where we illustrated how security forces originated and grew from independence until the end of the Cold War. The legacy of professionalization and politicization has made deep and comprehensive security sector reform difficult to achieve. Instead, as illustrated here, governments respond to real or perceived security issues by creating new, and more specialized, forces.

This chapter focuses on the creation and proliferation of state security forces across Latin America in the modern era. To illustrate this complexity, we draw from a new dataset that tracks the architecture of state violence by documenting the various tactical, counternarcotic, and border security units that have been created between 1990 and today. We also highlight how the proliferation of new security forces is, in part, due to the continued influence of the United States through ongoing financing and training operations, even during the post-Cold War democratic era. The chapter concludes by discussing challenges associated with these trends; the proliferation of forces makes abuses more likely while simultaneously complicating any efforts toward accountability or reform.

© The Author(s), under exclusive license to Springer Nature
Switzerland AG 2025
B. J. Kyle et al., *State Violence and Democracy in Latin America*,
Rethinking Political Violence,
https://doi.org/10.1007/978-3-032-06412-7_3

DEMOCRATIZATION IN LATIN AMERICA

From the late 1970s to the early 1990s, Latin American countries transitioned away from authoritarianism as part of a global trend termed the Third Wave of democratization (Huntington 1991).[1] Militaries in the region transferred power to elected civilian leaders, aiming to put an end to the state violence associated with military rule. The Andean countries of Ecuador and Peru were among the first in the region to democratize in this era. The reformist agendas that drove the militaries in both countries to seize power in the first place had largely failed by the mid-1970s. Ecuador held competitive multiparty presidential elections in two rounds between 1978 and 1979 (Corkill 1985). Peru democratized the following year, ending the military's experiment with controlled popular mobilization through state corporatism (Malloy 1974). In Bolivia, democracy was instituted in 1982 after several years of military infighting among competing factions and coups against appointed civilian presidents (Dunkerley 1990, 8–9).

The countries of the Southern Cone soon followed in their democratization. In Argentina, the 1982 debt crisis and unsuccessful war with the United Kingdom over the Falklands/Malvinas Islands led to the end of military rule in 1983 (Rock 1987, 383). In Paraguay, poor economic performance, combined with high levels of human rights violations, led to a loss of support for Alfredo Stroessner's dictatorship. A reformist faction of the military ousted him in a coup in 1989 and held democratic elections (Lambert and Nickson 1997). Internal regime divisions and popular activism pressured Brazil's military to democratize through gradual loosening of restrictions on political activity, finally resulting in direct elections for a civilian president in 1989 (Linz and Stepan 1996, 167–169). The Augusto Pinochet regime left power in Chile through the constitutionally mandated 1988 plebiscite and subsequent elections, which resulted in democratic victory and transition in 1990 (Barros 2002). In Uruguay, lengthy negotiations among traditional party leaders and hardliner and reformist factions of the military led to democratization in 1985 (Gillespie 1986).

In the rest of the region, democratization played out in myriad ways. In the Dominican Republic, gradual liberalization led to the electoral defeat of Joaquín Balaguer in 1978, who had dominated politics for two decades (Tillman 2021). After years of reform and growth of political opposition in the legislature, the peaceful election of Vicente Fox to the presidency in 2000 ended decades of one-party rule under the Institutional Revolutionary Party in Mexico (Greene 2007). In Central America, war played a large part in democratization. In El Salvador and Guatemala, turning power over to civilians in the 1980s was part of the counter-insurgency strategy to undermine support for communist revolutionaries (Schirmer 1998; Siegel and Hackel 1988). The revolutionary Sandinista government in Nicaragua, having taking power by force in 1979, pursued political opening in the late 1980s, culminating in opposition victory in 1990 (Williams 1990). A combination of domestic mobilization and pressure by the US led Honduras to democratize in 1982 (Schulz and Sundloff Schulz 1994, 55–72). In Panama, the United States invaded to end the rule of Manuel Noriega in 1989 (Woodward 1999, 304–305). As Table 3.1 shows, by the early 1990s the entire region was democratic.[2]

Most countries in the region have remained democratic.[3] Countries have carried out free and fair elections over many cycles, despite sometimes severe economic and political crises. The region has been more democratic in the post-Cold War period than at any point in its history. As noted above, high levels of state violence played a role in many democratic

Table 3.1 Democratic transitions in Latin America

Country	Year of most recent democratic transition
Argentina	1983
Bolivia	1982
Brazil	1985
Chile	1989
Colombia	1957
Costa Rica	1920
Dominican Republic	1978
Ecuador	1979
El Salvador	1984
Guatemala	1986
Honduras	1982
Mexico	1994
Nicaragua	1990
Panama	1989
Paraguay	1989
Peru	2001
Uruguay	1985
Venezuela	1958

transitions. Such abuses caused popular protests against authoritarian rule, the withdrawal of international support for these regimes, and intervention from the UN in the civil wars in Central America. New democracies made a concerted effort to dismantle and reform the state security apparatuses that existed at the time of their transitions. Yet, as we discuss below, these attempts were incomplete. Instead, many of the Cold War legacies among state security forces are still observed today.

INCOMPLETE SECURITY SECTOR REFORM

As discussed in Chapter 1, democratic political leaders successfully reduced the power and political influence of their militaries as they embarked on democratic transitions. They reduced the size of their country's security forces and budgets from their Cold War highs. El Salvador, for example, cut its military forces by more than half following the end of the civil war (Córdova Macías 2001, 27). The United States oversaw the abolition of the military in Panama after its invasion in 1989 (Sylvia and Danopoulos 2005, 89).

New governments also worked to increase oversight of security forces and clarify their missions. New civilian politicians, for example, created strict mission parameters for militaries (Martínez 2013, 68) and shifted police forces from ministries of defense to civilian ministries (Dammert 2007). The new constitution in El Salvador separated national defense from public security.[4] In Honduras, the government disbanded the secret police in 1993 and created a new civilian police force in 1997 to replace the one controlled by the military (Pérez and Pestana 2016, 11).

With additional oversight came an ambitious focus on human rights training for police forces and the adoption of community policing models (Arias and Ungar 2009; Bobea 2012). In Nicaragua, for example, police reform in the 1990s was heavily community-oriented. This included recruiting women in high numbers (approximately one-third of the force by 2009) and creating women-only police stations. Other specialized units were specifically created to engage with families and youth (Malone et al. 2023, 119–120). While Costa Rica did not undergo a democratic transition during this period, the end of the Cold War led to a similar reappraisal of the role of the security forces. The public viewed the police as overly militaristic, unprofessional, and corrupt (Eijkman 2006a, 149–150). This led to significant institutional reform, including the recentralization of security forces under one Public Force, an emphasis on community policing, and increased training (Dursun-Özkanca 2017), including in human rights (Eijkman 2006b). The state's intelligence service was rebranded the Directorate of Intelligence and National Security in 1994 and it was prohibited from conducting arrests or interrogations (Hernández-Naranjo et al. 2022, 194). The government launched a community policing program in 1998 (Malone et al. 2023).

Despite these efforts, security sector reform remained largely incomplete. Militaries often remained as a "shadow presence" in many countries (Koonings and Kruijt 2004, 17). They fought doggedly to prevent being held accountable for past human rights violations (Lessa et al. 2014) and clung to their legal prerogatives (Kyle and Reiter 2013). In Guatemala, the military blocked all attempts at reform in the late 1980s and early 1990s (Glebbeek 2001, 434–437). The peace agreement to end the war required the demobilization of the National Police and Treasury Guard, and the creation of a new National Civil Police. Yet, most ranks of the new force consisted of recycled members of the old ones, with little training or vetting (Stanley 1999, 126). Police reform in the Dominican Republic was impossible because retired military officers held high-ranking roles in the police and resisted reforms well into the 1990s (Bobea 2012, 60).

Moreover, due to their clandestine nature, it was very difficult for the new governments to exert authority over intelligence services. In Chile, for example, "the armed forces strongly held onto key prerogatives, such as the autonomy of their intelligence agencies from civilian oversight and control" (Oeffinger et al. 2022, 114). While the repressive National Information Center was disbanded following the transition in 1990, five intelligence agencies of the military and police remained. The Defense Information Service was the main intelligence agency of the military junta in Uruguay. It was renamed in 1986 and moved to the Ministry of National Defense, yet it continued to be led by the armed forces with little civilian oversight (Alvarez 2022, 170).

Overall, despite two decades of security sector reform, militaries still retained outsized influence given the lack of external threats to national security. They also retained significant political influence because of how entrenched they were from their time in power. In Chile, for example, though Pinochet was removed from power when the country transitioned to democracy, he remained a "senator for life" until he began to face accountability measures for the human rights abuses that occurred during his rule. Throughout the region, militaries continue to have expansive roles codified in national constitutions along with sizable budgets

(RESDAL 2024). In most countries, many of the same people from the repressive forces in the authoritarian era operated in renamed units with similar mandates, autonomy, and power.

Continued US Influence

Beyond the legacy of security forces from non-democratic periods, another factor that limited reform was the continued influence of the United States. While its military involvement in Latin America has waned since the Cold War, it still has an outsized impact on state security forces in the region.[5] It continues to deploy troops for joint operations, coordinate bilateral and multilateral training exercises, provide security assistance and advanced weaponry to allies in the region, and educate members of state security forces at US institutions.

As of March 2025, the United States deployed personnel from the military or Department of Defense in 17 of the 18 countries in our study, with Venezuela being the lone exception.[6] The largest deployment is in Honduras where US Joint Task Force-Bravo, the United States Southern Command's lead unit in the region, is housed at the Soto Cano Air Base.[7] From there, it coordinates United States and local forces in combatting drug trafficking and transnational crime. Following a push by President Daniel Noboa, the National Assembly in Ecuador approved a constitutional amendment in June 2025 to remove the ban on having foreign troops stationed in the country, which had been in place since 2009. This paves the way for US troops to be permanently housed in the country again (Valencia 2025). Beyond the main operating base in Honduras, the United States has 66 additional cooperative security locations and local bases in use (Kurylo 2024, 2–3).

The United States also regularly coordinates large-scale training exercises.[8] Most prominently, PANAMAX-Alpha, conducted with Panama and neighboring countries, has been held annually for a decade and now includes US special forces. In May 2025, the United States, Costa Rica, Dominican Republic, El Salvador, Guatemala, and Honduras participated in the fourth annual CENTAM Guardian, a multinational exercise involving land, air, and sea operations. The UNITAS maritime exercise, held annually since 1960, includes naval forces from the United States and nearly two dozen other countries.

At the same time, the United States has worked to strengthen bilateral partnerships. In 2024, the United States partnered with Brazil on

Exercise Formosa which included joint operations by the US Marine Corps Forces and the Brazilian Naval Infantry, among other units. That same year, it carried out exercise Southern Fenix with the Chilean army, which included soldiers from the US Army 11th Airborne Division and the deployment of the US Army M142 High Mobility Artillery Rocket System (HIMARS) that has been successful on the battlefield in Ukraine (Johnson 2025). Chile also hosts the annual Southern Start exercise focused on special forces that includes other Latin American countries and the United States. On a smaller scale, in February 2025, the Mexican Senate authorized a month-long training session of Mexican marines by US military personnel in San Luis Carpizo aimed at combatting drug trafficking organizations (LatinNews 2025). In Ecuador, Noboa signed a military cooperation agreement with the United States in 2024 to engage in joint operations (Zinevich 2024).

The United States also provides sizeable funding and equipment to the region. It exports arms to nearly every country in the region, about a quarter of which go to Colombia (Kurylo 2024, 8). Some of this is designed for conventional war-fighting. In 2023, for example, the United States approved a third-party transfer of F-16 Fighting Falcon fighter jets to Argentina and in June 2025 Argentina announced a purchase of Stryker infantry fighting vehicles from the US (Sanchez 2025). In 2022, US President Joe Biden designated Colombia a Major Non-NATO Ally, providing it with the ability to purchase more advanced weapons from the United States, among other military and economic privileges (Kyle and Reiter 2022).

Most of the security sector assistance from the United States, however, goes to strengthening the capabilities of the region's security forces to combat non-traditional threats, facilitating the transition to public order violence. From 2001 to 2023, US security sector aid averaged $887 million annually.[9] In fiscal year 2023, the bulk of the $604 million was allocated to Stabilization Operations and Security Sector Reform ($324 million) and Counternarcotics ($159 million). There has been growing support for combatting Transnational Crime, with allocations in that category rising from just $7 million in 2019 to $61 million in 2023. Colombia received over a third ($226 million) of total aid. The high level of support originated with Plan Colombia, a military and economic assistance package that provided over $10 billion in aid from 2000 to 2015, as the key component of the US "war on drugs" (Londoño 2015).

Yet this funding has always allowed state security forces to combat a variety of threats. While the funding provided under Plan Colombia was initially restricted to operations against drug trafficking organizations, within months this restriction was lifted following an attack by the Revolutionary Armed Forces of Colombia on a police station near Bogotá, the capital city (Trindade Viana 2022, 47–48). From then on, targets of state violence were referred to as narcoguerrillas or narcoterrorists, the latter of which was frequently invoked after the events of 9/11.

The focus on combatting internal threats to national security is reinforced by US training programs including "the Inter-American Air Force Academy, the Western Hemisphere Institute for Security Cooperation, the Inter-American Defense College, the US Naval Small Craft Instruction and Technical Training School and the Combating Terrorism Fellowship," many of which were used for similar purposes during the Cold War.[10] Because of incomplete security sector reforms and the influence of the United States, when internal security threats emerged, state security forces came to the fore, because they already had an orientation toward defending the nation from internal enemies with the use of violence.

THE EMERGENCE OF NEW SECURITY THREATS

Latin America is consistently ranked as the most violent region in the world when measured by intentional homicides (United Nations Office on Drug and Crime [UNODC] 2024). This has been driven by "a dense ecosystem of organized criminal groups, including hundreds of drug trafficking organizations, mafia syndicates, gangs and militia, that alternately cooperate, collude and compete for the control of illegal markets" (UNODC 2023, 3). A 2020 study identified at least 463 armed groups in Mexico alone (Esberg 2020). In 2023, Costa Rica's Security Minister Mario Zamora claimed that the number of criminal groups operating in the country had risen from 35 to 340 over the previous decade (Ruiz 2023). Increases in violent crime and homicide are often directly related to increased activity of such groups. In Ecuador, for example, homicides rose 407% from 2016 to 2022, attributable to conflict between rival gangs competing over control of the port of Guayaquil, a major transit hub in the drug trade (UNODC 2023, 7–9). The illicit drug trade continues to expand, with the most recent data showing an all-time high for coca production and cocaine seizures, which affects the entire region (UNODC 2025).

Violence and security concerns (real or perceived, as demonstrated in Chapter 4) have increased discontent within the population. In the 2023 Latinobarómetro regional survey, 59.2% of the respondents reported being worried about being a victim of violent crime "all" or "some" of the time.[11] In another survey in 2022, high percentages of respondents in the region named crime and violence as the biggest threats to their safety, including more than 40% in Venezuela, Ecuador, Argentina, Colombia, and Mexico. More than a third of respondents said they would permanently move to another country if they were able.[12]

Many people have chosen to leave or have been forced to flee from their homes. As of May 2025, nearly 7.9 million people have left Venezuela, most of whom (6.7 million) are living in neighboring Latin American or Caribbean countries.[13] At the end of 2022, there were 665,000 refugees and asylum seekers from Guatemala, El Salvador, and Honduras worldwide, with nearly 300,000 more internally displaced in those countries (International Organization for Migration 2024, 92). In 2023, more than half a million migrants crossed the Darién Gap between Colombia and Panama, moving north toward the United States (Roy 2024). These massive displacements and migrations have further stressed already weak democratic institutions, leading to increased dissatisfaction with those in power.

In short, the emerging security threats in the region have caused citizen dissatisfaction with democratic leaders. Politicians respond by securitizing many issues and by using violence motivated by a promise of public order. The homicide rates in Honduras and El Salvador have declined markedly in recent years with the governments claiming their success due to the use of states of emergency, security crackdowns, and mass incarcerations (Cavalari et al. 2025). As we show below, security threats—whether real or perceived—have caused a proliferation of forces and led to a complex architecture of state security.

THE ARCHITECTURE OF STATE SECURITY FORCES IN LATIN AMERICA TODAY

Working to curtail human rights violations at the hands of the state requires understanding who is committing state violence and under what mandates and supervision they are doing so. Yet to date, there has been no comprehensive accounting of state security forces in Latin America. Indeed, in studies of armed conflict, the government is often treated as a unitary actor. The most widely used dataset on armed conflict, the Uppsala Conflict Data Program's Armed Conflict Dataset, contains extensive information on non-state armed combatants (Davies et al. 2025). For Colombia, for example, it includes data on 28 rebel, paramilitary, and criminal groups, and drug trafficking organizations, but simply notes that they are combatting the "government of Colombia."[14]

Those studies that disaggregate the state are almost entirely focused on the military. Moreover, such studies measure the military in terms of its strength as a war-fighting force. Many rely on the International Institute for Strategic Studies (2025) Military Balance data, the Global Militarisation Index, which contains information on expenditures, personnel, and heavy weapons (von Boemcken et al. 2023), or the Correlates of War Arms Technology Data (Hariri and Wingender 2025). Other datasets focus on aspects of the military as an institution, including those on military recruitment (Upton Institute 2022a) and military education (Upton Institute 2022b). Several cross-national studies focus on the military's engagement in politics (Croissant et al. 2016; White 2017), the economy (Izadi 2022), and the justice system (Kyle and Reiter 2021). Yet the focus is still entirely on the military and it is treated as a unitary actor.

Several important studies have disaggregated state security forces in novel ways. The Pro-Government Militia Dataset has extensive data on militia groups, but only includes forces that are pro-government or government-sponsored and excludes official state forces (Carey et al. 2022). The M^3 Dataset is the most comprehensive cross-national dataset on material, political, and societal militarization, and includes "uniformed armed organizations such as presidential and coast guards, police, border security forces, and government militias," but only if they are under the commands of the Ministry of Defense (Bayer et al. 2023, 817). As we demonstrate in this chapter, this excludes a significant component of state security forces.

Erica De Bruin's State Security Forces dataset is the best effort so far to provide a more complete picture of state security forces. The data include information on "ground combat-compatible forces" outside of those of the traditional military (De Bruin 2021, 3). The dataset is limited though by the use of random sampling, which yielded 110 countries with no region fully examined, and it ends in 2010. Moreover, despite being a significant improvement over previous studies, the number of state security forces documented is minimal. For Colombia, for example, the dataset includes the National Police and two long-defunct groups (Special Vigilance and Private Security Services, and the Community Service Groups), yet today, there are more than 20 state security forces operating in Colombia, according to our dataset.

The dearth of data on state security forces in Latin America necessitated the creation of a new dataset on the creation and proliferation of these forces. Below, we describe how the dataset was completed and offer some preliminary findings.

State Security Forces Dataset

To better capture trends in the proliferation of state security forces, we created a new State Security Forces in Latin America dataset that contains detailed information on 286 active forces (as of spring 2025) across the 18 countries in our study.[15] These forces are official state-run, permanent organizations that have the ability and authorization to use violence against the civilian population, or are involved in gathering intelligence for such activities. This excludes temporary task forces formed by a collaboration of existing organizations and militias and it excludes paramilitary forces not officially operated by the state (Koonings and Kruijt 2004, 27). While some militaries do not currently have legal authorization to use force domestically, as we show in Chapter 7, all constitutions allow for this authorization to occur and these forces frequently operate domestically, and so they are included in our dataset.

For each force, we document their parent agencies and ministries of oversight, year of creation, type of force, and primary mission(s). In determining which forces to include as separate entries, we focus on their level of autonomy and the degree to which their mission is distinct when they are part of a larger umbrella force (such as the navy or national police). In Ecuador, for example, the General Directorate of Police Intelligence, General Directorate of Citizen Security and Public Order, and General Directorate of Investigation, are all under the control of the National Police of Ecuador, but are included as separate entries. Because our goal is to reveal the complexity of state security forces in the region, we erred on the side of disaggregation.

To create the dataset, we drew first from government websites. For traditional forces, such as the branches of the armed services and police, governments often have detailed information on specific forces and publish clear organizational charts.[16] We then searched all other ministries and government entities for security forces. Some government websites were incomplete, outdated, or unreliable, however, and so we confirmed the existence of, and details on, all forces through national legislation, government documents and press releases, news reports, coverage by nongovernmental organizations, and academic sources. Doing so also uncovered some forces, often those in the clandestine services, about which governments provide limited public information.

While most of the forces were situated in a Ministry of Defense (45%), many others were under ministries of the interior, justice, or peace and security (46%). The apparatus of state security forces is complex, however, and there are units (9%) in various other areas of government that also perpetrate state violence. The Customs Control Unit in Bolivia, for example, is an anti-smuggling police force situated in the Ministry of Finance. The Special Inspection Group of the Brazilian Institute of the Environment and Renewable Natural Resources is a police force under the Ministry of the Environment that combats organized crime, including illegal mining. Other units are under direct control of the president, such as the National Directorate for Drug Control and the National Intelligence Directorate in the Dominican Republic.

Besides creating a more complete picture of who is involved in state violence, the dataset also allows us to quantify the proliferation of state security forces: 49% predate the end of the Cold War, another 29% were created between 1990 and 2009, and 28% were created in the last 15 years. Below, we detail the creation of tactical forces, counternarcotics units, and forces associated with border security.

First, with the rise in criminal organizations and gang violence, we find a significant proliferation of tactical units: those designed for counter-insurgency, riot control, and high-risk policing situations. Table 3.2 shows the primary tactical units in the region, though many other state security forces participate in such operations, as well.

Honduras is emblematic of this trend of ever-expanding security forces in the context of high levels of societal violence. The murder rate doubled between 2005 and 2010; with 82.1 homicides per 100,000 people, the country had the highest rate in the world (United Nations Office on Drugs and Crime 2011). The increase in murders was driven, in part, by gang violence, including fighting between MS-13 and its archrival 18th Street. The government's response to rising crime was first to deploy the

Table 3.2   Primary tactical forces in Latin America

Country	Forces
Argentina	Joint Command of Special Operation Forces; Joint Operations Command
Bolivia	Blue Devils Special Task Force; General Directorate for the Special Force Against Crime; Special Force to Combat Violence; Anti-Terrorist Group
Brazil	National Public Security Force; Special Inspection Group
Chile	Special Police Operations Group
Colombia	Joint Special Operations Command; Military Unified Action Groups for Personal Freedom; Mobile Anti-Disturbance Squadron; National Police Unified Action Groups for Personal Freedom
Costa Rica	Public Force Reserves
Ecuador	General Directorate of Citizen Security and Public Order; Joint Command of Military Forces
El Salvador	Special Forces Command; Specialized Police Tactical Unit; Zeus Command
Guatemala	Special Battalion for Interdiction and Rescue; Special Forces Brigade
Honduras	Military Police of Public Order; Intelligence Troop and Special Security Response Groups; National Directorate for Special Forces; Special Operations Command
Mexico	24th Marine Infantry Battalion of the Presidential Guards; Special Reaction and Intervention Force; Special Forces; Special Reaction Force
Nicaragua	Patriotic Military Reserve; Special Operations Command
Paraguay	Joint Task Force
Peru	Directorate of Police Aviation; General Directorate Against Organized Crime; Joint Command of the Armed Forces
Uruguay	National Directorate of the Republican Guard
Venezuela	Bolivarian National Militia; Directorate of Strategic and Tactical Actions; National Anti-Extortion and Kidnapping Command

military in domestic policing. Since 2002, the military has participated in joint operations with the police.

In 2004, over 1,500 police and soldiers traveled aboard city buses to protect drivers and passengers. By 2014, over 7,000 soldiers were participating in public-safety operations (Flores-Macías and Zarkin 2021, 527). The army's 15th Battalion, which was trained by the US Army Rangers and Spanish and Israeli Special Forces, played a prominent role in policing rural areas, including the Bajo Aguan Valley where it worked closely with private security corporations to protect the interest of foreign companies and targeted environmental activists (Bird and Spring 2013, 13). In addition, in 2013 the government created the Military Police of Public Order as a fourth branch of the armed forces to replace the police in some areas of security. To speed up its creation, the first 1,000 members were drawn directly from the military (Ungar 2021, 284).

Moreover, Honduran government leaders created new state security forces specifically designed to combat organized crime and gangs. At one point there were as many as 15 different anti-gang units (Ungar 2021, 284). Most notable were the Intelligence Troop and Special Security Response Groups (TIGRES) and the Special Operations Command (COBRAS). The government created the TIGRES in 2013 and by June 2014 the first class of TIGRES graduated from a special training program with the US 7th Special Forces Group (Airborne) and Colombia's Jungle School. In March 2015, US Green Berets hosted members of the TIGRES at Eglin Air Force Base in Florida for additional training (Pérez and Pestana 2016, 23). The unit was implicated in the 2016 assassination of the indigenous environmental activist Berta Cáceres (Lakhani 2020). Prior iterations of the COBRAS were anti-guerrilla forces. The relaunched version in 2014 was modeled as a riot police, and has been used to "quell prison uprisings, coordinate anti-gang activities, disperse illegal land occupations, and bolster security in high-crime zones" (Ungar 2021, 284). These forces often deploy jointly and their operations are guided by intelligence gathered by the National Directorate of Intelligence.

A second area of proliferation of state security forces across the region is to engage in counternarcotics. The rise in crime has been driven, in part, by increased drug trafficking as cartels and gangs fight for control over parts of the supply chain where illicit drugs are grown, produced, and shipped. For several countries, counternarcotics operations are carried out by the regular military, police or border security forces. In others, as shown in Table 3.3, special dedicated units work to combat the threat.

The focus on counternarcotics began in the 1980s as the expanding cocaine trade drew increased attention from the United States. Interdicting drugs while in transit and eradicating coca crops in the Andean region became central foci of its heavily supply-side focused "war on drugs" (Crandall 2002). Colombia was the main source of cocaine consumed in the United States, and the Cali and Medellín cartels came to dominate the market (Thoumi 2002). The United States and Colombia signed the Treaty of Extradition in 1979 allowing for those involved in the drug trade captured in Colombia to be tried and imprisoned in the United States.[17] The Colombian government created the Search Bloc, an ad hoc special operations unit of the National Police, to locate and

Table 3.3 Primary counternarcotics forces in Latin America

Country	Forces
Bolivia	Amphibious Command Battalion; Blue Devils Special Task Force; General Directorate for the Special Force Against Drug Trafficking
Brazil	Directorate for Investigating and Combating Organized Crime and Corruption
Colombia	Anti-Narcotics Directorate; Military Unified Action Groups for Personal Freedom
Costa Rica	Drug Control Police
Dominican Republic	National Drug Control Directorate
El Salvador	Anti-Narcotics Division of the National Police
Guatemala	Special Battalion for Interdiction and Rescue; Subdirectorate General of Analysis of Anti-Narcotic Information
Mexico	The Special Forces
Nicaragua	National Commission for the Registration and Control of Toxic Substances
Paraguay	National Anti-Drug Secretariat
Peru	General Directorate Against Organized Crime
Uruguay	General Directorate for the Suppression of Illicit Drug Trafficking
Venezuela	National Anti-Drug Command

apprehend Pablo Escobar, the leader of the Medellín Cartel. A covert US Army signals intelligence unit, code-named Centra Spike, worked closely with the Search Bloc. Members of US Delta Force special operations later joined on the ground (Bowden 2021). Escobar was eventually killed in a fire-fight with the Search Bloc in 1993.

In conjunction with the increased US funding through Plan Colombia, the government created a Counternarcotics Battalion within the Army in 1999. This originally contained three brigades but has now expanded to five and is the key Army unit focused on counternarcotics. The Counternarcotics Battalion joined the existing Antinarcotic Division of the National Police in eradication and interdiction operations. The government also obtained 74 helicopters from the United States to improve its air power (Trindade Viana 2022, 219).[18] Concurrently, the army created the Rapid Deployment Force in 1999 that specializes in air assault. If narco-targets are involved in kidnapping and extortion, the Unified Action Groups for Personal Freedom of the various branches of the armed forces would get involved, and the Urban Anti-Terrorist Special Forces Group would be likely to participate, as well, in any urban missions against highly sought-after targets. Counternarcotics missions are informed by intelligence gathered by the National Intelligence Directorate as well as the Directorate of Police Intelligence and intelligence units in the branches of the armed forces. Colombia also cooperates with the US Drug Enforcement Administration in counternarcotics operations.

A third area of expansion of state security forces—in number and lethality—is to address border control. The high levels of migration across the region and illicit drug trade prompted states to securitize border policing. In a number of countries, as shown in Table 3.4, special dedicated units now seek to manage and secure national borders.

Panama provides a good illustration of this trend. After the United States invaded the country in 1989 and ousted Noriega, it oversaw the transformation of the Panamanian Defense Forces (PDF) into the Pana-manian Public Forces. The new government immediately reduced the force in size from 15,000 to 11,800 and purged the office corps of PDF loyalists (Sylvia and Danopoulos 2005, 89). A 1994 constitutional amendment formally abolished the military. The 1997 Organic Law on the National Police completed the civilianization of the security forces:

Table 3.4 Primary border control forces

Country	Forces
Argentina	Argentine Naval Prefecture; National Directorate of Migration
Bolivia	Customs Control Unit; General Directorate of Border Security Zones; General Directorate of Migration; Migratory Control Police Unit; National Customs
Colombia	Fiscal and Customs Police; Special Administrative Unit for Migration
Costa Rica	Border Police
Dominican Republic	General Directorate of Migration; Specialized Corps for Land Border Security
Guatemala	Division of Ports, Airports, and Border Posts; Territorial Control and Border Task Force
Ecuador	General Directorate of Citizen Security and Public Order; National Customs Service of Ecuador
El Salvador	Border Patrol
Panama	National Border Service
Paraguay	National Directorate of Migration
Peru	General Directorate of Captaincies and Coast Guard; National Superintendence of Migration
Uruguay	National Directorate of Migration
Venezuela	Bolivarian National Guard

replacing ranks with levels, clearly defining its mission, prohibiting political activities, and instituting a strict code of conduct (Caumartin 2007, 124).[19]

The exception to the civilianization of the security forces, however, were the border police, which were specially trained and heavily armed (Caumartin 2007, 125). This increased as the United States began to focus on combatting drug trafficking in the region. In the early 2000s, the United States provided the border police with jungle warfare training and donated several patrol boats to increase the capabilities of the naval police (Conniff and Bigler 2019, 147). After 9/11, the United States further increased its assistance, training upward of 1,000 police annually (Conniff and Bigler 2019, 175). The government created a special, US-trained Reconnoiter and Combat Unit to patrol the border in 2004. In 2008, facing increased spillover from the Colombian Civil War, the security forces were reorganized with the creation of the new National Intelligence Service, and the reorganization of other forces into the National Air-Naval Service and National Border Services (SENAFRONT).

With migrant flows across the Darién Gap increasing, SENAFRONT plays a prominent role and is usually the first point of contact for migrants who make it over the border. With such a highly militarized force, however, human rights abuses are more likely. Activist groups and victims have made complaints against SENAFRONT (Human Rights Watch 2024), particularly for its actions in the indigenous communities along the border (International Indian Treaty Council 2025). Moreover, there is risk of its mandate and reach being extended beyond the border. In 2010–11, for example, the Ngäbe-Buglé indigenous groups protested the creation of the Barro Colorado dam and the government sent in SENAFRONT to break up roadblocks and demonstrations (Conniff and Bigler 2019, 250–251).

Conclusion

As we have shown in this chapter, the architecture of state security forces in Latin America today is complex. This presents several distinct problems for reducing state violence. First, when human rights violations occur it is often extremely difficult to identify the perpetrators. Individuals from many units are deployed concurrently and many wear similar style camouflage uniforms. Moreover, public information about which security forces are engaged in particular operations is often limited.

Second, it is difficult to determine accountability since it is not always clear who has oversight over which aspects of each mission. The proliferation of security forces, combined with the fact that they are often working together, complicates determining hierarchy and responsibility in operations. The complex web of security institutions also challenges external oversight from legislatures or other democratic bodies by limiting their visibility in the security apparatus, thereby undermining the potential for accountability.

Finally, the trends outlined in this chapter also make meaningful reform extremely challenging. The government can retrain, purge, or disband one force, but multiple other forces continue to operate, focused on combatting each type of threat, and most have been trained at the same domestic and US-based institutions. In the following three chapters we explore the use of state security forces in the context of policing, controlling borders, and pursuing economic interests in Brazil, Mexico, and Peru, respectively, with reflections from across the region.

NOTES

1. Three countries in the region—Costa Rica, Colombia, and Venezuela—democratized prior to the Third Wave.
2. The years are taken from the Polity5 dataset's polity variable (Marshall and Gurr 2018). Peru transitioned to democracy in 1980, but reverted to authoritarianism in 1992 when President Alberto Fujimori orchestrated a "self-coup." It transitioned to democracy again in 2001.
3. Some countries, however, have become increasingly authoritarian in recent years (e.g., El Salvador, Nicaragua, and Venezuela) or have experienced notable disruptions to democratic practice, such as the 2009 coup in Honduras.
4. Article 159, El Salvador's Constitution of 1983 with Amendments through 2014, www.constituteproject.org/constitution/El_Salvador_2014. Copies of all primary documents cited in the book are available at www.andyreiter.com.
5. While the United States is central, it is important to note that, just like in the Cold War, Latin American countries also coordinate with one another. The Northern Triangle countries of El Salvador, Guatemala, and Honduras cooperate to combat gangs moving across their borders. They share intelligence and have created joint

forces to patrol the borders (Gagne 2016). Likewise, the Andean countries of Bolivia, Colombia, Ecuador, and Peru agreed in 2024 to launch an intelligence sharing network, as well as increase their coordination on border security (LatinNews 2024). Moreover, like Chile during the late 1800s and early 1900s and Argentina during the Cold War, Colombia plays an outsized role in training other Latin American security forces (Trindade Viana 2022, 224–27).

6. Number of Military and DoD Appropriated Fund (APF) Civilian Personnel, by Assigned Duty Location and Service/Component, March 31, 2025, https://dwp.dmdc.osd.mil/dwp/app/dod-data-reports/workforce-reports.

7. United States Southern Command, Joint Task Force-Bravo, https://www.jtfb.southcom.mil/.

8. Information on all of the training exercises discussed below can be found on the United States Southern Command's website: https://www.southcom.mil/.

9. This reflects disbursements and obligations to the 18 countries in our study in constant (2023) dollars in the peace and security sector. The data are available here: https://foreignassistance.gov/data.

10. United States Southern Command, Building Partner Capacity/Supporting Our Partners, https://www.southcom.mil/Commanders-Priorities/Strengthen-Partnerships/Building-Partner-Cap acity/.

11. The data are available at: https://www.latinobarometro.org/lat Online.jsp.

12. Lloyd's Register Foundation World Risk Poll, available at: https://www.lrfoundation.org.uk/news/latin-americans-fear-crime-and-violence-more-than-anyone-else-as-many-consider-leaving#:~:text=With%20much%20of%20Latin%20America,2019%20to%2034%25%20in%202021.

13. United Nations High Commissioner for Refugees, Emergency Appeal, Venezuela Situation, https://www.unhcr.org/us/emerge ncies/venezuela-situation.

14. Uppsala Conflict Data Program, Colombia, https://ucdp.uu.se/country/100.

15. The full dataset is available at https://www.andyreiter.com.

16. Examining police forces was most difficult in Argentina, Brazil, Venezuela, and Mexico, which are all federal systems of government and organize their police forces at national, regional, and local levels. In those cases, we document federal police forces and include a broad entry for department level police, without including a specific line for each department's force.

17. Treaty of Extradition Between the United States of America and the Republic of Colombia, signed at Washington on September 14, 1979.

18. As of 2022, across the armed services and police, security forces have 342 helicopters at their disposal. Authors' calculations from the Military Balance (International Institute for Strategic Studies 2022).

19. Ley orgánica de la Policía Nacional, N° 18, de 4 de junio de 1997.

REFERENCES

Alvarez, Nicolás. 2022. Uruguay. In *The Handbook of Latin American and Caribbean Intelligence Cultures*, eds. Florina Christiana Matei, Carolyn Halladay, and Eduardo E. Estévez, 169–187. Lanham, MD: Rowman & Littlefield.

Arias, Enrique Desmond, and Mark Ungar. 2009. Community Policing and Latin America's Citizen Security Crisis. *Comparative Politics* 41 (4): 409–429.

Barros, Robert. 2002. *Constitutionalism and Dictatorship: Pinochet, the Junta, and the 1980 Constitution*. Cambridge: Cambridge University Press.

Bayer, Markus, Aurel Croissant, Roya Izadi, and Nikitas Scheeder. 2023. Multidimensional Measures of Militarization (M3): A Global Dataset. *Armed Forces & Society* 51 (3): 815–839.

Bird, Annie, and Karen Spring. 2013. Human Rights Violations Attributed to Military Forces in the Bajo Aguán Valley in Honduras. Rights Action.

Bobea, Lilian. 2012. The Emergence of the Democratic Citizen Security Policy in the Dominican Republic. *Policing & Society* 22 (1): 57–75.

Bowden, Mark. 2021. The Story of the U.S. Role in the Killing of Pablo Escobar. In *Routledge Handbook of U.S. Counterterrorism and Irregular Warfare Operations*, eds. Michael A. Sheehan, Erich Marquardt, and Liam Collins, 203–211. New York: Routledge.

Carey, Sabine C., Neil J. Mitchell, and Katrin Paula. 2022. The Life, Death and Diversity of Pro-Government Militias: The Fully Revised Pro-Government Militias Database Version 2.0. *Research & Politics* 9 (1).

Caumartin, Corinne. 2007. 'Depoliticisation' in the Reform of the Panamanian Security Apparatus. *Journal of Latin American Studies* 39 (1): 107–132.

Cavalari, Marina, Juliana Manjarrés, and Christopher Newton. 2025. InSight Crime's 2024 Homicide Round-Up. February 26. https://insightcrime.org/news/insight-crime-2024-homicide-round-up/.

Conniff, Michael L., and Gene E. Bigler. 2019. *Modern Panama: From Occupation to Crossroads of the Americas*. New York: Cambridge University Press.

Córdova Macías, Ricardo. 2001. Demilitarizing and Democratizing Salvadoran Politics. In *El Salvador: Implementation of the Peace Accords*, ed. Margarita S. Studemeister, 27-32. Washington, DC: United States Institute of Peace.

Corkill, David. 1985. Democratic Politics in Ecuador, 1979–1984. *Bulletin of Latin American Research* 4 (2): 63–74.

Crandall, Russell. 2002. *Driven by Drugs: U.S. Policy Towards Colombia*. Boulder: Lynne Rienner.

Croissant, Aurel, Tanja Eschenauer, and Jil Kamerling. 2016. Militaries' Roles in Political Regimes: Introducing the PRM Data Set. *European Political Science* 16 (3): 400–414.

Dammert, Lucía. 2007. *Report on the Security Sector in Latin America and the Caribbean*. Santiago: Facultad Latinoamericana de Ciencias Sociales (FLACSO-Chile).

Davies, Shawn, Thérése Pettersson, Margareta Sollenberg, and Magnus Öberg. 2025. Organized Violence 1989–2024, and the Challenges of Identifying Civilian Victims. *Journal of Peace Research* 62 (4): 1223–1240.

De Bruin, Erica. 2021. Mapping Coercive Institutions: The State Security Forces Dataset, 1960–2010. *Journal of Peace Research* 58 (2): 315–325.

Dunkerley, James. 1990. *Political Transition and Economic Stabilisation: Bolivia, 1982–1989*. London: Institute of Latin American Studies.

Dursun-Özkanca, Oya. 2017. Pitfalls of Police Reform in Costa Rica: Insights into Security Sector Reform in Non-Military Countries. *Peacebuilding* 5 (3): 320–338.

Eijkman, Quirine A. M. 2006a. 'Around here I am the law!' Strengthening Police Officers' Compliance with the Rule of Law in Costa Rica. *Utrecht Law Review* 2 (2): 145–176.

Eijkman, Quirine. 2006b. To Be Held Accountable: Police Accountability in Costa Rica. *Police Practice and Research* 7 (5): 411–430.

Esberg, Jane. 2020. More Than Cartels: Counting Mexico's Crime Rings. International Crisis Group. May 8. https://www.crisisgroup.org/latin-america-caribbean/mexico/more-cartels-counting-mexicos-crime-rings.

Flores-Macías, Gustava A., and Jessica Zarkin. 2021. The Militarization of Law Enforcement: Evidence from Latin America. *Perspectives on Politics* 19 (2): 519–538.

Gagne, David. 2016. Northern Triangle Deploys Tri-National Force to Combat Gangs. InSight Crime. November 15. https://insightcrime.org/news/brief/northern-triangle-deploys-tri-national-force-to-combat-gangs/.

Gillespie, Charles G. 1986. Uruguay's Transition from Collegial Military-Technocratic Rule. In *Transitions from Authoritarian Rule: Latin America*, eds. Guillermo O'Donnell, Philippe C. Schmitter, and Laurence Whitehead, 173–195. Baltimore: The Johns Hopkins University Press.

Glebbeck, Marie-Louise. 2001. Police Reform and the Peace Process in Guatemala: The Fifth Promotion of the National Civilian Police. *Bulletin of Latin American Research* 20 (4): 431–443.

Greene, Kenneth F. 2007. *Why Dominant Parties Lose: Mexico's Democratization in Comparative Perspective*. Cambridge: Cambridge University Press.

Hariri, Jacob Gerner, and Asger Mose Wingender. 2025. A New Data Set on Arms Technology Adoption 1816–2023. Version 1.0. https://correlatesofwar.org/data-sets/arms-technology-data-v1-0/.

Hernández-Naranjo, Gerardo, Marco Vinicio Méndez-Coto, and Carlos Humberto Cascante-Segura. 2022. Costa Rica. In *The Handbook of Latin American and Caribbean Intelligence Cultures*, eds. Florina Cristiana Matei, Carolyn Halladay, and Eduardo E. Estévez, 189–207. Lanham, MD: Rowman & Littlefield.

Human Rights Watch. 2024. Neglected in the Jungle: Inadequate Protection and Assistance for Migrants and Asylum Seekers Cross the Darién. April 3. https://www.hrw.org/report/2024/04/03/neglected-jungle/inadequate-protection-and-assistance-migrants-and-asylum-seekers.

Huntington, Samuel P. 1991. *The Third Wave: Democratization in the Late Twentieth Century*. Norman: University of Oklahoma Press.

International Indian Treaty Council. 2025. The United Nations Special Rapporteur on the Rights of Indigenous Peoples, Dr. Albert Barume, made an academic visit to Panama from June 19 to 22, 2025. June 30. https://www.iitc.org/the-united-nations-special-rapporteur-on-the-rights-of-indigenous-peoples-dr-albert-barume-made-an-academic-visit-to-panama-from-june-19-to-22-2025.

International Institute for Strategic Studies. 2022. *The Military Balance: The Annual Assessment of Global Military Capabilities and Defence Economics*. London: Routledge.

International Institute for Strategic Studies. 2025. *The Military Balance: The Annual Assessment of Global Military Capabilities and Defence Economics*. London: Routledge.

International Organization for Migration. 2024. World Migration Report 2024. https://publications.iom.int/books/world-migration-report-2024.

Izadi, Roya. 2022. State Security or Exploitation: A Theory of Military Involvement in the Economy. *Journal of Conflict Resolution* 66 (4–5): 729–754.

Johnson, Reuben. 2025. Thanks to the Ukraine War, Everyone Now Wants HIMARS Missiles. *National Security Journal*. https://nationalsecurityjournal. org/thanks-to-the-ukraine-war-everyone-now-wants-himars-missiles/.

Koonings, Kees, and Dirk Kruijt. 2004. Armed Actors, Organized Violence and State Failure in Latin America: A Survey of Issues and Arguments. In *Armed Actors: Organized Violence and State Failure in Latin America*, eds. Kees Koonings and Dirk Kruijt, 5–32. London: Zed.

Kurylo, Benjamin. 2024. Comparative Analysis of U.S., Russian, and Chinese Military Cooperation with Latin America and the Caribbean. *Military Review*. July. https://www.armyupress.army.mil/Portals/7/military-review/ Archives/English/Online-Exclusive/2024/Kurylo-Comparative-Analysis/ Kurylo-Comparative-Analysis-UA.pdf.

Kyle, Brett J., and Andrew G. Reiter. 2013. Militarized Justice in New Democracies: Explaining the Process of Military Court Reform in Latin America. *Law & Society Review* 47 (2): 375–407.

Kyle, Brett J., and Andrew G. Reiter. 2021. *Military Courts, Civil-Military Relations, and the Legal Battle for Democracy: The Politics of Military Justice*. New York: Routledge.

Kyle, Brett J., and Andrew G. Reiter. 2022. For Hemispheric Unity, A Change in U.S. Foreign Policy is Needed. *NACLA*. April 8. https://nacla.org/hem ispheric-unity-change-us-foreign-policy-needed-latin-america/.

Lakhani, Nina. 2020. *Who Killed Berta Caceres?: Dams, Death Squads, and an Indigenous Defender's Battle for the Planet*. London: Verso.

Lambert, Peter, and Andrew Nickson, eds. 1997. *The Transition to Democracy in Paraguay*. New York: St. Martin's.

LatinNews. 2024. Latin American Weekly Report. January 25. https://www.lat innews.com/media/k2/pdf/WR-24-03.9874.pdf.

LatinNews. 2025. Latin American Weekly Report. February 13. https://www. latinnews.com/component/k2/item/104655.html.

Lessa, Francesca, Tricia D. Olsen, Leigh A. Payne, Gabriel Pereira, and Andrew G. Reiter. 2014. Overcoming Impunity: Pathways to Accountability in Latin America. *International Journal of Transitional Justice* 8 (1): 75–98.

Linz, Juan J., and Alfred Stepan. 1996. *Problems of Democratic Transition and Consolidation; Southern Europe, South America, and Post-Communist Europe*. Baltimore: The Johns Hopkins University Press.

Londoño, Ernesto. 2015. Taking Stock of the $10 Billion Washington Spent on Colombia's War. *New York Times*, November 16. https://archive.nytimes. com/takingnote.blogs.nytimes.com/2015/11/16/taking-stock-of-the-10-bil lion-washington-spent-on-colombias-war/.

Malloy, James M. 1974. Authoritarianism, Corporatism and Mobilization in Peru. In *The New Corporatism: Socio-Political Structures in the Iberian World*, eds. Frederick B. Pike and Thomas Stritch, 52–84. South Bend, IN: University of Notre Dame Press.

Malone, Mary Fran T., Lucía Dammert, and Orlando J. Pérez. 2023. *Making Police Reform Matter in Latin America*. Boulder: Lynne Rienner.

Marshall, Monty G., and Ted Robert Gurr. 2018. Polity5 Political Regime Characteristics and Transitions, 1800–2018. https://www.systemicpeace.org/polityproject.html.

Martínez, Rafael. 2013. Objectives for Democratic Consolidation in the Armed Forces. In *Debating Civil-Military Relations in Latin America*, eds. Rafael Martínez and David R. Mares, 43–95. Liverpool, United Kingdom: Liverpool University Press.

Oeffinger, John Clay, Shane Moran, and Florina Christiana Matei. 2022. Chile. In *The Handbook of Latin American and Caribbean Intelligence Cultures*, eds. Florina Christiana Matei, Carolyn Halladay, and Eduardo E. Estévez, 111–128. Lanham, MD: Rowman & Littlefield.

Pérez, Orlando J., and Randy Pestana 2016. Honduran Military Culture. Jack Gordon Institute Research Publications. https://gordoninstitute.fiu.edu/research/military-culture-series/orlando-j-perez-and-randy-pestana-2016-honduran-military-culture1.pdf.

RESDAL, Latin American Security and Defence Network. 2024. *A Comparative Atlas of Defence in Latin America and the Caribbean*. Montevideo, Uruguay: RESDAL Internacional.

Rock, David. 1987. *Argentina, 1516–1987: From Spanish Colonization to Alfonsín*. Berkeley: University of California Press.

Roy, Diana. 2024. Crossing the Darién Gap: Migrants Risk Death on the Journey to the U.S. Council on Foreign Relations. July 22. https://www.cfr.org/article/crossing-darien-gap-migrants-risk-death-journey-us.

Ruiz, Paula. 2023. En 10 años, Costa Rica pasó de 35 a 340 organizaciones criminales con sicarios dentro de sus estructuras. *El Observador*. October 3.

Sanchez, Wilder Alejandro. 2025. With Stryker Deal, Argentina Tightens US Defense Ties. Breaking Defense. July 10. https://breakingdefense.com/2025/07/with-stryker-deal-argentina-tightens-us-defense-ties/.

Schirmer, Jennifer. 1998. *The Guatemalan Military Project: A Violence Called Democracy*. Philadelphia: University of Pennsylvania Press.

Schulz, Donald E., and Deborah Sundloff Schulz. 1994. *The United States, Honduras, and the Crisis in Central America*. Boulder: Westview.

Siegel, Daniel, and Joy Hackel. 1988. El Salvador: Counterinsurgency Revisited. In *Low-Intensity Warfare: Counterinsurgency, Proinsurgency, and Antiterrorism in the Eighties*, eds. Michael T. Klare and Peter Kornbluh, 112–135. New York: Pantheon.

Stanley, William. 1999. Building New Police Forces in El Salvador and Guatemala: Learning and Counter-Learning. *International Peacekeeping* 6 (4): 113–134.

Sylvia, Ronald D., and Constantine P. Danopoulos. 2005. Civil-Military Relations in a Civilianized State: Panama. *Journal of Political & Military Sociology* 33 (1): 81–96.

Thoumi, Francisco E. 2002. Illegal Drugs in Colombia: From Illegal Economic Boom to Social Crisis. *The Annals of the American Academy of Political and Social Science* 582: 102–116.

Tillman, Ellen D. 2021. The Dominican Republic: From Military Rule to Democracy. In *Oxford Encyclopedia of the Military in Politics*, eds. William R. Thompson and Hicham Bou Nassif. Oxford: Oxford University Press. https://oxfordre.com/politics/display/10.1093/acrefore/9780190228637.001.0001/acrefore-9780190228637-e-1811.

Trindade Viana, Manuela. 2022. *Post-conflict Colombia and the Global Circulation of Military Expertise*. Cham, Switzerland: Palgrave Macmillan.

Ungar, Mark. 2021. The Police of Honduras. In *Global Perspectives in Policing and Law Enforcement*, ed. Josepter M. Mbuba, 281–294. Lanham, MD: Lexington.

United Nations Office on Drugs and Crime. 2011. 2011 Global Study on Homicide: Trends, Contexts, Data. https://www.unodc.org/documents/data-and-analysis/statistics/Homicide/Globa_study_on_homicide_2011_web.pdf.

United Nations Office on Drugs and Crime. 2023. UNODC Global Study on Homicide in 2023: Homicide and Organized Crime in Latin America and the Caribbean. https://www.unodc.org/documents/data-and-analysis/gsh/2023/GSH_2023_LAC_web.pdf.

United Nations Office on Drugs and Crime. 2024. United Nations Crime Trends Survey. https://dataunodc.un.org/dp-intentional-homicide-victims-est.

United Nations Office on Drugs and Crime. 2025. World Drug Report. https://www.unodc.org/unodc/en/data-and-analysis/world-drug-report-2025.html.

Upton Institute. 2022a. Military Recruitment Data Set, Version 2022. https://www.uptoninstitute.org/data.

Upton Institute. 2022b. Military Schools Data Set, Version 2022. https://www.uptoninstitute.org/data.

Valencia, Alexandra. 2025. Ecuador Legislature Backs Reform Allowing Foreign Military Bases. *Reuters*. June 3. https://www.reuters.com/world/americas/ecuador-legislature-backs-reform-allowing-foreign-military-bases-2025-06-03/.

von Boemcken, Marc, Max Mutschler, Markus Bayer, Rolf Alberth, Rodrigo Bolaños Suárez, Marius Bales, Carina Schlüsing, Paul Rohleder, Jürgen Brandsch and Stella Hauk. 2023. Global Militarization Index, Codebook, Version 3.0. https://gmi.bicc.de/#rank@2022.

White, Peter B. 2017. Crises and Crisis Generations: The Long-term Impact of International Crises on Military Political Participation. *Security Studies* 26 (4): 575–605.

Williams, Philip J. 1990. Elections and Democratization in Nicaragua: The 1990 Elections in Perspective. *Journal of Interamerican Studies and World Affairs* 32 (4): 13–34.

Woodward, Ralph Lee, Jr. 1999. *Central America: A Nation Divided*, 3rd ed. New York: Oxford University Press.

Zinevich, Benjamin. 2024. US Troops will Return to Ecuador, Decades After Removal by Correa. *Peoples Dispatch*. February 20. https://peoplesdispatch. org/2024/02/20/.us-troops-will-return-to-ecuador-decades-after-removal-by-correa/#.

CHAPTER 4

Violent Policing in Brazil: Brutality, Inequality, and Public Order

INTRODUCTION

On December 2, 2024, São Paulo Military Police broke up a street party in the Cidade Ademar neighborhood. Afterward, video was posted online of a police officer throwing a man off a bridge into the canal below. The action appeared completely unprovoked and unnecessary, given that the victim was surrounded by several police officers and not resisting; fortunately, he survived (Duran 2024). Public outcry was particularly strong because of the availability of video footage documenting the abuse and because it came on the heels of several other high-profile acts of police brutality, including the killing of an unarmed shoplifter in a supermarket and a medical student who police officers chased into a hotel after claiming he had hit their car (Latin American Weekly Report [LAWR] 2024a).

Policing in Latin America is often highly militarized, revolves around combatting drugs and organized crime, and impunity for excesses is widespread. In this chapter, we focus on Brazil because it is an extreme case. The shocking violence of events such as the assault described above, or the seven-hour gun battle in Bahia state between Military Police and suspected drug gangs on March 4, 2025 that left 12 people dead (Nascimento 2025), as well as national statistics, depict a pattern of policing that is a major source of state violence. In 2023, Brazilian police killed 6,393 people, an average of more than 17 people per day (Fórum Brasileiro de Segurança Pública [FBSP] 2024, 61). Fogo Cruzado, the civil society organization that tracks gunshots in Brazil, found that in 2024, police action was responsible for 29% of shootings nationwide. In Bahia state it was even more severe: police operations in 2024 accounted for 59% of mass shootings—incidents resulting in three or more deaths (Fogo Cruzado 2025).

Brazilian policing demonstrates the persistence of state violence in the democratic era and its troubling resurgence in recent years. State violence was at its worst during the military dictatorship (1964–85). Beginning with democratization in 1985, conditions of state violence improved significantly and held steady from the late 1980s through the 1990s. Further improvements came in the early 2000s. The positive developments of the 1990s–2000s in Brazil, however, were followed by a precipitous decline beginning in 2016, when state violence dramatically worsened in an era of punitive populism.[1]

We begin this chapter by outlining the normative ideals of policing and its importance to democracy. We then focus on police violence in Brazil, given the extreme nature of the problem there, placing it in historical and social context. We conclude by looking at selected examples throughout the region to demonstrate that Brazil is emblematic of a larger regional trend of (re)militarization of policing, *mano dura* ("iron fist") policies, and impunity for police violence.

Democratic Policing

Following David Bayley (1990), we define police as "people authorized by a group to regulate interpersonal relations within the group through the application of physical force" (7). In keeping with our understanding of state violence overall, as described in Chapter 1, policing is a function of the organized violence of the state and therefore involves the use of force or the anticipation of its use. The use of force in democratic policing must adhere to the principles of legality, necessity, and proportionality (Amnesty International [AI] 2016b).

Good policing lies at the heart of good democracy because "policing represents a people's use of force against itself" (Bayley 1990, 6). Though police use violence, at times, democratic policing is restrained, as the power of the state is dispersed among many actors. Police may apprehend a suspect, but it is not the job of police to be the proverbial judge, jury, and executioner. Determining guilt or innocence is up to other authorities—and the punishment of the guilty is up to still others. The rule of law requires that everyone is equal before the law and that people believe the system to be fair, rather than treating people differently based on social status or other circumstances that warps the law in their favor, exempts them from it, or prejudicially targets them in its application (Jackson et al. 2022). Moreover, when police engage in misconduct or violate the law themselves, their status as agents of the state should not exempt them from accountability. Policing based on the rule of law can be summed up as "enforcing the law while obeying the law" (Sozzo 2016, 339).

In addition to restraints on how police can engage in violence, democratic policing requires police to act as public servants, performing a duty for the fellow members of their community, as embodied in Peel's Principles.[2] These nineteenth-century ideals emphasize the importance of police legitimacy—that is, public acceptance of the lawful exercise of police power—through securing public cooperation in observing the law, equal application of the law regardless of one's social status, police adherence to the law independent of public opinion or government policy, and restraint in the use of physical force when it must be applied (Reith 1975, 149). Police and the public benefit from commitment to the ideal that "the police are the public and the public are the police; the police being only members of the public who are paid to give full-time attention to duties which are incumbent on every citizen, in the interests of community welfare and existence" (Reith 1975, 163–164). Police must protect the public so that citizens can exercise their democratic rights such as freedom of speech, assembly, organizing, protesting, and casting a vote. Likewise, police must protect elected leaders and other officials of the state so they can fulfill their duties on behalf of the people.

Ultimately, protection of human rights, minimal use of force, and accountability are essential components of ideal democratic policing (Prado et al. 2012). Democratic policing is vital for democracy to thrive. Policing after authoritarianism and in the highly unequal socioeconomic conditions of Latin America is fraught with problems that undermine these ideals. Ineffective policing results in constrained citizenship, reducing people's ability to participate in public life, and unequal policing results in stratified citizenship, in which existing inequalities are reinforced (González 2017, 495). Daniel Brinks and Sandra Botero (2014) summarize the troubling nature of post-dictatorship policing: "in spite of concerted efforts at legal reform, most police forces in the region no longer target political opponents but continue to torture and kill on a large scale in the interest of social order. The key to the failure is that these violations target one of the most economically, socially, and politically disadvantaged populations in the region: young urban males, often unemployed, often black, often suspected (or guilty) of petty crimes" (223).

This problem reflects and reinforces the challenges of weak rule of law and unequal citizenship rights in the region. Though electoral democracy has survived in recent decades, not everyone enjoys membership in the political community necessary for liberal democracy (Nord et al. 2025, 13). Democratic procedures, such as holding elections and transferring power between political parties are followed, but these amount to "democracies without citizenship" (Iturralde 2010, 310), given that people are not equal in the eyes of law enforcement—either to merit protection by police or from police. Socioeconomic inequalities and poor-performing institutions undermine faith in the system, thereby creating or reinforcing incentives to use violence for survival, protection, or gain (Caldeira and Holston 1999; Sanchez 2006). Rather than broad-based, egalitarian politics, democracy in these conditions can amount to a "dictatorship over the poor" (Wacquant 2003). In the next section, we examine the case of Brazil to demonstrate the causes and effects of police violence.

Violent Policing in Brazil

Throughout Brazil's history, policing has relied on physical violence to maintain the country's highly unequal social and economic systems. Policing is characterized by the uneven application of force against lower status groups rather than equal enforcement of the law. In the democratic era, violent policing has electoral appeal, resulting in a paradox of the co-existence of fear and outrage against police abuses alongside support and acceptance of them. There are near-constant police reform efforts, but these are often too small or limited in scope to bring widespread change.

The Origins of Violent Policing: From Empire to Military Rule (1822–1964)

As a colony of Portugal (1500–1822) and as an independent empire (1822–1889), slavery was legal in Brazil. Portuguese expeditions of *bandeirantes* (slave-hunters) in the São Paulo area took place in the

1600s–1700s, enslaving indigenous people (Hudson 1998, 12–13; Skidmore 1999, 10), and millions of Africans were brought to Brazil as slaves from the 1500s to the 1800s.[3] The plantation economy relied on slave labor, and in 1830, slaves outnumbered free persons (Skidmore 1999, 52). White Brazilian elites feared slave uprisings, and the earliest policing in Brazil revolved around controlling the slave population. In the empire, large landowners maintained and commanded units of state militias; there was no separation between the plantation owners and the violent force used to uphold the system (Keith 1976, 61). Nighttime curfews were in effect from the 1820s to 1870s, and while they formally applied to everyone, in practice they amounted to "a reign of selective policing" based on race (Chazkel 2020, 108). Thus, from the beginning of Brazil's modern history, the state used violence to control racialized underclasses while "high-status individuals saw themselves as immune" to it (Clark 2008, 96; Pereira 2000, 219).

The Rio de Janeiro police, established in 1831, recaptured escaped slaves and participated in the disciplining of slaves by whipping them "for a fee, at the request of the slave owners" (Pereira 2019, 150). On patrol, rather than carrying out arrests and turning suspects over to other state authorities for trial and punishment, police would immediately whip slaves they perceived as disrespectful or posing a danger to public order (Holloway 1993, 138). Similarly, one of the main functions of the state militia of São Paulo was to recapture runaway slaves (Dallari 1976, 85). By the 1870s, almost 75% of blacks and *pardos* (people of mixed ancestry) were free (Chalhoub 2011, 408). Nevertheless, police treated free blacks and *pardos* with hostility, presuming them to be fugitive slaves, leading to hundreds of racially motivated arrests in Rio in the 1860s and 1870s and many cases of illegal enslavement after arrest (Chalhoub 2011, 432–433).

In 1888, Brazil finally abolished slavery, but social stratification by race remained (Skidmore 1995, 97), and the state enacted new vagrancy laws that expanded public order offenses and established agricultural penal colonies where arrested former slaves were sent to work (Huggins 1985, 62). With the arrival of new immigrant laborers, landowners used "the militia in the solution of social conflicts....as if they were the guardians of the planters' special interests, practicing every kind of violence against the immigrants and their families" (Dallari 1976, 86). Moreover, the São Paulo state forces violently put down railway strikes and suppressed other popular political activity in the early 1900s (Dallari 1976, 89–90).

The United States began training Brazilian police in the 1950s, aimed at countering communism during the Cold War (Huggins 1998, 95–96). Among the developments of this era was the creation of special elite patrol squads tasked with "hunting down and disposing of Rio's bandits by any and all means...[and] it was not long before bodies with signs of torture and marked with skull and crossbones began appearing in Rio slums, fields, and ditches" (Huggins 1998, 97). Meanwhile, the federal army grew in size and political ambition, assuming a significant role in Brazil's modernization and economic development (Ronning 1976, 216). By the time of the 1964 coup d'etat, the military and its extensive intelligence apparatus had a thoroughly anti-communist mission and worked along-side the police to carry out politically motivated repression against the civilian population (Stepan 1988).

Military Dictatorship and the Institutionalization of Police Violence (1964–85)

During the military dictatorship (1964–85), state forces were responsible for disappearances, arbitrary detentions, and arrests on national security charges. Habeas corpus rights were formally still in effect under the constitution, but Institutional Act 5 overrode this protection for national security-related cases (Comissão Nacional da Verdade [CNV] 2014, 304). People were often held in detention for long periods without being brought to trial. When trials did take place, they were held in military courts because the dictatorship was relying on the 1953 Law of National Security as the legal basis for its actions (Pereira 1998).[4] Detainees were held incommunicado, denied access to defense counsel, and frequently subjected to torture (CNV 2014; Pereira 2005). There was near-total impunity for police violence, with the conduct being dismissed as the result of "over-enthusiastic new recruits who [had] not undergone sufficient training" (LAWR 1980).

Police operations relied heavily on extreme violence. This era saw the creation of new special units such as the Rondas Ostensivas Tobias de Aguiar (ROTA) of the São Paulo Military Police to fight urban guer-rillas (Barcellos 1992). In their targeting of journalists, lawyers, and members of political parties and labor unions, Brazilian police carried out armed operations that resulted in the death of those they were meant to arrest. The Military Police, for example, reported the deaths of 363 criminal suspects from January to August 1982, with "most...said to have happened during arrest" (AI 1983, 117). State authorities fabricated claims about how victims died, often stating they were killed while trying to escape arrest or as a result of an armed confrontation, regardless of evidence to the contrary (AI 1977, 127; CNV 2014, 447–455). In 1969, for example, when police killed Carlos Marighella, the former Brazilian Communist Party member of the Chamber of Deputies, they claimed he died in a shootout. However, there was no evidence that Marighella fired a weapon, and at least one of the gunshots inflicted on his body was fired at close range, consistent with an execution (CNV 2014, 448). These violent policing operations also led to the arrest of large numbers of people. The initial post-coup Operation Cleanup resulted in tens of thousands of arrests (Huggins 1998, 121–122). From January to February 1977, police in São Paulo detained 28,000 people on suspicion of ordinary crime (AI 1977, 128).

While in detention, state authorities subjected prisoners to physical and psychological torture to extract confessions from them (AI 1976, 90). Methods of torture included the infamous "parrot's perch," which "consists of an iron bar wedged behind the victim's knees and to which his wrists are tied; the bar is then placed between two tables, causing the victim's body to hang some 20 or 30 centimeters from the ground" (Dassin 1998, 16). Prisoners were also subject to electrocution, drowning, sexual abuse, beatings, extreme cold, loud noises, sleep deprivation, and withholding of food and water (CNV 2014, 335; Dassin 1998). Prisoners were also tormented with snakes, alligators, and cockroaches (Dassin 1998, 21–22). Reported cases of torture were at their highest in 1969 and 1970 (CNV 2014, 349), but the practice was widespread throughout the dictatorship, and it went uninvestigated by the judiciary (Pereira 2005, 76). Many people died in state custody as a result of torture. The authorities often covered up their responsibility for these deaths by calling them suicides (AI 1980, 115; CNV 2014, 468–477).

These abuses took place in clandestine facilities operated by the military and police. Army officers commanded the Department of Information Operations-Command for Internal Defense Operations (DOI-CODI), Brazil's internal intelligence agency during the dictatorship (Dassin 1998, 78). DOI-CODI operated out of army bases and carried out their abuses in these "joint facilit[ies] for civilian and military torturers" (CNV 2014, 728). Military and police installations across the country served as torture centers (CNV 2014, 831–833)—one of the most notorious of these sites was an army barracks in São Paulo at the headquarters of Brazil's Second Army (AI 1976, 91; CNV 2014, 755). The government applied this system of violent policing to counter demonstrations over prosaic issues such as public services and cost of living. For example, in 1968, when protestors objected to the end to a restaurant subsidy in Rio, police "fired indiscriminately" at the group, killing a high school student. When mourners and demonstrators gathered in the ensuing days, they too were attacked by police, including with a cavalry charge of Military Police on horseback (Huggins 1998, 141). Police violently suppressed riots by poor housewives over shortages of black beans in Rio de Janeiro in 1976 (LAWR 1976). In 1979, police injured hundreds of people in Maranhão when they attacked demonstrators who had been demanding affordable bus service for students (LAWR 1979). In 1981, police in São Paulo injured and arrested many people who were protesting poor train service (LAWR 1981).

In rural areas, violent policing occurred in the context of conflict over land. Landowners targeted indigenous groups and the landless. Local police failed to protect them from violence and were often suspected of involvement in kidnappings and killings (AI 1981, 120; 1985, 129). Countering land occupations by landless peasants, police worked in conjunction with hired gunmen to evict them, such as the 1979 expulsion in Pará state of 400 families from land owned by a São Paulo bank, or the 1985 killing of a 78-year-old man "when a force of 80 military police fired into peasants' houses while evicting them" from a settlement in the state of Maranhão (AI 1986, 132).

Those who protested police misconduct were also subject to a violent response. For example, police in Mato Grosso shot and killed a Jesuit priest when he and a bishop went to the police station "to plead for clemency for two women who were being tortured there" (AI 1977, 128). Journalists investigating state abuses were targeted, as with the high-profile killing in police custody of Vladimir Herzog in 1975 and the shooting death of Mario Eugênio de Oliveira in 1984 (AI 1985, 128; Dávila 2013, 143). Overall, violent policing in Brazil during the military regime involved meting out arbitrary violence to impose social order, rather than genuine enforcement of the law (Willis 2016, 480).

State Violence in Transition (1980s)

Brazil began its long road back to democracy in 1979 with the installation of General João Figueiredo as president, congressional elections, repeal of Institutional Act No. 5, and the restoration of habeas corpus (Bacchus 1987, 157–162; Hudson 1998, 82). The transitional era was a period of institutional change and attempts at human rights reforms, but violent policing persisted, and simultaneous economic crises and proliferation of societal violence meant that harsh policing methods in pursuit of public order continued. Improvements in legal protections under the new 1978 Law of National Security were minimal and often violated by the authorities.[5] For example, the law only reduced the number of days a detainee could be held incommunicado from 10 to 8, rather than abolishing the practice altogether. Some military judges simply rejected the law's mandate to reduce prison sentences for political crimes (AI 1979, 51–52). Moreover, the law still allowed the military government to curtail political and civil rights, which it used to arrest and imprison labor leaders and journalists who published information critical of the regime (AI 1980, 114; 1981, 119). Military courts retained jurisdiction over national security crimes and were known to hold suspects incommunicado (AI 1988, 97; Andreu-Guzmán 2018).

Growing opposition to military rule, uneven economic performance, and a mounting debt crisis kept the transition on track in the early 1980s. The military government cut back on its outright repression of political opposition. Amendments to the National Security Law in 1983 reduced the time a suspect could be kept in custody before their trial, nearly halved the number of offenses that could be prosecuted as national security crimes, moved many cases to civilian courts, and lessened the permissible sentences for those convicted (AI 1984, 132; Bacchus 1990, 122).[6]

The political transition also involved efforts to civilianize public security. The Military Police, the uniformed branch responsible for day-to-day policing, were state-level institutions, but they came under the direct control of the armed forces during the dictatorship. In 1966, the Institutional Act No. 3 banned the direct election of state governors, but the democratization process reestablished gubernatorial elections in 1982.[7] Newly elected governors sought to reassert their control over policing (Hudson 1998, 278; Hunter 1997, 50). Reform-minded governors in the most populous states of Rio de Janeiro and São Paulo took a lead role in wresting control of the Military Police from the army. Beginning in 1983, governors had the power to select the commander of their state's Military Police, and the commander no longer had to be an army officer (Hunter 1997, 50–51). The 1988 constitution reiterated the division of labor between the Military Police, responsible for "policing and preserving public order," and the Civil Police, responsible for criminal investigations, both answering to elected governors.[8] These moves reversed the centralization of control over policing that took place early in the dictatorship through the 1967 Police Organic Law, which placed police forces under the authority of each state's military-appointed secretary of public security (Huggins 1998, 130).[9]

Now responsive to electoral demands, governors also sought to make good on their campaign promises to enhance public security, including safety from violent and arbitrary policing. In São Paulo, Governor André Franco Montoro implemented reforms aimed at reducing torture and shootings of not only political dissidents but also ordinary citizens (Chevigny 1995, 146). He placed the Civil Police, in charge of the station houses where torture was typically carried out, under the leadership of station chiefs with law degrees. To deal with the worst abuses of street policing, Montoro also targeted specialized tactical units, such as the notorious Rondas Ostensivas de Tobias Aguiar (ROTA), and "dismiss[ed] the most violent members," ultimately resulting in the firing of over 1,800 Military Police between 1983 and 1986 (Chevigny 1995, 153).[10] Additionally, a new method of tracking police weapons was introduced—firearms would now be issued daily to individual officers, rather than as a group, thereby making it possible to connect specific weapons to shootings in a manner that had not been possible before (Caldeira 2000, 167).

While these reform efforts were positive developments, they had limited success. Torture and extrajudicial execution of criminal suspects and ordinary civilians was still a common occurrence. São Paulo Military Police "shot dead 220 people in the first nine months of 1986" (AI 1987, 139). The repeated use of grotesque torture methods to punish prisoners was common at the 6,000-inmate Casa de Detencão at Carandiru Prison in São Paulo, as well as at individual police stations. For example, after an attempted escape from the 42nd police precinct station, officers crammed over 50 prisoners into a small cell with no ventilation, resulting in 18 deaths by asphyxiation. Police interfered with investigations into these types of abuses. After the incident at the 42nd precinct station, two police officers were suspended for 30 days but then "were transferred to active duty at the Police Disciplinary Board, which was investigating the case" (AI 1988, 99; 1990, 48).

The new political and police leadership also struggled to reorient policing toward public service in its new mandate to refer to members of the public as *cidadão* (citizen) and to protect labor demonstrations rather than reflexively responding to them with violent repression (Caldeira 2000, 167; Chevigny 1995, 151). Police violence against striking workers and peasant leaders, however, continued. In 1986, police fired on a group of striking sugar workers in Leme, São Paulo, killing one and wounding seven (AI 1987, 139). In Marabá, Pará, in 1987, Military Police killed 20 people when they forcibly cleared protestors from a bridge who were demonstrating against dangerous working conditions at a local mine (AI 1988, 98). In 1988, when the army responded with force to a strike at the Volta Redonda steel mill, three workers were killed and more than 40 wounded (AI 1989, 110). Military Police in Rio Grande do Sul carried out a large-scale expulsion of 600 peasant families in 1989, firing indiscriminately into the crowd and wounding at least 14 people, followed by the detention and torture of peasant leaders (AI 1990, 47–48).

Moreover, reform efforts proved unpopular with both the police and the public. Police were accustomed to being autonomous and thus opposed scrutiny over their actions. They saw legal oversight as a hindrance to fighting crime (Caldeira 2000, 166–167) and resisted reforms through slowdowns in their work (Chevigny 1995, 151). Meanwhile, the public, faced with economic crisis and rising crime in the early 1980s, interpreted police reforms and a focus on human rights as "privileges for bandits" (Caldeira 2000, 159). They embraced harsh police responses to criminality, especially because of an overriding feeling that the legal system did not work and therefore the informal justice of violent policing and vigilantism was necessary for public order (Chevigny 1995, 158; Willis 2016). In a poll taken in 1982, 85% of respondents opposed disbanding ROTA (Caldeira 2000, 171). Governor Montoro in São Paulo lost reelection in 1986, and his successors reversed his reforms, including removing reformist secretaries of public security and reinstating dismissed members of ROTA (Caldeira 2000, 174; Chevigny 1995, 146). Police violence worsened in the ensuing years. In the first half of 1989, police in Rio de Janeiro were believed to be responsible for over 1,000 killings, many carried out by "'extermination groups' made up of civilian vigilantes and members of the civil and military police" (AI 1990, 48). São Paulo police killed hundreds of people every year in the 1980s–90s, with a peak in 1991–92 at over 1,000 deaths each year (Chevigny 1996, 26; Caldeira 2000, 162), accounting for as much as 15% of homicides in the São Paulo metro area (Chevigny 1995, 148).

To summarize, reform efforts in the transitional period had some short-lived positive effects, and state violence directly motivated by partisanship came to an end. Policing in Brazil, however, continued its long-standing practice of targeting marginalized populations in pursuit of public order in a society with deep racial, economic, social, and geographic divisions (Caldeira 2000; Pereira 2000; Costa and Thompson 2011; Willis 2015).

Reduced but Persistent State Violence (1990s–2000s)

Brazil's democracy stabilized in the late 1980s and early 1990s. The country held direct presidential elections in 1989, went through multiple electoral cycles, and successfully transferred power from one political party to another, even weathering an impeachment crisis in 1992 (Weyland 2005). Elected civilian governments also reduced the political power of the military (Hunter 1997). Stabilization and survival, however, did not translate to high-quality democracy. Instead, the new system was a "partial regime," characterized by growing inequalities and shortcomings in the rule of law that undermined democratic practice (Kingstone and Power 2000, 4–8). Civil rights continued to be violated, even as political rights were renewed in the democratic era (Caldeira and Holston 1999). Nowhere was this disjunction more evident than through the actions of police forces (Pinheiro 1997, 262).

Formally, the state made important commitments to reduce violence and strengthen the rule of law. The 1988 constitution guaranteed basic physical integrity rights, such as placing prohibitions on torture, slavery, and cruel treatment.[11] It also established due process rights, including the right to a fair, public trial by jury, and guaranteed habeas corpus rights, seeking to prevent unlawful detention by the state. Moreover, it specified that "no one shall be arrested unless *in flagrante delicto* or by written and substantiated order of a competent judicial authority"—that is, for police to make an arrest, a person would either have to be caught in the act of committing a crime or would need to be served with a warrant issued by a judge.[12] In 1989, Brazil ratified the United Nations Convention against Torture and Other Cruel Inhuman or Degrading Treatment or Punishment.[13] In 1998, the country accepted the jurisdiction of the Inter-American Court of Human Rights (Pinheiro 2000, 134). The 1988 constitution also empowered the federal Public Prosecutor's Office in the Public Ministry to conduct oversight of the police (Lemgruber 2002, 12–13). States created their own Offices of the Police Ombudsman, which "systematically documented and published reports on police violence" (Mesquita Neto 2006a, 164).

With the goal of improving police performance and winning public trust, states also established new programs and partnerships. Many states began human rights awareness training in conjunction with the National Secretariat of Human Rights and local human rights organizations (United States Department of State [USDS] 1999). They created women's police stations (Hautzinger 2007) and Police Stations of Racial Crimes (Santos 2005, 138). Multiple states experimented with community policing, which as practiced in Brazil in the 1990s, was a form of policing involving "participation by the community and by local state agencies in designing ways to reduce crime rates, reduce the sense of citizen insecurity, and increase public acceptance of the police, while also improving social monitoring of police actions" (Smulovitz 2006, 207).

Yet, for a variety of reasons, new formal rules and institutions, experiments in new policing models, and efforts to reform police structures, were largely ineffective in changing the violent nature of policing in Brazil. First, many of the partnerships and community policing efforts were short-lived, experimental pilot programs, and they remained separate from the existing Military Police. For example, the Neighborhood Policing program under Governor Leonel Brizola in Rio de Janeiro in 1991 lasted only two months and was undertaken in only a few neighborhoods. It was often difficult to engage the public effectively because even while improvements could be seen, abuses and corruption remained high (Arias and Ungar 2009, 422). These limitations made it difficult from the outset to achieve real change and ensured police and political leaders who opposed these programs could simply wait them out. One of the lessons of these shortcomings was the need to mobilize many government agencies to improve conditions and to engage in reform of more than just the police (Muniz et al. 1997; Mesquita Neto 2006b, 45).

Second, many reform efforts in the democratic era were reactions to major incidents of state violence and reflected crisis management more than concerted long-term strategies to confront systemic abuses. For example, in 1992, in response to a fight among prisoners at the Carandiru prison, São Paulo Military Police massacred over 100 inmates (Human Rights Watch [HRW] 1992). This led to the creation of a police-civilian working group the following year (Caldeira 2000, 177; Mesquita Neto 2006b, 48). As noted above, this prison had been the site of consistent abuses for years, and despite the attention the horrific 1992 massacre brought, torture and other abuses there continued (USDS 1997). Similarly, the community policing initiatives in São Paulo emerged in response to protests over videotapes of police abuses and a subsequent police strike, rather than through proactive reform efforts (Mesquita Neto 2006b, 48).

The national government was similarly motivated by reaction to crisis, instead of forethought. President Fernando Henrique Cardoso announced his National Plan for Public Security (PNSP) in 2000, one week after the high-profile hijacking of Bus 174 in Rio de Janeiro in which one woman was killed and the hostage taker later died in police custody. The PNSP outlined many laudable principles of public security, including countering impunity, integrating social policies with public safety, and calling for multifaceted government reform, but it was far from an actionable plan (Dellasoppa and Branco 2006). Brazil's federal system further complicated these efforts. Because police forces are state-level institutions, the national government's power was limited to providing guidance, coordination, and incentives for reform. States thus opted out of the PNSP.

Finally, police and their political allies rejected major reforms (Smulovitz 2006). Constitutional changes would have been necessary to alter the fundamental structure of police forces, and proposals to civilianize the Military Police or to merge the Civilian Police and Military Police "were systematically blocked by the congressional lobbies of the armed forces and the military police" (Mesquita Neto 2006b, 47). Reformers found that police would not buy in to small programmatic changes like community policing because those infringed on their turf (Smulovitz 2006, 219), and major institutional changes put them on the defensive, leading to outright resistance (Ward 2006, 180).

Together, the short-termism of pilot programs, the reactionary crisis-management nature of political attention to policing, and resistance from police to major changes meant "the Brazilian democratic state [was] not able to reform the police structure inherited from dictatorship" (Pinheiro 2002, 117). Consequently, despite democratization, state violence continued in a context of high levels of crime and public fear of crime, socioeconomic inequality, and systemic prejudice in society that meant police violence persisted, especially targeting people marginalized by race, geography, and socioeconomic status (Chevigny 1996; Costa and Thompson 2011; Huggins 2010). Police continued to arbitrarily arrest people in sweeps through public spaces or in raids on people's homes (HRW 1994, 22–23; USDS 1997). Police killings were common (AI 2015; HRW 1994, 80; 1997, 43) and police continued to use torture in questioning suspects as well as to extract payment to let them go (HRW 1994; USDS 2006).

In the urban favelas, the absence of the state left residents at the mercy of growing criminal enterprises such as drug gangs and paramilitary *milicias* (self-defense militias) that developed in response (Wolff 2019; Zaluar 2004). The government implemented a "border patrol" model of policing that maintained the literal and figurative boundaries between social groups in Brazil's highly segregated cities (Caldeira 2000; Pinheiro 2002, 117). Police operations took on the military character of periodic *blitz* raids into favelas (HRW 1996). At times, even units of the regular army were deployed to favelas as in Operation Rio in 1994 (Koonings 1999, 229). In these raids, heavily armed police, supported by helicopters, entered a favela and fired indiscriminately, "killing possible suspects or just (young black) males who happened to be in the wrong place at the wrong time" (Kruijt and Koonings 2015, 39).

In rural areas, police violence continued against squatters and those fighting for land reform. In 1996, for example, police in the state of Pará responded to a protest march by landless workers by firing tear gas at them and machine-gunning the crowd (USDS 1997). Nineteen people were killed, with evidence that at least 10 of them were executed after the confrontation (USDS 1997). A similar massacre of squatters was perpetrated by state forces in Rondônia in 1995, with the wounds on the victims' bodies indicating they "had been killed from behind while kneeling" (USDS 1997). Civil Police killed the founder of the Movement of Rural Workers in 2000 in Mato Grosso do Sul and reported it as a "resistance death" (USDS 2002). When violently evicting 500 members of the Landless Rural Workers Movement in Rio Grande do Sul in 2009, police shot and killed one man and tortured others by tying them up "for hours with their hands behind their necks, some on top of ant hills" (USDS 2010).

Surge in State Violence (2016–22)

As illustrated above, policing in the 1990s–2000s continued to be very violent, yet it represented a dramatic decrease from the even higher levels of violence that characterized the 1964–85 military regime. Without a qualitative shift to better practices, however, improvements are fragile and can be reversed quickly. Beginning in the mid-2010s, Brazil experienced political turmoil, severe economic downturn, the spotlight of hosting major international sporting events, followed by the Covid-19 pandemic in 2020–22, which increased government pressure for quick fixes and violent responses to the problems of crime and social disorder. As a result, in this era of punitive populism, public order violence grew much worse, returning to levels not seen since the mid-1980s.[14]

In Rio de Janeiro, beginning in 2008, the government implemented yet another experimental reform—Police Pacification Units (UPPs), which were intended to provide a consistent police presence in the favelas along with renewed efforts at providing infrastructure and social services such as health care and education (Felbab-Brown 2011). The program had some success in reducing crime and violence in the first few years but ultimately suffered from the same challenges as previous reform efforts—lack of political commitment, failure of the social policies to fully materialize, divisions within the police over this encroachment on traditional Military Police, as well as ongoing violence from UPPs in the favelas (Salem 2017; Washington Office on Latin America 2016). Overall, policing continued to rely on the performance of "violent spectacle," especially through highly militarized units such as Special Operations Battalion (Larkins 2013; Meira 2016). Large-scale armed invasions of favelas, utilizing heavy weaponry such as armored personnel carriers and helicopters continued, reflecting the overwhelming view that police are at war with the population (FBSP 2016, 28–29). Instead of policing being understood as one part of the law enforcement process, geared toward crime prevention and apprehending suspects to be prosecuted and punished by other state institutions, police continue to be employed as an "agent of social control" (Willis 2016). Police and the public are skeptical of the ability of courts and lawyers to enforce the law, and they favor violence against marginalized populations (Goldani 2021; Jackson et al. 2022, 126).[15] Paradoxically, the public supports violent policing, even

while fearing it (FBSP 2016, 6).[16] Ultimately, police violence dispropor-
tionately affects black male adolescents, especially in favelas (FBSP 2024;
USDS 2018; Vargas and Alves 2010).

In 2011, Dilma Rousseff succeeded Luiz Inácio Lula da Silva as president of Brazil. Lula was a very popular president who oversaw a period of
economic growth. Within the next few years, however, both Dilma and
Lula were embroiled in corruption scandals that eventually led to Dilma's
removal from office and Lula's imprisonment. In addition to this political
turmoil, Brazil experienced one of the worst economic contractions in its
history. Poverty, which had been declining in the early 2010s, increased
significantly after 2014, and unemployment exploded, rising from 6.8% in
2014 to 13.7% in 2020.[17] Majorities of Brazilians reported fearing being
the victim of crime and changing daily behavior, such as limiting recre-
ation, because of concerns over insecurity (Muggah and Aguirre Tobón
2018, 11).[18]

This period of political and economic crisis coincided with Brazil's
hosting of major international sporting events—the Confederations Cup
in June 2013, the World Cup in June 2014, and the Rio Olympics in
August 2016. In the lead up to the Confederations Cup, there were
nationwide protests over poor public services in the face of wasteful
spending on hosting duties. The government violently suppressed these
demonstrations (HRW 2014, 216). During the games themselves, violent
policing continued, as the country sought to make itself presentable to
international audiences (USDS 2014). These practices repeated themselves in the following years, with detentions and police use of excessive
force against protests before and during the World Cup and Rio Olympics
(AI 2014, 2016a). Overall, police violence in Brazil increased significantly
during this period of upheaval. Beginning in 2013, deaths resulting from
police interventions increased every year until 2021.[19] Over the decade
there was a 188.9% increase in deaths caused by police (FBSP 2024, 22).
On average, killings by police account for 13% of total intentional violent
deaths in the country (FBSP 2020, 84; 2022, 14).

In 2019, former army captain and long-time right-wing member of
congress, Jair Bolsonaro, was inaugurated as president. Illustrating the
dynamic of punitive populism in democracy, he campaigned on a platform of nationalism and divisive rhetoric pitting "good citizens" against
"bandits" who he encouraged Brazilians to see as an internal enemy to
be destroyed, especially through police violence (Machado and Pimenta
2022). This viewpoint only reinforced the state-level problems that

emerged under President Michel Temer, who succeeded Rousseff after her impeachment. Through the increased use and expanded scope of Guarantee of Law and Order operations, which involve deploying the army in policing duties, the federal government assumed a larger role in policing and increased impunity for state violence (Harig 2020). In 2017, for example, the congress passed a new law ensuring that military personnel would not be subjected to the jurisdiction of civilian courts.[20] Moreover, in response to an increase in violence in the state of Rio de Janeiro, in early 2018 President Temer took the extraordinary step of giving the military command over public security there (Latin American Security and Strategic Review 2019). When Bolsonaro came into office, he expanded the use of GLOs and their scope (Akkoyunlu and Lima 2022, 44), as well as attempting many executive actions to give police and others a free hand to use violence against people he declared to be criminals (LAWR 2019). The continued role of the United States is evident here in joint Federal Bureau of Investigation (FBI) police training, US State Department funding, and reliance of the Brazilian police on US weapons, ranging from firearms to armored vehicles (Bouchard 2025).

There have been some limited successes in combatting state violence. High courts played an important role, an avenue for reform that we discuss in more detail in Chapter 7. In the state of Rio de Janeiro, a coalition of civil society organizations, along with the Brazilian Socialist Party and the Rio state Public Defender's Office, brought an Action for Breach of a Fundamental Precept to the Federal Supreme Court in 2020 (Conectas 2020; FBSP 2020, 92). The measure was granted, temporarily suspending regular police operations in Rio de Janeiro. Instead, police were restricted to actions only in "exceptional cases," which they would have to "justify in writing…to the Public Prosecutor's Office," which is responsible for police oversight (FBSP 2020, 92).[21] In 2022, in conjunction with the ruling of the Inter-American Court of Human Rights in *Favela Nova Brasilia* v. *Brazil*, the supreme court required Rio to develop a Police Lethality Reduction Plan.[22] These were positive developments for the state of Rio, which experienced a 34.5% drop in killings attributed to police from 2022 to 2023 (FBSP 2024, 57). Action by the Supreme Court has also been responsible for holding the government accountable for deaths and injuries caused by stray bullets. After a long legal fight, the Supreme Court issued a landmark ruling in April 2024 that requires the state to compensate victims and their families of this form of unintentional police violence.[23] Overall, however, police lethality has grown enormously over the last decade, and the small improvements observed in these success stories have been offset nationwide by a large increase in state violence in Bahia, the northeastern states, and states of the Amazon. As in earlier periods, the public is wary of police violence, but putting an end to it, even in a democratic context, is very difficult. As Ronald Ahnen (2007) writes about the relationship between state violence and democracy, "the impact of democracy on respect for basic rights...depends on the social, political, and economic context in which it operates" (144). As illustrated by Brazil's experience, fear of crime and social disorder can lead to the paradoxical public disapproval and fear of police violence, along with its widespread use and acceptance. High levels of crime and violence can make harsh policing appealing. Brazil accounts for only 3% of the global population yet accounts for over 10% of homicides worldwide (FBSP 2024, 26). Especially where faith in the justice system is weak, violent policing is seen as an acceptable option in pursuit of public order (Jackson et al. 2022). Moreover, politicians vow to direct this violence at an otherized enemy, intentionally mobilizing voters behind a promise to reward them with security while punishing the opposition (Bonner 2019). Politicians find little benefit from pursuing police reform (González 2019). It is electorally a riskier proposition than violent policing when restraint in the face of high crime is perceived as capitulation to the forces of disorder. The underlying political, social, and economic conditions driving the problems with policing in Brazil will not be sufficiently addressed anytime soon and thus this form of state violence will likely continue at high levels into the foreseeable future.

Re-Militarization, *Mano Dura*, and Impunity in Violent Policing

While extreme, Brazil is not unique. Across Latin America, state violence through policing is a serious problem. Governments respond violently to issues as varied as gangs and organized crime preying on citizens to landless squatters and labor unions carrying out protests. They have adopted measures that (re-)militarize public security, turn policing into repression, and perpetuate impunity for abuses.

Elected presidents often emphasize military support in moments of political crisis and use the armed forces to put down protests or respond to overwhelming security challenges. During the 2019 protests in Chile, for example, President Sebastián Piñera went on television gratuitously surrounded by military personnel to sign the orders extending his state of emergency. While security forces fired on the public in the streets, it was an unmistakable signal to any public or partisan opposition that he maintained the support of the military (Fisher 2019). At the same time, in Peru, while at an impasse with congress over calling new legislative elections, President Martín Vizcarra released images of himself seated with the chiefs of the army, navy, and national police (Perú21 2019). In Ecuador, when President Guillermo Lasso invoked the *muerte cruzada* (crossed death) clause of the constitution to call early presidential and legislative elections in 2023, the military announced its support and "warn[ed] that the armed forces would crack down on any violence" (Garcia Cano and Solano 2023).

When faced with security crises, governments empower their militaries to take on regular policing duties. Faced with a dramatic increase in violence from drug trafficking organizations in Ecuador in 2024, President Noboa put the army on the streets and gave it control over prisons, which immediately led to allegations of torture and other abuses against those who were detained (LAWR 2024c). He used states of exception to suspend civil liberties and to give security forces extraordinary powers including executing warrantless raids (LatinNews Daily 2024e). He also approved the establishment of new military bases to expand the army's physical presence (LAWR 2025c). Military units now man checkpoints and patrol the streets, which has produced appalling acts of violence. In December 2024, a military patrol in Guayaquil, for example, forcibly disappeared four children on their way home from a football game. No formal arrest was made, nor were they charged with any crime. Instead, they were reportedly taken to an air force base, and their bodies were discovered over two weeks later, on Christmas Eve (LatinNews Daily 2025d). This shocking case led to public protests, but the expansion of military operations continued.

Argentina has similarly militarized policing. When criminal violence surged in Rosario in 2023, President Alberto Fernández sent federal police and gendarmes (militarized national guard) to the city (LAWR 2023).[24] The following year, with security problems escalating, new right-wing populist President Javier Milei added "naval prefecture, airport security police, and federal police" to the deployment as well as more "logistical support" from the armed forces (LatinNews Daily 2024b). President Milei also proposed new security legislation that would have allowed the use of the military in regular policing; when his proposal stalled out in congress, he issued two executive decrees that gave the Minister of Security the authority to use the military "to guard any strategic objective or any asset considered of national interest" without the declaration of a state of emergency (LAWR 2025a; LatinNews Daily 2024c).[25]

In Mexico, President Felipe Calderón deployed the army in 2006 to fight organized crime. Demonstrating one of the dangers of using the regular army for policing duties, this was meant to be a temporary measure, but by the time Calderón left office in 2012, the armed forces were "effectively substituting for—rather than merely supporting—the police" (HRW 2018). Moreover, when President Andrés Manuel López Obrador came into office in 2018, he created the new National Guard as a civilian institution, specifically to reduce the militarization of public security (Washington Office on Latin America 2020). Nevertheless, it was staffed with police and military transferred from other units, and eventually it came fully under the control of the armed forces (Washington Office on Latin America 2022).

Leaders of the left and right in Latin America have turned to the military in recent years, and the move enjoys popular support (Kyle and Reiter 2019, 21–22). Fear of crime and a lack of confidence in regular police and judiciaries to tackle insecurity has led voters and their governments to embrace *mano dura* (iron fist) approaches to policing, which focus on punitiveness and repression, typically through militarization; fewer restraints on the use of force; and mass incarceration (Rosen and Cutrona 2021; Singer et al. 2020). Punitive populism has proven a popular political strategy in many countries.

President Nayib Bukele introduced an extreme form of *mano dura* policing in El Salvador in 2022, arresting and imprisoning tens of thousands of people and keeping them in inhumane conditions without ever bringing them to trial (AI 2024). At least 261 people died in custody between 2022 and 2024, with many deaths caused by asphyxiation, trauma, or illnesses, including those such as kidney failure and malnutrition that indicate severe deprivation of food and water (Cristosal 2024b, 9). Prison authorities conceal information about deaths in custody and thwart any investigation that would make it possible to determine responsibility (Cristosal 2024b). President Bukele has also used the police and military to intimidate civil society and arrest critics, including human rights defenders and journalists investigating the regime's corruption and abuses (Janetsky and Alemán 2025; Cristosal 2024a; LatinNews Daily 2025e).

The decline in national homicide rates has kept Bukele's popularity high and has led many other countries to believe they can follow the "Bukele model" of mass arrests. Peru's Justice Minister, Eduardo Arana, visited El Salvador in February 2024 to meet with Salvadoran officials and learn about their prison system and how to implement it in Peru (LatinNews Daily 2024g). Bukele traveled to Costa Rica in November 2024 to encourage President Rodrigo Chaves to adopt hardline security policies, including the construction of a massive new prison (LatinNews Daily 2024d). This is an especially troubling development for Costa Rica, since it overturned the public security policies introduced at the beginning of Chaves' term that were oriented toward crime prevention and bolstering social programs (LatinNews Daily 2025c). It also comes at a time when several police officers stand accused of beating a suspect to death in their custody (LAWR 2025b). As a promise to the "Bukele lovers" in Ecuador, President Daniel Noboa promised at the beginning of 2024 to build two mega-prisons exactly like El Salvador's 40,000-inmate capacity Terrorism Confinement Center (LatinNews Daily 2024f).[26] In Argentina, under President Milei, prisons have adopted the performative aspects of the Bukele model such as shaving prisoners' heads and positioning them seated shirtless against one another with their heads bowed for degrading photo ops (LatinNews Daily 2024a).

Once governments use heavy-handed police tactics to combat violence caused by organized crime, drug trafficking, and gangs, they can easily be applied to suppress political opposition. In Chile in 2019, as noted earlier, the government of Sebastian Piñera used the police and military to respond violently to protests over socioeconomic inequality. Police beat protestors with batons, intentionally hit them with their vehicles, and used conventional firearms as well as "less-lethal weapons" such as rubberized buckshot to fire at civilians, causing severe injuries and multiple deaths (AI 2020). Austerity measures in many countries have led to public protests, which police and military put down with force. In Panama, police and protestors clashed in February 2025 over proposed changes to social security, including raising the retirement age, resulting in many police injured and hundreds of protestors arrested (LatinNews Daily 2025f). In Argentina, President Milei's massive cuts to government services prompted major protests. Security forces responded with violent crackdowns, firing canisters of tear gas into crowds and shooting protestors with rubber bullets, causing serious injury. In both of these cases, cuts to government services were accompanied by new laws to criminalize protest, effectively legalizing public order violence and more readily putting civilians in violent conflict with the state (Associated Press 2024; Kane 2024; LatinNews Daily 2025a, 2025b).

Exacerbating the crisis of police violence in Latin America is a culture of impunity. As we discuss in more detail in Chapter 7, there is an elaborate legal framework that prevents accountability for abuses committed by state security forces. On March 7, 2025, President Noboa in Ecuador announced "preemptive pardons for police and military personnel responding to an armed attack that killed at least 22" people in Guayaquil (Canizares et al. 2025). In Peru, congress passed the Police Protection Act in March 2020 in the early days of the Covid-19 pandemic, providing legal immunity for military and police personnel for any abuses they committed while enforcing quarantine and curfews (HRW 2020).[27] Years after the 2019 protests in Chile, there were only 27 convictions from the more than 10,000 complaints filed against military and police personnel (AI 2023).

CONCLUSION

Providing public safety is an important role of the state, yet the variability of state institutions makes effective policing a major challenge across Latin America. Policing that can lawfully provide security is essential to high-quality democracy by making it possible for people to participate in politics, civil society, and the economy. Police cannot provide this on their own, however. The broader state apparatus must be oriented toward the public interest, adhering to the rule of law and instilling legitimacy in the state's exercise of its power. Full and equal citizenship is crucial to democratic success, as it instills a sense of belonging and literal membership in the group making decisions on questions as crucial as the use of force within the community. As we explore in Chapter 5, violence directed outward, in the management of international borders and movement across them, is also a major source of state violence in Latin America today.

NOTES

1. The V-Dem "Physical violence index" gives Brazil nearly the worst score possible (0.02) for the first decade of the 1964–85 military regime. Conditions improved marginally from 1975 to 1978 (0.02 to 0.07), followed by a greater positive change, to 0.21, in 1979. From 1984 to 1987, Brazil's score jumped from 0.21 to 0.61. During the 2000s, Brazil consistently scored 0.73 before dropping to 0.44 beginning in 2016 (Coppedge et al. 2025). We discuss the term punitive populism (Bonner 2019) and its role in state violence at length in Chapter 1.
2. Robert Peel was Home Secretary of the United Kingdom when Parliament passed the Metropolitan Police Act of 1829, establishing the Metropolitan Police in London. The new civilian police were a departure from the "militiamen and soldiers" who were otherwise responsible for keeping order (Roth 2001, 259). In contemporary terms, there was popular pressure to *de-militarize* policing after the 1818 Peterloo Massacre, in which British cavalry charged a crowd of 60,000 workers and their families in Manchester, killing 11 people and wounding at least another 500 (Reith 1975, 142–143). An essential change was the orientation of policing toward crime prevention, rather than being primarily reactionary (Roth 2001). The first two commissioners who Peel appointed, Charles Rowan and Richard Mayne, developed the nine principles (Reith 1975, 155–167).
3. Slave Voyages, Trans-Atlantic Slave Trade – Database, https://www.slavevoyages.org/assessment/estimates/.
4. Lei Nº 1.802, de 5 de janeiro de 1953, "Define os crimes contra o Estado e a Ordem Política e Social, e dá outras providências." Copies of all primary documents cited in the book are available at www.andyreiter.com.
5. Lei Nº 6.620, de 17 de dezembro de 1978, "Define os crimes contra Segurança Nacional, estabelece sistemática para o seu processo e julgamento e dá outras providências."
6. Lei Nº 7.170, de 14 de dezembro de 1983, "Define os crimes contra a segurança nacional, a ordem política e social, estabelece seu processo e julgamento e dá outras providências."
7. Ato Institucional Nº 3, de 5 de fevereiro de 1966.

8. Chapter III, Article 144, §6, Brazil's Constitution of 1988 with Amendments through 2017, https://www.constituteproject.org/ constitution/Brazil_2017. The federal government still has the power to mobilize state-level police as auxiliary units of the national armed forces.

9. Decreto-Lei No 317, de 13 de março de 1967, "Reorganiza as Polícias e os Cargos de Bombeiros Militares dos Estagiados, dos Territórios e do Distrito Federal e dá outras providências."

10. From January to September 1981, ROTA was responsible for shooting 136 people, killing 129 of them (Chevigny 1995, 152).

11. Chapter I, Article 5, III and XLVII, Brazil's Constitution of 1988 with Amendments through 2017, https://www.constituteproject. org/constitution/Brazil_2017.

12. Chapter I, Article 5, LXI, Brazil's Constitution of 1988 with Amendments through 2017, https://www.constituteproject.org/ constitution/Brazil_2017.

13. UN Treaty Body Database, Ratification Status for Brazil, https:// tbinternet.ohchr.org/_layouts/15/TreatyBodyExternal/Treaty. aspx?CountryID=24&Lang=en.

14. Brazil's score on the V-Dem "Physical violence index" reached its best performance in the period from 2005 to 2016 (0.73 for each year). The country then experienced a dramatic worsening after 2017, when the score fell to 0.64 in 2018, 0.5 in 2019, and reached its nadir of 0.44 in 2021 and 2022. The last time the score had been below 0.5 was 1985, the last year of the military regime (Coppedge et al. 2025).

15. In 2023, large percentages of respondents in Brazil in the Latinobarómetro survey reported "Little" (38.8%) or "No trust" (21.9%) in the judiciary. See: https://www.latinobarometro.org/ latOnline.jsp.

16. FBSP survey data show that a majority (57%) agree with the statement, "*Bandido bom é bandido morto*" (A good bandit is a dead bandit). Majorities also express sympathy with the police, recognizing that they are targeted by criminal violence and that their working conditions are poor. Meanwhile, majorities also fear being victims of violence from the Military Police (59%) or Civil Police (53%) and believe that the police use excessive force (70%) (2016, 6).

17. World Bank, "Poverty headcount ratio at $3.00 a day (2021 PPP) (% of population) – Brazil," World Development Indicators database, https://data.worldbank.org/topic/poverty?locations=BR; World Bank, "Unemployment, total (% of total labor force) (national estimate)—Brazil," World Development Indicators database, https://data.worldbank.org/indicator/SL.UEM.TOTL.NE.ZS?locations=BR.
18. In response to the question, "How frequently do you worry about being the victim of violent crime?" 66.4% of those surveyed by Latinobarómetro in Brazil said "All or almost all of the time" and 16.6% said "Sometimes." Only 9.4% said "Never." See: https://www.latinobarometro.org/latOnline.jsp.
19. From 2009 to 2015, there were 17,688 deaths resulting from police interventions (FBSP 2016, 6). From 2016 to 2023, there were 47,341 deaths (authors' calculation from FBSP 2017–24 reports).
20. Lei no 13.491, de 13 de outubro de 2017.
21. ADPF 635, Arguição de Descumprimento de Preceito Fundamental, Liminar referendada, Supremo Tribunal Federal (August 5, 2020), https://portal.stf.jus.br/processos/detalhe.asp?incidente=5816502.
22. *Favela Nova* v. *Brazil*, Preliminary Exceptions, Merits, Reparations and Costs, Inter-Am. Ct. H.R. (ser. C) No. 333 (February 16, 2017), https://www.corteidh.or.cr/docs/casos/articulos/seriec_333_ing.pdf; ADPF 635, Arguição de Descumprimento de Preceito Fundamental, Embargos recebidos em parte, Supremo Tribunal Federal (February 3, 2022), https://portal.stf.jus.br/processos/detalhe.asp?incidente=5816502.
23. ARE 1385315, Recurso Extraordinário com Agravo, Julgada mérito de tema con repercussão geral, Supremo Tribunal Federal (April 11, 2024), https://portal.stf.jus.br/processos/detalhe.asp?incidente=6411925.
24. Argentina's 1991 Internal Security Law (Seguridad Interior, Ley Nº 24.059) prohibits direct military policing operations.
25. Decreto 1107/2024, Boletín Oficial Nº 35.571 (December 18, 2024); Decreto 1112/2024, Boletín Oficial Nº 35.572 (December 19, 2024).
26. By the end of the year, however, this promise was significantly scaled back and the government abandoned plans to build a

new prison in the Amazonian province of Napo after sustained indigenous-led protests against it (LAWR 2024b).
27. Law No. 31012, El Peruano Diario Oficial del Bicentenario (March 28, 2020).

REFERENCES

Ahnen, Ronald E. 2007. The Politics of Police Violence in Democratic Brazil. *Latin American Politics and Society* 49 (1): 141–164.
Akkoyunlu, Karabekir, and José Antonio. Lima. 2022. Brazil's Stealth Military Intervention. *Journal of Politics in Latin America* 14 (1): 31–54.
Amnesty International. 1976. *The Amnesty International Report 1 June 1975–31 May 1976*. London: Amnesty International Publications.
Amnesty International. 1977. *Amnesty International Report 1977*. London: Amnesty International Publications.
Amnesty International. 1979. *Amnesty International Report 1979*. London: Amnesty International Publications.
Amnesty International. 1980. *Amnesty International Report 1980*. London: Amnesty International Publications.
Amnesty International. 1981. *Amnesty International Report 1981*. London: Amnesty International Publications.
Amnesty International. 1983. *Amnesty International Report 1983*. London: Amnesty International Publications.
Amnesty International. 1984. *Amnesty International Report 1984*. London: Amnesty International Publications.
Amnesty International. 1985. *Amnesty International Report 1985*. London: Amnesty International Publications.
Amnesty International. 1986. *Amnesty International Report 1986*. London: Amnesty International Publications.
Amnesty International. 1987. *Amnesty International Report 1987*. London: Amnesty International Publications.
Amnesty International. 1988. *Amnesty International Report 1988*. London: Amnesty International Publications.
Amnesty International. 1989. *Amnesty International Report 1989*. London: Amnesty International Publications.
Amnesty International. 1990. *Amnesty International Report 1990*. London: Amnesty International Publications.
Amnesty International. 2014. Brazil: Protests During the World Cup 2014: Final Overview: No Foul Play, Brazil! Campaign. London: Amnesty International. https://www.amnesty.org/en/documents/amr19/008/2014/en/.

Amnesty International. 2015. You Killed My Son: Homicides by Military Police in the City of Rio de Janeiro. London: Amnesty International. https://www.amnesty.org/en/documents/amr19/2068/2015/en/.

Amnesty International. 2016a. Brazil: A Legacy of Violence: Killings by Police and Repression of Protest at the Rio 2016 Olympics. https://www.amnesty.org/en/documents/amr19/4780/2016/en/.

Amnesty International. 2016b. Use of Force: Guidelines for Implementation of the UN Basic Principles on the Use of Force and Firearms by Law Enforcement Officials: https://policehumanrightsresources.org/content/upl oads/2015/01/ainl_guidelines_use_of_force_0.pdf.

Amnesty International. 2020. Eyes on Chile: Police Violence and Command Responsibility During the Period of Social Unrest. https://www.amnesty.org/en/documents/amr22/3133/2020/en/.

Amnesty International. 2023. Chile: Four Years on From the Social Unrest, Impunity and a Lack of Comprehensive Reparations Persist. October 17. https://www.amnesty.org/en/latest/news/2023/10/chile-four-years-social-unrest-impunity/.

Amnesty International. 2024. El Salvador: The Institutionalization of Human Rights Violations after Two Years of Emergency Rule. March 27. https://www.amnesty.org/en/latest/news/2024/03/el-salvador-two-years-emerge ncy-rule/.

Andreu-Guzmán, Federico. 2018. *Fuero militar y Derecho internacional: Los civiles ante los tribunales militares. Vol 2. of Military Jurisdiction and International Law*. Geneva: International Commission of Jurists. https://www.icj.org/wp-content/uploads/2018/05/Universal-Tribunales-Militares-Vol-II-Publications-Reports-Thematic-reports-2018-SPA.pdf.

Arias, Enrique Desmond, and Mark Ungar. 2009. Community Policing and Latin America's Citizen Security Crisis. *Comparative Politics* 41 (4): 409–429.

Associated Press. 2024. Argentina's Police Step Up Response to Growing Anti-Government Protests. April 15. https://apnews.com/article/protests-milei-rightwing-argentina-hunger-poverty-crackdown-fb43ffa829d56854d6ffc 77b12caf3f2.

Bacchus, Wilfred A. 1987. Controlled Political Transition in Brazil: *Abertura* as a Process for a Gradual Sharing of Political Power. In *Liberalization and Redemocratization in Latin America*, eds. George A. Lopez and Michael Stohl, 137–171. New York: Greenwood.

Bacchus, Wilfred A. 1990. *Mission in Mufti: Brazil's Military Regimes, 1964–1985*. New York: Greenwood.

Barcellos, Caco. 1992. *ROTA 66: A História da Polícia que Mata*. São Paulo: Globo.

Bayley, David. 1990. *Patterns of Policing: A Comparative International Analysis*. New Brunswick, NJ: Rutgers University Press.

Bonner, Michelle D. 2019. *Tough on Crime: The Rise of Punitive Populism in Latin America*. Pittsburgh: University of Pittsburgh Press.

Bouchard, Joseph. 2025. The U.S. Is Helping Brazilian Police Kill. *NACLA*. January 7. https://nacla.org/us-helping-brazilian-police-kill/.

Brinks, Daniel, and Sandra Botero. 2014. Inequality and the Rule of Law: Ineffective Rights in Latin American Democracies. In *Reflections on Uneven Democracies: The Legacy of Guillermo O'Donnell*, eds. Daniel Brinks, Marcelo Leiras, and Scott Mainwaring, 214–239. Baltimore: Johns Hopkins University Press.

Caldeira, Teresa Pires do Rio. 2000. *City of Walls: Crime, Segregation, and Citizenship in São Paulo*. Berkeley: University of California Press.

Caldeira, Teresa Pires do Rio, and James Holston. 1999. Democracy and Violence in Brazil. *Comparative Studies in Society and History* 41 (4): 691–729.

Canizares, Ana Maria, Mauricio Torres, Ivonne Valdés, and Max Saltman. 2025. Ecuadorian President Offers Carte Blanche to Police and Military after Attack Kills 22 in Guayaquil. *CNN*. March 7. https://www.cnn.com/2025/03/07/americas/ecuador-noboa-pardons-attack-latam-intl/index.html.

Chalhoub, Sidney. 2011. The Precariousness of Freedom in a Slave Society. *International Review of Social History* 56 (3): 405–439.

Chazkel, Amy. 2020. Toward a History of Rights in the City at Night: Making and Breaking the Nightly Curfew in Nineteenth-Century Rio de Janeiro. *Comparative Studies in Society and History* 62 (1): 106–134.

Chevigny, Paul. 1995. *Edge of the Knife: Police Violence in the Americas*. New York: The New Press.

Chevigny, Paul. 1996. Changing Control of Police Violence in Rio de Janeiro and São Paulo, Brazil. In *Policing Change, Changing Police: International Perspectives*, ed. Otwin Marenin, 23–35. New York: Garland.

Clark, Timothy W. 2008. Structural Predictors of Brazilian Police Violence. *Deviant Behavior* 29 (2): 85–100.

Comissão Nacional da Verdade. 2014. Relatório da Comissão Nacional da Verdade. December 10. https://cnv.memoriasreveladas.gov.br/.

Conectas. 2020. STF Upholds Suspension of Police Operations in Rio de Janeiro Favelas During the Pandemic. August 4. https://conectas.org/en/noticias/stf-upholds-suspension-of-police-operations-in-rio-de-janeiro-favelas-during-the-pandemic/.

Coppedge, Michael, John Gerring, Carl Henrik Knutsen, Staffan I. Lindberg, Jan Teorell, David Altman, Fabio Angiolillo, Michael Bernhard, Agnes Cornell, M. Steven Fish, Linnea Fox, Lisa Gastaldi, Haakon Gjerløw, Adam Glynn, Ana Good God, Sandra Grahn, Allen Hicken, Katrin Kinzelbach, Kyle L. Marquardt, Kelly McMann, Valeriya Mechkova, Anja Neundorf, Pamela Paxton, Daniel Pemstein, Johannes von Römer, Brigitte Seim, Rachel Sigman,

Svend-Erik Skaaning, Jeffrey Staton, Aksel Sundström, Marcus Tannenberg, Eitan Tzelgov, Yi-ting Wang, Felix Wiebrecht, Tore Wig, and Daniel Ziblatt. 2025. "V-Dem Codebook v15" Varieties of Democracy (V-Dem) Project.

Costa, Arthur Trindade Maranhão, and Timothy Thompson. 2011. Police Brutality in Brazil: Authoritarian Legacy or Institutional Weakness? *Latin American Perspectives* 38 (5): 19–32.

Cristosal. 2024a. Cristosal Raises the Alarm about Militarization and Arrest of People Involved in Community Organizations. March 25. https://cristosal.org/EN/2024/03/25/cristosal-raises-the-alarm-about-militarization-and-arrest-of-people-involved-in-community-organizations/.

Cristosal. 2024b. *El silencio no es opción: Investigación sobre las prácticas de tortura, muerte y justicia fallida en el regimen de excepción.* San Salvador: Cristosal Derechos Humanos. https://cristosal.org/ES/el-silencio-no-es-opcion-informe-completo/.

Dallari, Dalmo de Abreu. 1976. The *Força Pública* of São Paulo in State and National Politics. In *Perspectives on Armed Politics in Brazil*, eds. Henry H. Keith and Robert A. Hayes, 79–112. Tempe: Center for Latin American Studies, Arizona State University.

Dassin, Joan, ed. 1998. *Torture in Brazil: A Shocking Report on the Pervasive Use of Torture by Brazilian Military Governments, 1964–1979.* Austin: University of Texas Press.

Dávila, Jerry. 2013. *Dictatorship in South America.* Chichester, UK: Wiley-Blackwell.

Dellasoppa, Emilio Enrique, and Zoraia Saint'Clair Branco. 2006. Brazil's Public-Security Plans. In *Public Security and Police Reform in the Americas*, eds. John Bailey and Lucía Dammert, 24–43. Pittsburgh: University of Pittsburgh Press.

Duran, Pedro. 2024 PM que jogou homem de ponte é preso em São Paulo. *CNN Brasil.* December 5. https://www.cnnbrasil.com.br/nacional/pm-que-jogou-homem-de-ponte-e-preso-em-sao-paulo/.

Felbab-Brown, Vanda. 2011. *Bringing the State to the Slum: Confronting Organized Crime and Urban Violence in Latin America. Lessons for Law Enforcement and Policymakers.* Washington, DC: The Brookings Institution. https://www.brookings.edu/wp-content/uploads/2016/06/1205_latin_america_slums_felbabbrown.pdf.

Fisher, Max. 2019. 'A Very Dangerous Game': In Latin America, Embattled Leaders Lean on Generals. *New York Times.* October 31. https://www.nytimes.com/2019/10/31/world/americas/latin-america-protest-military.html.

Fogo Cruzado. 2025. *Relatório Anual 2024.*

Fórum Brasileiro de Segurança Pública. 2016. *Anuário Brasileiro de Segurança Pública: 2016.* https://publicacoes.forumseguranca.org.br/handle/123456789/65.

Fórum Brasileiro de Segurança Pública. 2017. *Anuário Brasileiro de Segurança Pública: 2017.* https://publicacoes.forumseguranca.org.br/handle/123456 789/94.

Fórum Brasileiro de Segurança Pública. 2020. *Anuário Brasileiro de Segurança Pública: 2020.* https://publicacoes.forumseguranca.org.br/handle/123456 789/61.

Fórum Brasileiro de Segurança Pública. 2021. *Anuário Brasileiro de Segurança Pública: 2021.* https://publicacoes.forumseguranca.org.br/handle/123 456789/60.

Fórum Brasileiro de Segurança Pública. 2022. *Anuário Brasileiro de Segurança Pública: 2022.* https://publicacoes.forumseguranca.org.br/handle/123 456789/58.

Fórum Brasileiro de Segurança Pública. 2023. *Anuário Brasileiro de Segurança Pública: 2023.* https://publicacoes.forumseguranca.org.br/handle/123456 789/229.

Fórum Brasileiro de Segurança Pública. 2024. *Anuário Brasileiro de Segurança Pública: 2024.* https://publicacoes.forumseguranca.org.br/handle/123456 789/253.

Garcia Cano, Regina, and Gonzalo Salano. 2023. Ecuador's President Dismisses Legislature as it Tries to Oust Him, in a Move that Promises Turmoil. *Associated Press.* May 17. https://apnews.com/article/ecuador-president-dissolves-national-assembly-impeachment-ec47b677d44a7e0105959ecde8963ec0.

Goldani, Julia Maia. 2021. Notes on Law and Police Occupational Culture in Brazil's Military Polices: An Explorative Study. *Oñati Socio-Legal Series* 11 (6): 1463–1491.

González, Yanilda María. 2017. 'What Citizens Can See of the State': Police and the Construction of Democratic Citizenship in Latin America. *Theoretical Criminology* 21 (4): 494–511.

González, Yanilda María. 2019. The Social Origins of Institutional Weakness and Change: Preferences, Power, and Police Reform in Latin America. *World Politics* 71 (1): 44–87.

Harig, Christoph. 2020. Soldiers in Police Roles. *Policing and Society* 30 (9): 1097–1114.

Hautzinger, Sarah L. 2007. *Violence in the City of Women: Police and Batterers in Bahia, Brazil.* Berkeley: University of California Press.

Holloway, Thomas H. 1993. *Policing Rio de Janeiro: Repression and Resistance in a Nineteenth-Century City.* Stanford, CA: Stanford University Press.

Hudson, Rex A., ed. 1998. *Brazil: A Country Study,* 5th ed. Washington, DC: Library of Congress.

Huggins, Martha K. 1985. *From Slavery to Vagrancy in Brazil: Crime and Social Control in the Third World.* New Brunswick, NJ: Rutgers University Press.

Huggins, Martha K. 1998. *Political Policing: The United States and Latin America*. Durham, NC: Duke University Press.

Huggins, Martha K. 2010. Systemic Police Violence in Brazil. In *Police Use of Force: A Global Perspective*, eds. Joseph B. Kuhns and Johannes Knutsson, 73–82. Santa Barbara, CA: Praeger.

Human Rights Watch. 1992. Brazil: Prison Massacre in São Paulo. Vol. IV, Issue 10.

Human Rights Watch. 1994. *Final Justice: Police and Death Squad Homicides of Adolescents in Brazil*. New York: Human Rights Watch.

Human Rights Watch. 1996. Brazil: Fighting Violence with Violence: Human Rights Abuse and Criminality in Rio de Janeiro. Vol. 8, No. 2 (B).

Human Rights Watch. 1997. *Police Brutality in Urban Brazil*. New York: Human Rights Watch.

Human Rights Watch. 2014. *World Report 2014: Brazil*. New York: Human Rights Watch.

Human Rights Watch. 2018. Mexico: The Militarization of Public Security. October 5. https://www.hrw.org/news/2018/10/05/mexico-militariz ation-public-security.

Human Rights Watch. 2020. Peru: Law Protects Abusive Policing. May 12. https://www.hrw.org/news/2020/05/12/peru-law-protects-abu sive-policing.

Hunter, Wendy. 1997. *Eroding Military Influence in Brazil: Politicians Against Soldiers*. Chapel Hill: University of North Carolina Press.

Iturralde, Manuel. 2010. Democracies without Citizenship: Crime and Punishment in Latin America. *New Criminal Law Review: An International and Interdisciplinary Journal* 13 (2): 309–332.

Jackson, Jonathan, Krisztián Pósch, Thiago R. Oliveira, Ben Bradford, Sílvia. M. Mendes, Ariadne Lima Natal, and André Zanetic. 2022. Fear and Legitimacy in São Paulo, Brazil: Police-Citizen Relations in a High Violence, High Fear City. *Law and Society Review* 56 (1): 122–145.

Janetsky, Megan, and Marcos Alemán. 2025. With Trump as Ally, El Salvador's President Ramps Up Crackdown on Dissent. *Associated Press*. June 12. https://apnews.com/article/trump-bukele-el-salvador-crackdown-dissent-el-faro-7e54e98156ec1954f7de7c578ca94427.

Kane, Corey. 2024. The Iron Fist of José Raúl Mulino, Panama's New President. *NACLA*. June 11. https://nacla.org/iron-fist-jose-raul-mulino-pan amas-new-president.

Keith, Henry H. 1976. Armed Federal Interventions in the States During the Old Republic. In *Perspectives on Armed Politics in Brazil*, eds. Henry H. Keith and Robert A. Hayes, 51–78. Tempe: Center for Latin American Studies Arizona State University.

Kingstone, Peter R., and Timothy J. Power. 2000. Still Standing or Standing Still? The Brazilian Democratic Regime Since 1985. In *Democratic Brazil: Actors, Institutions, and Processes*, eds. Peter R. Kingstone and Timothy J. Power, 3–13. Pittsburgh: University of Pittsburgh Press.

Koonings, Kees. 1999. Shadows of Violence and Political Transition in Brazil: From Military Rule to Democratic Governance. In *Societies of Fear: The Legacy of Civil War, Violence and Terror in Latin America*, eds. Kees Koonings and Dirk Kruijt, 197–234. London: Zed.

Kruijt, Dirk, and Kees Koonings. 2015. Exclusion, Violence and Resilience in Five Latin American Megacities: A Comparison of Buenos Aires, Lima, Mexico City, Rio de Janeiro and São Paulo. In *Violence and Resilience in Latin American Cities*, eds. Kees Koonings and Dirk Kruijt, 30–52. London: Zed.

Kyle, Brett J., and Andrew G. Reiter. 2019. A New Dawn for Latin American Militaries. *NACLA Report on the Americas* 51 (1): 18–28.

Larkins, Erika Robb. 2013. Performances of Police Legitimacy in Rio's Hyper Favela. *Law and Social Inquiry* 38 (3): 553–575.

Latin American Security and Strategic Review. 2019. Brazil: Rio de Janeiro: Life After Military Intervention. January.

Latin American Weekly Report. 1976. Brazil. October 22.

Latin American Weekly Report. 1979. Brazil. September 28.

Latin American Weekly Report. 1980. Society: The Poor Seek Redress through Violent Crime. January 4.

Latin American Weekly Report. 1981. Brazil. February 13.

Latin American Weekly Report. 2019. Brazil: Tough-on-Crime Talk Takes Center Stage. November 28.

Latin American Weekly Report. 2023. Send in the Army—Really? March 9.

Latin American Weekly Report. 2024a. Brazil: São Paulo Police under Pressure Over Alleged Brutality. December 5.

Latin American Weekly Report. 2024b. Ecuador: Government Backtracks on Amazon Prison. December 19.

Latin American Weekly Report. 2024c. Ecuador: Torture Allegations Heighten Scrutiny on Gang Crackdown. February 15.

Latin American Weekly Report. 2025a. Argentina: Milei's Chainsaw Still Revving in Second Year. January 9.

Latin American Weekly Report. 2025b. Costa Rica: Worries over Crime. February 20.

Latin American Weekly Report. 2025c. Ecuador: A Violent Start to the Year. February 27.

LatinNews Daily. 2024a. Argentina: Gov't Cracks Down on Prisoners. March 7.

LatinNews Daily. 2024b. Argentina: Gov't Responds to Rosario Violence. March 13.

LatinNews Daily. 2024c. Argentina: Milei Wants Military Role in Public Security. August 19.

LatinNews Daily. 2024d. Costa Rica/El Salvador. November 13.

LatinNews Daily. 2024e. Ecuador: Noboa Announces 'Phase Two' of Crackdown. May 23.

LatinNews Daily 2024f. Ecuador: Noboa Promises New Prisons for 'Bukele lovers.' January 5.

LatinNews Daily. 2024g. Peru: Plans to Imitate El Salvador's Prison Model. February 23.

LatinNews Daily. 2025a. Argentina: Pensions Protest Turns Violent. March 13.

LatinNews Daily. 2025b. Argentina: Tensions Build as More Protests Loom. March 19.

LatinNews Daily. 2025c. Costa Rica: Gov't Moving on El Salvador-Inspired Jail. April 10.

LatinNews Daily. 2025d. Ecuador: Outrage Over Murder of Arrested Children. January 2.

LatinNews Daily 2025e. El Salvador: Arrest and Disappearance of Leading Activist Draws Outrage. May 20.

LatinNews Daily. 2025f. Panama: Protests Turn Violent Over Proposed Social Security Reform. February 13.

Lemgruber, Julita. 2002. *Civilian Oversight of the Police in Brazil: The Case of the Ombudsman's Offices*. Rio de Janeiro: Center for Studies on Public Security and Citizenship. https://biblioteca.cejamericas.org/bitstream/handle/2015/1045/cescec-civilian-oversight.pdf.

Machado, Marta Rodriguez de Assis, and Raquel de Mattos Pimenta. 2022. Authoritarian Zones within Democracy. *Verfassung und Recht in Übersee/Law and Politics in Africa, Asia and Latin America* 55 (4): 441–458.

Meira, Breno Luna. 2016. Brazilian Military Police: A Culture of Brutality. *Revista da Faculdade de Direito de São Bernardo do Campo* 22 (2).

Mesquita Neto, Paulo de. 2006a. Paths toward Police and Judicial Reform in Latin America. In *Toward a Society under Law: Citizens and Their Police in Latin America*, eds. Joseph S. Tulchin and Meg Ruthenburg, 153–170. Washington, DC: Wilson Center.

Mesquita Neto, Paulo de. 2006b. Public-Private Partnerships for Police Reform in Brazil. In *Public Security and Police Reform in the Americas*, eds. John Bailey and Lucía Dammert, 44–57. Pittsburgh: University of Pittsburgh Press.

Muggah, Robert, and Katherine Aguirre Tobón. 2018. Citizen Security in Latin America: Facts and Figures. Igarapé Institute, Strategic Paper 33, April. https://igarape.org.br/wp-content/uploads/2018/04/Citizen-Security-in-Latin-America-Facts-and-Figures.pdf.

Muniz, Jacqueline, Sean Patrick Larvie, Leonarda Musumeci, and Bianca Freire. 1997. Resistências e dificuldades de um programa de policiamento comunitário. *Tempo Social* 9 (1): 197–213.

Nascimento, Luciano. 2025. Instituto Fogo Cruzado alerta para violência policial na Bahia. *Agência Brasil*. March 5. https://agenciabrasil.ebc.com.br/direitos-humanos/noticia/2025-03/instituto-fogo-cruzado-alerta-para-violen cia-policial-na-bahia.

Nord, Marina, David Altman, Fabio Angiolillo, Tiago Fernandes, Ana Good God, and Steffan I. Lindberg. 2025. *Democracy Report 2025: 25 Years of Autocratization – Democracy Trumped?* V-Dem Institute: University of Gothenburg.

Pereira, Anthony W. 1998. 'Persecution and Farce': The Origins and Transformation of Brazil's Political Trials, 1964–79. *Latin American Research Review* 33 (1): 43–66.

Pereira, Anthony W. 2000. An Ugly Democracy? State Violence and the Rule of Law in Postauthoritarian Brazil. In *Democratic Brazil: Actors, Institutions, and Processes*, eds. Peter R. Kingstone and Timothy J. Power, 217–235. Pittsburgh: University of Pittsburgh Press.

Pereira, Anthony W. 2005. *Political (In)Justice: Authoritarianism and the Rule of Law in Brazil, Chile, and Argentina*. Pittsburgh: University of Pittsburgh Press.

Pereira, Anthony W. 2019. The Police Ombudsman in Brazil as a Potential Mechanism to Reduce Violence. In *The Politics of Violence in Latin America*, ed. Pablo Policzer, 143–170. Calgary: University of Calgary Press.

Perú21. 2019. Fuerzas Armadas Respaldan a Presidente Martín Vizcarra. September 30. https://peru21.pe/politica/martin-vizcarra-fuerzas-armadas-acuden-a-palacio-de-gobierno-para-reunion-noticia/.

Pinheiro, Paulo Sérgio. 1997. Popular Responses to State-Sponsored Violence in Brazil. In *The New Politics of Inequality in Latin America: Rethinking Participation and Representation*, eds. Douglas A. Chalmers, Carlos M. Vilas, Katherine Hite, Scott B. Martin, Kerianne Piester, and Monique Segarra, 261–280. New York: Oxford University Press.

Pinheiro, Paulo Sérgio. 2000. Democratic Governance, Violence, and the (Un)Rule of Law. *Daedalus* 129 (2): 119–143.

Pinheiro, Paulo Sérgio. 2002. The Paradox of Democracy in Brazil. *The Brown Journal of World Affairs* 8 (2): 113–122.

Prado, Mariana Mota, Michael Trebilcock, and Patrick Hartford. 2012. Police Reform in Violent Democracies in Latin America. *Hague Journal on the Rule of Law* 4 (2): 252–285.

Reith, Charles. 1975. *The Blind Eye of History: A Study of the Origins of the Present Police Era*. Montclair, N.J.: Patterson Smith Publishing Corporation.

Ronning, C. Neal. 1976. The Military and the Formulation of Internal and External Policy in Brazil in the Twentieth Century. In *Perspectives on Armed Politics in Brazil*, eds. Henry H. Keith and Robert A. Hayes, 207–224. Tempe: Center for Latin American Studies Arizona State University.

Rosen, Jonathan D., and Sebastián Cutrona. 2021. Understanding Support for *Mano Dura* Strategies: Lessons from Brazil and Colombia. *Trends in Organized Crime* 24 (3): 324–342.

Roth, Mitchel P. 2001. *Historical Dictionary of Law Enforcement*. Westport, CT: Greenwood.

Salem, Tomas. 2017. Diplomats or Warriors? The Failure of Rio's Pacification Project. *NACLA Report on the Americas* 49 (3): 298–302.

Sanchez, Magaly R. 2006. Insecurity and Violence as a New Power Relation in Latin America. *The Annals of the American Academy of Political and Social Science* 606 (1): 178–195.

Santos, Cecília MacDowell. 2005. *Women's Police Stations: Gender, Violence, and Justice in São Paulo, Brazil*. New York: Palgrave Macmillan.

Singer, Alexa J., Cecilia Chouhy, Peter S. Lehmann, Jessica N. Stevens, and Marc Gertz. 2020. Economic Anxieties, Fear of Crime, and Punitive Attitudes in Latin America. *Punishment and Society* 22 (2): 181–206.

Skidmore, Thomas E. 1995. Fact and Myth: Discovering a Racial Problem in Brazil. In *Population, Ethnicity, and Nation-Building*, ed. Calvin Goldscheider, 91–117. Boulder, CO: Westview.

Skidmore, Thomas E. 1999. *Brazil: Five Centuries of Change*. New York: Oxford University Press.

Smulovitz, Catalina. 2006. Citizen Participation and Public Security in Argentina, Brazil, and Chile: Lessons from an Initial Experience. In *Toward a Society under Law: Citizens and Their Police in Latin America*, eds. Joseph S. Tulchin and Meg Ruthenburg, 206–242. Washington, DC: Wilson Center.

Sozzo, Máximo. 2016. Policing after Dictatorship in South America. In *The Sage Handbook of Global Policing*, eds. Ben Bradford, Beatrice Jauregui, Ian Loader, and Jonny Steinberg, 337–355. London: Sage.

Stepan, Alfred. 1988. *Rethinking Military Politics: Brazil and the Southern Cone*. Princeton, NJ: Princeton University Press.

United States Department of State. 1997. Brazil: Country Reports on Human Rights Practices 1996.

United States Department of State. 1999. Brazil: Country Reports on Human Rights Practices 1998.

United States Department of State. 2002. Brazil: Country Reports on Human Rights Practices 2001.

United States Department of State. 2006. Brazil: Country Reports on Human Rights Practices 2005.

United States Department of State. 2010. Brazil: Country Reports on Human Rights Practices 2009.
United States Department of State. 2014. Brazil: Country Reports on Human Rights Practices 2013.
United States Department of State. 2018. Brazil: Country Reports on Human Rights Practices 2017.
Vargas, João Costa., and Jaime Amparo Alves. 2010. Geographies of Death: An Intersectional Analysis of Police Lethality and the Racialized Regimes of Citizenship in São Paulo. *Ethnic and Racial Studies* 33 (4): 611–636.
Wacquant, Loïc. 2003. Toward a Dictatorship over the Poor? Notes on the Penalization of Poverty in Brazil. *Punishment and Society* 5 (2): 197–205.
Ward, Heather H. 2006. Police Reform in Latin America: Brazil, Argentina, and Chile. In *Toward a Society under Law: Citizens and Their Police in Latin America*, eds. Joseph S. Tulchin and Meg Ruthenburg, 171–205. Washington, DC: Wilson Center.
Washington Office on Latin America. 2016. What Can be Learned from Brazil's 'Pacification' Police Model? March 11. https://www.wola.org/analysis/what-can-be-learned-from-brazils-pacification-police-model/.
Washington Office on Latin America. 2020. One Year After National Guard's Creation, Mexico is Far from Demilitarizing Public Security. May 26. https://www.wola.org/analysis/one-year-national-guard-mexico/.
Washington Office on Latin America. 2022. Mexico Deepens Militarization, But Facts Show it is a Failed Strategy. September 2. https://www.wola.org/analysis/mexico-deepens-militarization-but-facts-show-failed-strategy/.
Weyland, Kurt. 2005. The Growing Sustainability of Brazil's Low-Quality Democracy. In *The Third Wave of Democratization in Latin America: Advances and Setbacks*, eds. Frances Hagopian and Scott P. Mainwaring, 90–120. Cambridge: Cambridge University Press.
Willis, Graham Denyer. 2015. *The Killing Consensus: Police, Organized Crime, and the Regulation of Life and Death in Urban Brazil.* Berkeley: University of California Press.
Willis, Graham Denyer. 2016. Police, 'Police' and the Urban. In *The Sage Handbook of Global Policing*, eds. Ben Bradford, Beatrice Jauregui, Ian Loader, and Jonny Steinberg, 479–496. London: Sage.
Wolff, Michael Jerome. 2019. Organized Crime and the State in Brazil. In *The Criminalization of States: The Relationship between States and Organized Crime*, eds. Jonathan D. Rosen, Bruce Bagley, and Jorge Chabat, 323–339. London: Lexington.
Zaluar, Alba. 2004. Urban Violence and Drug Warfare in Brazil. In *Armed Actors: Organised Violence and State Failure in Latin America*, eds. Kees Koonings and Dirk Kruijt, 139–154. London: Zed.

CHAPTER 5

Violence at Mexican Borders: Sovereignty, Drugs, and Migration

INTRODUCTION

On October 1, 2024, Mexican soldiers in the southern state of Chiapas, which borders Guatemala, opened fire on a group of 33 migrants, killing 6 and wounding 10 more (Rodriguez Mega and Wagner 2024). This tragedy was repeated one month later—this time at the northern border—when Mexican National Guard troops in Baja California shot and killed two migrants from Colombia and wounded another four (Latin American Weekly Report [LAWR] 2024a). The statements issued by the Ministry of Defense after each case followed a familiar pattern—their forces were on patrol, encountered "suspicious vehicles" or "heard explosions," and responded by firing on the vehicles, successfully repelling an attack (Rodriguez Mega and Wagner 2024; LAWR 2024a). Meanwhile, they offered no evidence that the victims were armed, and beyond temporarily suspending from duty the officers who fired their weapons, there was no immediate further action; any potential investigation would be handled by the military. This kind of routine use of extreme state violence, and the impunity associated with it, is an example of the pernicious effect of securitization of borders—whereby transnational issues are treated as national security threats to be met with violence followed by impunity.

We focus in this chapter on Mexico, because of its high levels of overall state violence and its centrality in transnational issues in the Americas such

© The Author(s), under exclusive license to Springer Nature Switzerland AG 2025
B. J. Kyle et al., *State Violence and Democracy in Latin America*, Rethinking Political Violence, https://doi.org/10.1007/978-3-032-06412-7_5

as migration and drug trafficking. The United States is a major consumer of illicit drugs (e.g., marijuana, cocaine, and synthetics) that are grown, manufactured, or produced in Mexico or other Latin American countries and trafficked into Mexico on their way to the United States. The so-called "war on drugs" since the 1970s has focused on reducing the supply and movement of drugs through eradication and interdiction (Crandall 2020). These efforts have failed, while being extremely costly both in lives lost and in dollars spent. Meanwhile, the brutality of the drug trade conditions a violent response from the state.

Mexico also plays a central role in migration, again partly due to its geographic proximity to the United States. Mexico is a major migrant-sending country as well as being a transit and destination country, given its position in the "North American corridor," which stretches from Central America to Canada and accounts for the largest move-ment of people in the world (Feldmann et al. 2018, 6). The state often fails to protect migrants from criminal gangs and corrupt officials, and responding to migration through a threat lens, it frequently targets migrants with violence, making this an important source of state violence to consider.

In this chapter, we first discuss borders in Latin America and the state violence associated with monitoring or defending them. Securiti-zation of cross-border phenomena such as drug trafficking and migration is partly produced by and reinforces uneven state capacity, weak rule of law, and inequality. Second, through a case study of Mexico, we illus-trate the prevalence of state violence on the country's northern and southern borders, related to issues of drugs and migration. Mexico is not an isolated case, and so we conclude by illustrating the alarming pattern of militarization of borders and surging state violence against migrants in countries across the region.

Borders, Democracy, and State Violence in Latin America

Controlling who and what crosses a border is a basic function of the state, in which border control is "concerned with regulating entry and exit into the country and implementing immigration law and policy" through "pre-entry level controls, detecting entry into state territory, monitoring and ensuring migrant compliance with the conditions of their visitor's visas, and address the (legal) situation of migrants by reacting to or providing ways out of so-called 'irregularity'" (Gundhus and Franko 2016, 498). The policing of mobility has become especially salient in an era of globalization, which increased trade and population flows while diluting the traditional power of state sovereignty (Weber 2013). Increased attention to borders amounts to a "strategy for expanding and reasserting state sovereignty" (Gundhus and Franko 2016, 498). Mobility policing, however, reaches far beyond a literal international border to create a "ubiquitous border," in which people and goods may be policed by many state and private actors (Weber 2013, 206). As we showed with our discussion of ordinary policing in Chapter 4, the state is meant to be a guarantor of human rights, yet it is often the source of violations due to limited or uneven state capacity, shortcomings in the rule of law, and inequality.

Borders in Latin America have often been among the "ungoverned spaces" that evince a lack of full Weberian monopoly on organized violence in a country's territory (Marcella et al. 2022, 2). The "fragments of empire" that emerged as the region's first states in the early nineteenth century were large confederations (e.g., Gran Colombia, United Provinces of Central America, Peru-Bolivia) that dissolved into smaller entities over the ensuing decades (Loveman 1999, 28–29). The intense conflicts of the region's history have mostly been internal struggles "about the distribution of national riches between classes, individuals, institutions, and regions" that did not warrant the attention of the state to focus on its neighbors nor develop robust institutions to control borders between them (Centeno 2002; Centeno and Ferraro 2013). Central governments, instead, negotiate control with local intermediaries over distant lands in a form of "hybrid sovereignty" (Hochmüller and Idler 2025). The apparent lack of major external threats in the form of dangerous neighboring states has meant a history of relatively few major wars but unresolved competing territorial claims and militarized interstate disputes—the threat, display, or use of force in an international disagreement—along with tensions over cross-border crime and migration (Mares 2012).[1]

The lack of border control combined with weak rule of law have produced a turn toward securitization of borders and cross-border activity—viewing the mobility of people and illegal goods as a threat to national security. Securitization is permitted by weak rule of law and reinforces it, because the threat lens allows governments to "break rules that otherwise would be observed and to resort to extraordinary measures to confront the threat" (Vorobyeva 2015, 44). Governments in the region have also securitized the issue of drugs, often with the aid and influence of the United States. US-led programs such as the Andean Regional Initiative (1989), Plan Colombia (1999–2000), and the Mérida Initiative (2007) have directed billions of dollars to "fighting" the production and trafficking of drugs across borders in the region (Vorobyeva 2015, 50–55). Simultaneously, the securitization of the issue of migration in recent decades has given rise to the notion of "crimmigration"—the criminalization of immigration (Stumpf 2006).

Securitization and criminalization of immigration contributed to the development of the imperfect democracies of the contemporary era. While democracy depends on the idea of political equality and inclusion in decision-making, that equality and participation is extended only to those whom the elite consider to belong to the political community, making democracy "inherently exclusionary" (Barker 2013, 238), overlapping with the mission of borders to distinguish belonging to one state or another. Political mobilization of nationalist sentiment under punitive populism treats migration as a "threat to national identity...presented, and often accepted, as a justification for restrictive and harsh measures that are aimed at protecting the economic or security interests of 'native' inhabitants against those of immigrants, the potential dangerous other" (Koulish and van der Woude 2020, 10). This punitive approach in which criminal sanctions are applied to migration has the dangerous effect of granting governments greater license to use extraordinary measures against people the state deems an "internal enemy" (Stumpf 2006, 419).

Border control therefore demonstrates how state power—including the exercise of state power through democracy—and human rights can be in tension with one another. Borders divide jurisdictions, defining separate political communities and membership within them. The human right of national self-determination permits "the polity [to] be self-governing" (Schmitter and Karl 1991, 81–82), while implying boundaries on the political community—who is included in the collective self and empowered to participate in democracy. At the same time, there is a need to balance the sovereign right of control over territory with the individual human right to cross borders to seek refuge or asylum (Benhabib 2004).

As with democratic policing, "democratic border enforcement" would amount to the state enforcing the border while obeying the law. Securitization of borders, like other uses of public order violence, does not address the underlying drivers of cross-border issues such as migration and drugs, while intensifying state violence and further undermining rule of law. In the next section, we present the case study of Mexico, illustrating the policing of borders as a source of state violence, especially in relation to the issues of drugs and migration.

VIOLENCE AND BORDERS IN MEXICO

Throughout Mexico's history, borders have been poorly controlled. The recent rise in migration and drug trafficking has further challenged that control. This has led to increased securitization of cross-border phenomena, leading to high levels of state violence in the grey area where Mexican sovereignty begins and ends.

Colonial Legacies and International Conflict (1800s–1900s)

In the colonial era, the Viceroyalty of New Spain (1535–1821) claimed land from Central America to northern California, an immense territory. The northern lands were far removed from the seat of power in Mexico City and had only a sparse Spanish presence in the form of missions, army outposts, mining camps, and settlements (Barrett 2012; Jones 1996). Actual colonial occupation of the land was far short of claims on the map (Ganster and Lorey 2016, 27). When Mexico won its independence from Spain in 1821, the newly sovereign state inherited these vast, yet weakly held, territories.[2]

Mexico's 1824 Constitution provided for the establishment of a "permanent army and navy" and assigned it the duty of internal security as well as external defense.[3] In the 1820s, Mexico also established the Civic Militia, a voluntary and unpaid national guard tasked with helping to "preserve domestic order and security...and curb the army's political strength until civil power could be consolidated" (Santoni 2008, 68). Unsurprisingly, few people joined this force (Santoni 2008, 68). There was difficulty filling the ranks of the army as well, leading Mexico to resume the Spanish colonial practice of pressing men into service, which the government had initially banned (Merrill and Miró 1997, 283). By the mid-1800s, the army included at least "22,000 men who had been forcibly rounded up" (Santoni 2008, 66–67).

By the mid-1800s, Mexico's territory had also changed considerably. In the south, Mexico gained territory when the state of Chiapas separated from the newly formed United Provinces of Central America in 1821

140 B. J. KYLE ET AL.

and joined Mexico (Kenyon 1961, 177). Conflict with Guatemala over Chiapas continued until 1842, when Mexico prevailed definitively with a military occupation and annexation of the disputed area of Soconusco (Slade 1917, 260).[4] To the north, conflict with the United States resulted in major losses. Already concerned about US expansionism in the 1820s, Mexico sought to increase the settler population of Texas and use this remote territory as a buffer state with the United States (Ganster and Lorey 2016, 30). This plan backfired. US immigration far outpaced that of Mexican settlers to the state, and "by 1830 Anglos outnumbered Mexicans in Texas by more than five to one" (Mirandé 1987, 7). Mexico "began to take measures to stem the tide of illegal aliens" coming from the United States, including sending the army to Texas "to enforce Mexican laws" (Mirandé 1987, 7). Tensions over a variety of issues, including Mexico's abolition of slavery, led Texas to rebel and gain its independence from Mexico with the defeat of General Antonio López de Santa Anna's army in 1837. Though the fighting stopped, Mexico did not formally recognize Texas' independence. As a result, the US annexation of Texas in 1846 prompted war with Mexico over disputed territory (Griswold del Castillo 1990, 8; Mirandé 1987, 7–8).

The US-Mexican War concluded in 1848 with the signing of the Treaty of Guadalupe Hidalgo, which ceded almost one-third of Mexico's territory to the United States and—along with Gadsden Purchase (1853)—established the modern-day border between the two countries (Ganster and Lorey 2016, 33). The changes on the map were a great shock to the estimated 300,000 people who "lived in the ceded territories and Texas" (Ganster and Lorey 2016, 33). Some people migrated south voluntarily, encouraged by a Mexican repatriation campaign that provided families with free land across the border (Ganster and Lorey 2016, 33), but many more were dispossessed of their land by force or denial of land titles by new US authorities (Mirandé 1987, 39–44). Though the war was formally over, episodic violence continued. In 1859, for example, Juan Cortina, a caudillo whose lands were split in two by the new border, invaded Brownsville, TX (Mirandé 1987, 19). US state and federal forces responded, decisively defeating Cortina's forces in a battle several months later (Manning 2013).

The border remained mostly a formality in this period; people could freely come and go. The significance of the border changed due to the repressive dictatorship of Porfirio Diaz (1876–1911), revolutionary violence, and the response by the United States. For example, in 1906, a strike at a mine near Cananea, Sonora became violent, and the US owners called on US forces to respond. An ad hoc army of federal and Arizona state forces subsequently invaded Mexico. After the incident, the United States and Mexico deployed forces along their border. Revolutionary groups such as the Mexican Liberal Party (PLM) used the sanctuary of the United States to organize raids into Mexico. The US and Mexican armies in turn began more actively patrolling border areas. The US expulsion of PLM members in 1908 was the first major US deportation of Mexicans (Hernández 2022).

Revolutionary conflict continued to impact US-Mexican relations and border areas. During the Mexican Revolution (1910–20), rebels in south Texas created the 1915 Plan of San Diego, which sought to recapture territory lost in 1848 (Sandos 1972). Hundreds of people were killed and thousands displaced by the fighting and reprisals by state and non-state actors (Ganster and Lorey 2016, 69–70). In 1916, Pancho Villa's rebel army attacked a US Army base and the town of Columbus, New Mexico. The United States responded with the year-long Punitive Expedition into Mexico in an ultimately unsuccessful attempt to capture Villa (Britton 2013). It was also in this context that the US "Immigration Service constructed the first border fence to hold back the surge of refugees" fleeing the violence of the revolution (Hernández 2022, 298).

One can also see the origins of the modern pattern of labor migration from this period. "The supply of Mexican labor has been likened to a 'faucet' that can be readily turned 'on' or 'off,' depending on prevailing economic conditions" (Mirandé 1987, 21), and thus, in the economic boom of the early 1900s, border state populations grew significantly as people fled the violence of the Mexican Revolution and found opportunity on the US side of the border. Immigrants and temporary workers contributed to the growing agricultural, mining, and construction sectors (Ganster and Lorey 2016). With the onset of the economic crisis of the Great Depression, however, the United States repatriated over 420,000 people between 1929 and 1934 (Enciso 2017, 16). When World War II increased labor demand, the United States brought in hundreds of thousands of Mexican workers through the Bracero program beginning in 1942, only to be followed by more mass expulsions in the 1960s, along with the construction of border fencing between El Paso and Ciudad Juarez (Walker 1985).

Drugs, Central American Civil Wars, and Economic Change (1960s–90s)

Beginning in the 1960s, illicit drugs became a major source of tension on the US-Mexico border. Mexico had long taken a prohibitionist stance on illicit drugs, viewing them as a threat to individual health and national progress (Kloppe-Santamaria 2022). Nevertheless, Mexico became a major producer of, and transit country for, drugs into the United States. In 1969, US President Richard Nixon launched Operation Intercept, which was the first major effort to stop drug traffic at the border. By 1973, he had fully launched the "war on drugs," which targeted drugs as an external threat to be fought at US borders, and across Latin America as a mission of Operation Condor, the multinational anti-communist alliance among military dictatorships in the region (Crandall 2020, 149–150; Kloppe-Santamaria 2022, 226). Within Mexico, violent anti-drug operations especially impacted the states of Guerrero, Oaxaca, and Morelos where the military took over policing (Amnesty International [AI] 1978). The militarized approach to drugs became a routine source of US-backed state violence, overlapping with counter-insurgency operations carried out by the military and the Federal Security Directorate, Mexico's internal intelligence agency in the 1960s (AI 1991; Gomez-Cespedes 1999, 359–360), and set in motion the idea of "fighting" drugs that continues today.[5]

At Mexico's southern border, the Central American civil wars of the 1980s demonstrated Mexico's lack of border control and its failure to protect its own citizens as well as people fleeing conflicts in Nicaragua, El Salvador, and Guatemala. Escaping the genocidal campaign of the Guatemalan military regime, an estimated 40,000 Guatemalans fled to Mexico in the early 1980s (AI 1983, 158). Mexico refused to give them refugee status and even withdrew its army from the Guatemalan border, leaving people at the mercy of the Guatemalan Army, which raided refugee camps in Mexico at least 64 times between 1981 and 1984 (Rettie 1985, 201–202).[6] Mexican citizens were also killed in these attacks (AI 1985, 171; AI 1992, 187), while Mexico also forcibly repatriated thousands of Guatemalans (AI 1982, 142–143).

The cross-border violence in Chiapas is an illustration of state violence against rural communities, in particular. For example, in June 1980, Mexican troops "use[d] teargas [and] fired upon a group of peasants, killing 12 and wounding many more" (AI 1981, 169). Conflict in Chiapas spiked in 1994. The Zapatista Army of National Liberation, a far-left, primarily indigenous political and militant group, launched a rebellion against the government on January 1, the same day the North American Free Trade Agreement went into effect. At least 145 people were killed in the initial fighting. By the end of the year, at least 40,000 Mexican troops were operating in the state, with widespread abuses reported (AI 1995, 210). The economic disruption of the new free trade agreement across Mexico spurred migration to the United States and set the stage for another round of migration to economic opportunity and, in turn, a securitized US response (Rochlin 1997).

Drugs, Migration, and State Violence in the Democratic Era (2000s–20s)

Mexico democratized in 2000 with the election of Vicente Fox, the first president from a party other than the Institutional Revolutionary Party since the Mexican Revolution. Despite democratization, state violence remains a serious problem.[7] The Mexican state adopted many reforms in the 1990s–2000s, yet they did little to change the overall problems of widespread misconduct and impunity in border policing, which is the focus here, or in regular policing, which we discuss at length in Chapter 4. The government established a border office of the National Commission of Human Rights (CNDH) in Chiapas, specifically to "receive and attend to complaints of human rights violations from migrants" (United States Department of State [USDS] 2002). A new Migration Law was passed in 2011 to protect the rights of migrants, but little changed in practice (AI 2012, 236). Similarly, in 2016, President Enrique Peña Nieto's government created a Unit for the Investigation of Crimes against Migrants in the Attorney General's office, but abuses are common, and impunity remains high (AI 2017, 252).

Mexico created new police forces during this period, as well. Meaningful change, however, has been elusive in part because each force has been staffed largely by military personnel. In 1999, for example, the Federal Highway Police, the Fiscal Police, and the Migration Police Mexico were combined into the new Federal Preventive Police (PFP), but "nearly half of the roughly 10,000 members of the new force were military police" who were meant to be replaced by civilians, but never were (Meyer 2014, 6). A National Gendermerie was created in 2013 within the Federal Police. It too, was comprised of army and navy personnel and was assigned policing duties (AI 2015, 248; Guevara Moyano 2020, 10). The PFP was replaced by the new National Guard, established in 2019. Again, even though it was originally created as a *civilian* internal security force, it was led by a general and the army was in charge of vetting members of the Federal Police to join (AI 2019, 60–61). Military personnel made up 86% of its members, and it is now fully under military control (Brewer and Verduzco 2023, 11).[8] Institutional reforms in the democratic era have not led to fundamental improvements. Migration flows and conflict over illicit drugs became even more prominent in this era, adding to Mexico's challenges. These transnational issues are frequently met with force, often with the aid, assistance, and demands of the United States.

The illegal drug business is lucrative. Fighting production and movement of drugs, as the United States and others have been doing since the 1970s, does not change the underlying driver of the industry—demand for drugs. Effectively confronting production and trafficking is often only a "partial victory" because of well-known phenomena such as the "balloon effect" (in which eradicating production in one area only moves it to another) and the "cockroach effect" (in which shutting down one trafficking route only leads traffickers to open another route). Moreover, successfully dismantling one drug trafficking organization often leads to a proliferation of groups and more violence, as they compete for market share (Bagley 2015; Guerra 2022, 298). The severity of the challenge in Mexico in the democratic era reflects a "security failure," whereby the state has not failed completely, yet is not able to meet its obligation to provide security for its citizens (Kenny and Serrano 2012, 10).

Drug Violence

In attempting to combat drugs, Mexico employs harsh measures that ratchet up state violence with no improved protections for public safety. In the 1990s, federal police routinely arrested and tortured people to force confessions for drug offenses (AI 1991, 1992). Police and military forces even executed suspected drug traffickers (AI 1994). Overlapping with counter-insurgency operations, the government approached counternarcotics operations as a military-style campaign, carrying out attacks on towns, such as the March 2001 operation in Guardados de Abajo, Tamaulipas in which "the military sealed off the village...[and] broke into houses and carried out arbitrary detentions, reportedly torturing several of those detained" (AI 2002, 172). In 2006, President Felipe Calderón increased the militarization of the fight against drugs, giving the armed forces a "central role in the anti-crime strategy" (Brewer and Verduzco 2023, 9). By 2009, 50,000 soldiers were operating in 10 states (USDS 2010). As we observed in Chapter 4 regarding policing in general, militarizing policing—making the police a weapon of war, rather than law enforcement—generates an inherently violent relationship between authorities and the population. In Tijuana, for example, motivated by combatting drugs, police and other authorities adopted "zero-tolerance policing" in 2007–2012, which involved conceptualizing those they targeted as "a foreign other who does not belong to society" while justifying state violence as necessary "to accomplish a greater good" (Passos 2022, 223). "Zero-tolerance policing" also shows the danger of securitization because of its reliance on emergency powers that undermine the rule of law (Vorobyeva 2015). The military used preventive detention (*arraigo*), holding people "within military headquarters, where intelligence groups tortured them until they confessed their guilt" (AI 2005; Passos 2022227). Under President Calderón (2006–12), militarization did not improve public safety or police effectiveness—drug-related violence resulted in over 60,000 deaths, with near-total impunity for these crimes (AI 2013, 177).

The US role in framing, and responding to, drug and migration issues is significant. In 2008, the US-backed Mérida Initiative authorized a $400 million funding package for "equipment and training to the Mexican police and army as well as justice and immigration officials" (AI 2009, 224). This was followed by an additional $486 million the following year (AI 2010, 224), and in 2016, the United States provided $75 million for "'security and migration enforcement' on Mexico's southern border" as part of the Mérida Initiative (AI 2017, 252). The militarized approach to drugs has made the borders the location of the greatest number of confrontations involving security forces as well as the highest number of civilian casualties from 2007 to 2023 in the country (Seguridad Ciudadana 2024). Conditions are at their worst in Tamaulipas, particularly in the municipalities of Nuevo Laredo, Reynosa, and Matamoros (Seguridad Ciudadana 2024).

Violence Against Migrants

Overall violence in Mexico increased in the 2000s, "in particular affecting migrants in transit" (Consejo Ciudadano del Instituto Nacional de Migración 2017). The Mexican state fails to effectively protect migrants, who regularly face harassment, robbery, abduction, and murder from criminals, and there is widespread impunity for these crimes (AI 2010, 223, 2016, 252; USDS 2019). At times, police and immigration officials are directly implicated in crimes against migrants (AI 2012, 18; Red de Documentación de las Organizaciones Defensoras de Migrantes 2019). Violence characterizes the overall experience of migrants, from transit to detention to deportation.

The militarized fight against drugs and migrants encourages the blind use of violence from troops on patrol, as highlighted at the beginning of this chapter. Police and military forces firing on vehicles has been a long-standing practice. For example, in March 1998, federal police in Tamaulipas state fired at a vehicle with 45 migrants in it and wounded four of the passengers. A similar incident took place in May 1998, when the same police unit fired on a van carrying 23 people, killing one of the migrants (USDS 1999). In 2002, a Mexican Army unit in Baja California fired on a vehicle carrying 36 migrants when the driver failed to stop at a checkpoint (Comisión Nacional de los Derechos Humanos [CNDH] 2004, 111–112). In 2009, state police in Chiapas "shot and killed three irregular migrants and wounded others while pursuing [their] vehicle" (AI 2010, 225). The following year, in Tamaulipas, the army shot and killed two children who were "traveling by car with their family… Military and civilian authorities denied responsibility [and]…crime scenes had been altered and evidence ignored" (AI 2011, 225). In March 2021, the army shot and killed a Guatemalan citizen who approached a checkpoint in Chiapas (Ferri 2021). In October 2021, National Guard troops in Chiapas "fired on a truck carrying migrants," killing two (AI 2022, 253).

Migrants also often travel by rail, so trains have been a site of extreme state violence. For example, in July 2000, an auxiliary police unit in Ecatepec de Morelos, on the outskirts of Mexico City, "discovered four Central American migrants hiding in a rail car," and proceeded to beat and torture them while in custody (USDS 2001). One officer involved in the Ecatepec beating incident was detained in 2001 but then released without charge (USDS 2002). In May 2002, private security guards ordered a group of young migrants off a freight train heading to Saltillo, Coahuila. Mexican soldiers caught up with them in a vacant lot, firing at the group and killing two 16-year-old Honduran migrants and wounding two Salvadorans. In a rare instance of consequences for state violence, one of the soldiers was arrested and charged with murder (USDS 2003; World Organization Against Torture 2002). In 2010, federal police attacked migrants on freight trains in Oaxaca, resulting in at least three deaths (USDS 2011).

Migrants are not safe in custody either; detention is akin to imprisonment, and authorities do not adequately communicate with migrants or asylum seekers. The Consejo Ciudadano del Instituto Nacional de Migración (2017) reports that 61% of detainees did not know why they were being held and 74% did not know how long they would be there (102–103). Further abuses occur when migrants are apprehended and taken into custody. In August 2001, local police in Cristobal Garcia, Sonora, attacked a group of migrants and tortured them in detention (USDS 2002). In 2001, federal police tortured two migrant workers, trying to force a confession to human trafficking (AI 2002, 171). In Baja California, in 2003, soldiers in Rumorosa detained a group of 13 migrants and in an attempt to beat a confession out of them in detention, "kicked and placed plastic bags over their heads" (USDS 2004). In 2004, navy personnel detained and beat a Honduran migrant in Chiapas. The navy is not authorized to ask for immigration documents or detain people when they do not have them (CNDH 2005, 135). In Coahuila in April 2005, migration authorities beat a group of Central American migrants and forced them to "remove their shoes and walk one mile to a waiting vehicle" (USDS 2007). In 2007, the military "raided migrant camps in Chiapas and abused residents" (USDS 2008). In 2008, widely published photos showed the Mexican Navy and migration officials beating migrants in Oaxaca; even with this evidence, they "denied that abuses took place" (AI 2009, 227). In 2014, the Attorney General of Mexico "released documents…that revealed municipal police were complicit in the 2010 killing of 72 migrants in San Fernando, Tamaulipas. The documents also showed police involvement in the deaths of 193 other victims found in mass graves in Tamaulipas in 2011" (USDS 2015). In 2020, police in Quintana Roo used excessive force when arresting a Salvadoran refugee, breaking her neck (USDS 2021). In short, abuses by security forces are excessively violent and ubiquitous.

The surge in migration in recent years has added more strain to the system and encouraged even more forceful responses. Mexico detained 127,149 migrants at its southern border in 2014, 178,254 in 2015, and 174,526 in 2016, while very few people are granted asylum (AI 2016, 252, 2017, 252). In 2016, for example, only 2,162 people were granted asylum out of an estimated 200,000 migrants in the country who may have qualified (AI 2017, 252). Similarly, very few people are given refugee status; the majority of claims are denied (AI 2018a, 259). Mexico deported more Central American migrants than the United States in 2015 (AI 2016, 252). Moreover, US demands and pressure on Mexico to curb immigration have notably complicated the response to the most recent migration crisis.

Mexico and the United States

When President Andrés Manuel Lopez Obrador (AMLO) came into office in December 2018, he promised a more humane approach to migration. The intractable problems described above, along with US pressure, made this very difficult to achieve. In coordination with the Economic Commission for Latin America and the Caribbean, Mexico proposed a $30 billion regional development plan for Central America to address the underlying economic challenges that lead people to migrate in search of opportunity elsewhere. The Mexican government also sought to provide more "work opportunities for Central American migrants in Mexico" (Isacson and Meyer 2019). At the same time, however, the United States was pushing its "Remain in Mexico" policy, forcing people who arrived at the US-Mexico border to stay in Mexico while the United States processed their asylum claims. In 2018, the United States returned 60,000 asylum seekers to Mexico (AI 2019, 63), increasing the strain on Mexico and endangering migrants who were vulnerable to attack and exploitation by criminal gangs in northern Mexico (AI 2018a; b).

The United States also pressured Mexico to prioritize addressing the migration issue by threatening to impose trade tariffs on Mexican imports to the United States. In 2019, AMLO reversed his policy of humanitarian visas for Central American migrants and sent thousands of troops from the newly formed National Guard to the northern and southern borders (AI 2019), a move that undermined AMLO's overall security strategy by diverting the National Guard from its intended role as an internal police force meant to combat organized crime (Justice in Mexico 2021).

National Guard members are legally permitted to ask for migration papers while local police cannot, but as noted above, the National Guard is composed of military personnel who lack training in how to interact with migrants, refugees, and asylum seekers. These forces were also engaged in patrols far from the border, notably in "the *colonias* (poor neighborhoods), carrying heavy weapons" (Isacson and Meyer 2019). In the south, these deployments have added to the conflict associated with the joint US-Mexico-Guatemala Plan Frontera Sur (Southern Border Plan) operations that began in 2014 (Seguridad Ciudadana 2018). Forces in the region target migrants as they organize into caravans—seeking safety in numbers for the dangerous journey to the United States. For example, in October 2019, "members of the National Guard, Federal Police, and the INM blocked [a] caravan in the area around Huixtla, Chiapas, to impede them from moving, even though many had documents that allowed them to legally be in Chiapas" (Isacson and Meyer 2019). In 2020, Mexican forces broke up a caravan "of approximately 500 migrants" that was forming in Tapachula, Chiapas (USDS 2021). Faced with a renewed tariff threat from the United States in February 2025, President Claudia Sheinbaum deployed 10,000 National Guard troops to the northern border (Storr 2025).

Mexico and Guatemala

In Chiapas, the governor established a new 500-member state police force, the Pakal Immediate Reaction Force (FRIP), in December 2024, aimed at "pacifying" the state. It is a militarized unit, and the personnel are former members of the Mexican armed forces, National Guard, and Federal Police. They have an expansive mission to monitor highways and keep them unblocked, combat armed robberies, and patrol in remote areas (Jiménez 2025). Tensions rose on the border when members of this force "crossed into Guatemalan territory after killing four suspected criminals in Mexico," and the governor of Chiapas accused the Guatemalan Army of collaborating with drug trafficking organizations, because the unit present failed to respond (LatinNews Daily 2025f).

On the Guatemalan side, the Guatemalan army patrols the border, deployed to the western departments of San Marcos and Huehuetenango as well as Petén in the north. In 2023, it carried out 900 border operations and established checkpoints along the border with

Mexico (RESDAL 2024, 179). In total, the Guatemalan Army "conducted 31,364 binational patrols" to control land and water crossings, in conjunction with authorities of El Salvador, Honduras, and Mexico (RESDAL 2024, 179). In addition to coordinating with its immediate neighbors, the Guatemalan military engages in training operations organized by the United States, such as CENTAM Guardian, an annual multinational training operation that brings together forces from Guatemala, Costa Rica, the Dominican Republic, El Salvador, and Honduras (United States Southern Command 2025). In the 2025 operation, US National Guard forces carried out infantry and medical training missions near the border with El Salvador (Baribeau 2025), and US Army, US Navy, Department of Homeland Security, Drug Enforcement Administration, and Federal Bureau of Investigation personnel worked with their Latin American counterparts on a variety of programs, including those focused on border control "in the tri-border area of Guatemala, Honduras and El Salvador" (United States Southern Command 2025). Responding to the surge of migration northward through Central America in recent years, the United States has pressured Guatemala to conduct more interdiction of migrants and illegal activity at its border with Mexico. In 2024, Guatemala and Mexico began Operation Ring of Fire West, with air, land, and sea units patrolling border areas (Rodríguez 2025), especially because of the uptick in fighting among drug trafficking organizations in Chiapas, Mexico, and fears it could "spill over" into Guatemala (Guerrero de León 2025). When US Secretary of State Marco Rubio visited Guatemala in February 2025, Guatemalan President Bernardo Arévalo announced more troops and National Police would be deployed to this effort and that "Guatemala would form a new border force to patrol its borders with Honduras and El Salvador, as well" (Associated Press 2025a; LatinNews Daily 2025f). At the same time, Guatemala agreed to accept an increased number of deportation flights from the United States and announced the establishment of a new Migrant Return Center in San Marcos to receive migrants being deported by land from Mexico (Associated Press 2025b; c).

MILITARIZATION AND HARDENING OF BORDERS THROUGHOUT LATIN AMERICA

Across Latin America, countries are hardening their borders, deploying military units along their frontiers, and tightening migration controls. Coinciding with the rise of populist presidents mobilizing support through nationalist sentiment, governments demonize migrants and conflate immigration with security threats. In Argentina in December 2024, the government of President Javier Milei launched Plan Güemes, which focused on increasing border enforcement on Salta province's border with Bolivia. Visiting the border town of Aguas Blancas, Minister of Security Patricia Bullrich announced the plan and declared it was motivated by a war on crime, encompassing everything from combatting smuggling, narcotrafficking, human trafficking, terrorism, and hitmen (Ministerio de Seguridad Nacional 2024). Bolivian police have traditionally patrolled the area, while enforcement on the Argentine side has been lax. Plan Güemes deployed the Argentine Naval Prefecture (coast guard) to patrol the Bermejo River and the Argentine Federal Police to patrol nearby Highway 34 (Ministerio de Seguridad Nacional 2024).

In January 2025, the mayor of Aguas Blancas went even further, with the announcement that the town would build a barbed wire fence, 2.5 meters high, to stretch 200 meters along the river (Buenos Aires Herald 2025; LatinNews Daily 2025a). Bolivia's Foreign Ministry objected to the fact that Argentina did not consult with them on these deployments or coordinate the new border enforcement initiatives. Moreover, as former Argentine government officials pointed out in criticizing their successors' program, a 200-meter fence is only symbolic, given that Argentina and Bolivia share a 770-km border. Moreover, a fence of any length does nothing to stop smuggling by air—that would require investment in "helicopters and radars and other equipment to monitor air traffic" (Latin American Security and Strategic Review 2025). The technology that is being brought to bear on the border are biometric scanners, donated by US Homeland Security Investigations, to collect data on migrants for the US-run Biometric Identification Transnational Migration Alert Program (Latin American Security and Strategic Review 2025). Overwhelmingly, efforts in Salta are about being more hostile to migrants, because they coincide with the governor's elimination of health care for foreigners in the province, and encouraging President Milei to do so at the national level, which he subsequently did. In May 2025,

Milei issued a Decree of Necessity and Urgency requiring "transitory, temporary, and irregular residents" to pay for health care and higher education and ramping up deportations (LatinNews Daily 2025d).[9] In January 2025, the government further expanded Plan Güemes with the deployment of 300 federal police to Misiones province at the Triple Frontier with Paraguay and Brazil (LatinNews Daily 2025b). Underscoring the performative nature of these efforts, Argentina coordinated with the rightist government in Paraguay while ignoring the leftist government in Brazil, just as they had ignored Bolivia's government. The Argentine and Paraguayan Defense Ministers signed a joint agreement on combatting organized crime in February 2025 (LatinNews Daily 2025c).[10]

In Chile, the government has turned to the military for border enforcement in recent years, using it to support police in fighting drug trafficking, and gradually expanding its role to migration, as well. In July 2019, President Sebastián Piñera issued Decree 265, which permitted the military to "provide logistical, transport and technological support to the security forces in border areas...in specific locations along the border and for a determined length of time" (Latin American Security and Strategic Review 2019).[11] The initial decree was meant to address drug trafficking, but by 2021, Piñera expanded the military mission to counter migration, allowing the air force to carry out large-scale deportation flights (Latin American Security and Strategic Review 2021). The *carabineros* (militarized police) also forcibly removed migrants from encampments in the city of Iquique and anti-immigrant protestors burned their belongings (LatinNews Daily 2021). Serious anti-immigrant demonstrations continued in subsequent years, and a change in administration to the socialist president, Gabriel Boric, saw the continued use of the military in a border enforcement role. In February 2023, the army was deployed to the northern border to "carry out identity checks, searches of personal effects, and detain any migrants who have entered the country through unauthorized border points" (LatinNews Daily 2023a).[12] Notably, Boric did not declare a state of emergency. Instead, he relied on the legal authority provided by the 2023 critical infrastructure law that permits internal military deployments to strategic areas and allows the military to detain people for as long as 12 hours before turning them over to regular police authorities (Gobierno de Chile 2023).[13] At the same time, President Dina Boluarte deployed the armed forces to support the police in seven border departments on the Peruvian side of the border (Amnesty International 2023).

Brazil has similarly empowered its military in recent years to engage in border control and confront other challenges such as deforestation and illegal mining in border areas. For example, in 2023, the armed forces conducted a series of exercises under Operation Agata. Over 37,000 military personnel were deployed to Roraima state on the border with Venezuela. On the border with Peru and Colombia, the Air Force carried out surveillance operations, while the Navy took the lead on the border with Bolivia and Paraguay in Mato Grosso and Mato Grosso do Sul. In the south, the armed forces "carried out preventive and repressive actions against cross-border and environmental crimes," including joint operations with Paraguay and Uruguay (RESDAL 2024, 116). In the permanent mission of Operation Ostium, the Brazilian Air Force conducts air patrols to interdict air traffic that may be involved in drug trafficking (RESDAL 2024, 115). At times, this results in the Brazilian Air Force shooting down aircraft, as in the February 2025 downing of a drug-trafficking plane from Venezuela (MercoPress 2025).

In the Dominican Republic, in addition to militarization and building physical barriers on the border with Haiti, the government has "codified exclusion" through denaturalization (Hunter and Reece 2022, 595). Beginning in 2004, the Dominican Republic classified new Haitian immigrants as well as potentially hundreds of thousands of Dominicans of Haitian descent as "nonresidents," effectively stripping them of legal status in the country.[14] The law was born of a swell of nationalism and President Luis Abinader's rhetoric claiming "people of Haitian ancestry as a 'threat to national security'" (Hunter and Reece 2022, 595). Constitutional changes in 2010 did away with the automatic granting of birthright citizenship, and in 2013, the Constitutional Court ruled that the provision applied retroactively to anyone born between 1929 and 2010.[15] The Dominican Republic responded to international condemnation with a new Naturalization Law, which gave the appearance of creating a pathway back to citizenship, but in reality the process amounted to "administrative obstructionism," which kept all but 750 people affected by the denaturalization from successfully obtaining citizenship (Hunter and Reece 2022, 601).[16] Migration from Haiti has nevertheless continued in recent years due to economic and political conditions, extreme levels of violence, and natural disasters, such as the devastating 2010 earthquake. The Dominican Republic has responded with continued harsh anti-migrant measures, including immediate deportation if someone who is undocumented tries to access public services such as health care (LatinNews Daily

2025e). In 2025, President Abinader promised more anti-immigrant measures, including mass deportations of 10,000 people per week, adding 13 km of border wall to the existing 54 km, and sending more soldiers to the border to bring the total number of personnel deployed there to 11,000 (LatinNews Daily 2025e; Latin American Weekly Report 2025).

The Venezuelan crisis has led millions of people leave the country, with many crossing into neighboring Colombia (International Organization for Migration 2018). Those heading north over land encounter the harsh jungle terrain of the Darién Gap that makes up the Colombia-Panama border. Three binational surveillance posts were established in 2013–15 (Crítica 2022), but otherwise state presence in this area is traditionally minimal due to its remoteness, the inhospitable landscape, and because much of the land is designated as indigenous territories (International Crisis Group 2023). It is a largely ungoverned space that leaves migrants at the mercy of criminal bands and human traffickers (Isacson 2024). For example, the municipality of Acandí on the Colombian side only has "a total of 20 police to patrol its 600 square miles" (Isacson 2024, 21). Migration through this area was uncommon until 2021, when numbers rose dramatically from the usual hundreds to nearly 150,000; in 2023, an unprecedented 500,000 migrants traversed the Darién Gap (Isacson 2024, 8). In response, with the help of the United States, Colombia created a new joint military command that deployed to the western departments of Antioquia, Córdoba, Chocó, Sucre, and Bolívar to combat drug trafficking and other organized crime such as illegal gold mining (Caicedo 2023). In Antioquia, the military, police, and local government undertook an information campaign to warn migrants of the dangers of attempting the journey through the Darién (Méndez 2023). Even so, there are consistent reports of abuse (Human Rights Watch 2023).

On the Panamanian side, the 5th Brigade of the National Border Service is permanently stationed in the area, and since 2018 has worked in conjunction with the Aero-Naval Service, National Police, and the National Migration Service "to coordinate and cooperate on migratory flow issues" (RESDAL 2024, 211–212). Since 2015, Panama's migration policy has restricted the number of people who can pass through the Migration Reception Stations (Pappier and Yates 2023). Restricting migrants' movement leaves them vulnerable to abuses from border agents such as extracting bribes (International Crisis Group 2023). The extreme number of migrants transiting the country in 2023 led Panama to adopt new measures such as stepping up aerial surveillance, establishing additional camps where migrants would be "kept separate from local residents," and attempting to deport people from the country more quickly, rather than allowing them to continue on their journey north (LatinNews Daily 2023b). President José Mulino, who came into office in July 2024, went even further, closing multiple points of entry on the Colombian border, installing barbed wire fencing, as well as signing an agreement with the United States in which the United States helped deport people from Panama (LAWR 2024c).

Conclusion

Maintaining control over national borders is a central component of being a state. In Latin America, this control is elusive in most places. States have little capacity in border regions, leading to heightened levels of migration and cross-border trafficking of drugs and other illicit goods. The state response has been to securitize these issues, resulting in an increased militarization of border areas and more state violence. This state violence is driven by external factors and disproportionality affects migrants, indigenous groups, and the rural poor. In Chapter 6, we examine how those same issues play out in the area of economic development, where the state uses violence against their citizens to protect economic actors' investments.

Notes

1. Though enduring fewer major land wars than more conflictual world regions—notably Europe—Latin America experienced numerous border changes through war (e.g., US-Mexico, 1845–48; War of the Triple Alliance, 1864–70; War of the Pacific, 1879–83; Chaco War, 1929–35; and Peru-Ecuador, 1941) in the nineteenth and twentieth centuries (Loveman 1999, 45; Masterson and Sotelo 2007).
2. The Caribbean territories of New Spain (e.g., Cuba, Puerto Rico) remained under Spanish control.
3. Article 110, Federal Constitution of the United Mexican States, October 4, 1824, https://tarltonapps.law.utexas.edu/imgs/con stitutions/documents/mexican1824_english/mexican1824_eng lish.pdf. Copies of all primary documents cited in the book are available at www.andyreiter.com.

4. Mexican control over Chiapas was affirmed by the Treaty of Limits signed on September 27, 1882 (Rettie 1985, 196).

5. The Federal Security Directorate was established in 1947, "constructed out of the elite military of the Presidential Guards Brigade," and dissolved in 1986 due to corruption and alleged involvement in drug trafficking (Gomez-Cespedes 1999, 359–360). We discuss intelligence agencies and their role in state violence in more depth in Chapters 2 and 3.

6. Mexico was not a signatory to the 1951 Convention Relating to the Status of Refugees until 2000, See: https://treaties.un.org/doc/Publication/MTDSG/Volume%20I/Chapter%20V/V-2.en.pdf.

7. Mexico's V-Dem "Physical violence index" score has changed little in recent decades. There was marginal improvement in the lead up to democratization—from 0.47 in 1990 to 0.57 in 2000. From that height in 2000, the index fell to scores around 0.5 in the years after, with minimal fluctuations, followed by a drop to 0.42 in 2024 (Coppedge et al. 2025).

8. Mexico's 1917 Constitution allows the president to use the armed forces "for homeland security and defense of the federation against foreign threats." Article 89, VI, Mexico's Constitution of 1917 with Amendments through 2015, https://www.constituteproject.org/constitution/Mexico_2015.

9. Decreto 366/2025, de 28 mayo de 2025, https://www.argentina.gob.ar/normativa/nacional/decreto-366-2025-413297.

10. Coordination among neighboring countries and international authorities can be valuable in addressing cross-border crime. Paraguay, for example, has been working with Brazil in recent years to reduce trafficking of weapons that are imported legally to Paraguay and then smuggled to criminal gangs in Argentina and Brazil. The efforts have involved investigating and removing corrupt officials as well as better tracking of weapons imports, given that in the 2022–23 period, of 60,000 weapons imported to Paraguay, the government "lost track of 17,300 of them" (LAWR 2024b). In December 2024, in conjunction with Interpol, Paraguay carried out a major operation in the Triple Frontier against criminal networks trafficking illegally harvested timber (Grattan 2024; Interpol 2024). In response to criminal gangs carrying out "commando-style assaults" on branches of the

National Development Bank and police stations in the border province of Itapúa in April 2024, Paraguay deployed the army to Itapúa, and Ñeembucú and Misiones, the other two provinces bordering Argentina (La Nación 2024; LatinNews Daily 2024).

11. Decreto Núm 265, 9 de julio de 2019, "autoriza colaboración y delega en el ministro de defensa nacional las facultades en materia que indica."

12. Decreto 78, 24 de febrero de 2023, "Delimita Áreas de Zonas Fronterizas a Resguardar por Parte de las Fuerzas Armadas y de Orden y Seguridad Pública, Designa a Oficiales Generales Que Señala e Instruye lo Que Indica."

13. Ley 21,542, de febrero 3 de 2023, "Modifica la Carta Fundamental con el Objeto de Permitir la Protección de Infraestructura Crítica por Parte de las Fuerzas Armadas, en Caso de Peligro Grave o Inminente."

14. Ley No. 285-04, del 27 de agosto de 2004, "General de Migración."

15. Dominican Republic's Constitution of 2015, https://www. constituteproject.org/constitution/Dominican_Republic_2015; República Dominicana Tribunal Constitucional, Sentencia TC/ 0168/13, https://www.tribunalconstitucional.gob.do/consultas/ secretaría/sentencias/tc016813/.

16. Ley No. 169-14, el Congreso Nacional, https://migracion.gob. do/transparencia/wp-content/uploads/2019/10/Ley-No-169-14-de-Naturalización.pdf.

References

Amnesty International. 1978. *Amnesty International Report 1978*. London: Amnesty International Publications.

Amnesty International. 1981. *Amnesty International Report 1981*. London: Amnesty International Publications.

Amnesty International. 1982. *Amnesty International Report 1982*. London: Amnesty International Publications.

Amnesty International. 1983. *Amnesty International Report 1983*. London: Amnesty International Publications.

Amnesty International. 1985. *Amnesty International Report 1985*. London: Amnesty International Publications.

Amnesty International. 1991. *Amnesty International Report 1991*. London: Amnesty International Publications.

Amnesty International. 1992. *Amnesty International Report 1992*. London: Amnesty International Publications.

Amnesty International. 1994. *Amnesty International Report 1994*. London: Amnesty International Publications.

Amnesty International. 1995. *Amnesty International Report 1995*. London: Amnesty International Publications.

Amnesty International. 2002. *Amnesty International Report 2002*. London: Amnesty International Publications.

Amnesty International. 2005. Mexico: Eliminating Arraigo Will Be An Important Step Towards Protecting Human Rights. September 22.

Amnesty International. 2009. *Amnesty International Report 2009*. London: Amnesty International Publications.

Amnesty International. 2010. *Amnesty International Report 2010*. London: Amnesty International Publications.

Amnesty International. 2011. *Amnesty International Report 2011*. London: Amnesty International Publications.

Amnesty International. 2012. *Amnesty International Report 2012*. London: Amnesty International Publications.

Amnesty International. 2013. *Amnesty International Report 2013*. London: Amnesty International Publications.

Amnesty International. 2015. *Amnesty International Report 2014/15*. London: Amnesty International Publications.

Amnesty International. 2016. *Amnesty International Report 2015/16*. London: Amnesty International Publications.

Amnesty International. 2017. *Amnesty International Report 2016/17*. London: Amnesty International Publications.

Amnesty International. 2018a. *Amnesty International Report 2017/18*. London: Amnesty International Publications.

Amnesty International. 2018b. USA: 'You Don't Have Any Rights Here': Illegal Pushbacks, Arbitrary Detention & Ill-Treatment of Asylum-Seekers in the United States. https://www.amnesty.org/en/documents/amr51/9101/2018/en/.

Amnesty International. 2019. *Amnesty International Report 2019*. London: Amnesty International Publications.

Amnesty International. 2022. *Amnesty International Report 2021/22*. London: Amnesty International Publications.

Amnesty International. 2023. Open Letter to the President of Peru and the President of Chile Regarding the Protection Crisis at the Border. May 4.

Associated Press. 2025a. Guatemala Steps Up Patrols Along Border as US Extends Border Security Goals South. March 13.

Associated Press. 2025b. Guatemala Gives Rubio a Second Deportation Deal for Migrants Being Sent Home from the US. February 5.

Associated Press. 2025c. Guatemala Anuncia Construcción de Nuevo Centro Para Recepción de Deportados en Frontera con México. March 12.

Bagley, Bruce M. 2015. Drug Trafficking and Organized Crime in Latin America and the Caribbean in the Twenty-First Century: Challenges to Democracy. In *Drug Trafficking, Organized Crime, and Violence in the Americas Today*, ed. M. Bruce Bagley and Jonathan D. Rosen, 1–24. Gainesville: University Press of Florida.

Baribeau, Rowdy. 2025. Arkansas Air and Army National Guardsmen Recap CENTAM Guardian Guatemala Excursion. *KATV*. May 30.

Barker, Vanessa. 2013. Democracy and Deportation: Why Membership Matters Most. In *The Borders of Punishment: Migration, Citizenship, and Social Exclusion*, eds. Katja Franko Aas and Mary Bosworth, 237–254. Oxford: Oxford University Press.

Barrett, Elinore M. 2012. *The Spanish Colonial Settlement Landscapes of New Mexico, 1598–1680*. Albuquerque: University of New Mexico Press.

Benhabib, Seyla. 2004. *The Rights of Others: Aliens, Residents, and Citizens*. Cambridge: Cambridge University Press.

Brewer, Stephanie, and Ana Lucía Verduzco. 2023. Militarized Transformation: Human Rights and Democratic Controls in a Context of Increasing Militarization in Mexico. Washington Office on Latin America. September 2023. https://www.wola.org/wp-content/uploads/2023/09/Militarized-Transformation_Abridged_.pdf

Britton, John A. 2013. Punitive Expedition, Mexico (1916). In *Encyclopedia of U.S. Military Interventions in Latin America*, ed. Alan McPherson, 538–542. New York: ABC-CLIO.

Buenos Aires Herald. 2025. Argentina to Build Short Fence at Bolivian Border to Control Crossings. January 27

Caicedo, Luis. 2023. Colombia Busca Apoyo de EE.UU para Combatir al Clan del Golfo en el Darién. *Caracol Radio*. December 5.

Centeno, Miguel Angel. 2002. *Blood and Debt: War and the Nation-State in Latin America*. University Park: Pennsylvania State University Press.

Centeno, Miguel A., and Agustin E. Ferraro. 2013. Historical Legacies and State Strength in Contemporary Latin America and Spain. In *State and Nation Making in Latin America and Spain: Republics of the Possible*, eds. Miguel A. Centeno and Agustin E. Ferraro, 399–416. Cambridge: Cambridge University Press.

Comisión Nacional de los Derechos Humanos México (CNDH). 2004. *Informe de Actividades 2003*. Mexico, D.F.: Comisión Nacional de los Derechos Humanos.

Comisión Nacional de los Derechos Humanos México (CNDH). 2005. *Informe de Actividades 2004*. Mexico, D.F.: Comisión Nacional de los Derechos Humanos.

Consejo Ciudadano del Instituto Nacional de Migración. 2017. Personas en Detención Migratoria en México: Misión de Monitoreo de Estaciones Migratorias y Estancias Provisionales del Instituto Nacional de Migración. July. https://www.gob.mx/cms/uploads/attachment/file/281218/CCINM-Informe_Final_Monitoreo.pdf.

Coppedge, Michael, John Gerring, Carl Henrik Knutsen, Staffan I. Lindberg, Jan Teorell, David Altman, Fabio Angiolillo, Michael Bernhard, Agnes Cornell, M. Steven Fish, Linnea Fox, Lisa Gastaldi, Haakon Gjerløw, Adam Glynn, Ana Good God, Sandra Grahn, Allen Hicken, Katrin Kinzelbach, Kyle L. Marquardt, Kelly McMann, Valeriya Mechkova, Anja Neundorf, Pamela Paxton, Daniel Pemstein, Johannes von Römer, Brigitte Seim, Rachel Sigman, Svend-Erik Skaaning, Jeffrey Staton, Aksel Sundström, Marcus Tannenberg, Eitan Tzelgov, Yi-ting Wang, Felix Wiebrecht, Tore Wig, and Daniel Ziblatt. 2025. *V-Dem Codebook v15*. Varieties of Democracy (V-Dem) Project.

Crandall, Russell C. 2020. *Drugs and Thugs: The History and Future of America's War on Drugs*. New Haven: Yale University Press.

Crítica. 2022. No Existe Ninguna Base Militar Colombiana en Panamá. May 18. https://www.critica.com.pa/sucesos/no-existe-ninguna-base-militar-colombiana-en-panama-427614.

Enciso, Alanís, and Fernando Saúl. 2017. *They Should Stay There: The Story of Mexican Migration and Repatriation During the Great Depression [Translated by Russ Davidson]*. Chapel Hill: University of North Carolina Press.

Feldmann, Andreas E., Xóchitl. Bada, and Stephanie Schütze. 2018. Introduction: New Mobility Patterns in the Americas. In *New Migration Patterns in the Americas: Challenges for the 21st Century*, eds. Andreas E. Feldmann, Xóchitl. Bada, and Stephanie Schütze, 1–24. New York: Springer International Publishing.

Ferri, Pablo. 2021. La Muerte a Balazos de Un Migrante a Manos del Ejército Mexicano Eleva la Tensión en la Frontera Sur. *El País*. March 30. https://elpais.com/mexico/2021-03-30/la-muerte-a-balazos-de-un-migrante-a-manos-del-ejercito-mexicano-eleva-la-tension-en-la-frontera-sur.html.

Ganster, Paul with David E. Lorey. 2016. *The U.S.-Mexican Border Today: Conflict and Cooperation in Historical Perspective*, 3rd ed. Lanham, MD: Rowman & Littlefield.

Gobierno de Chile. 2023. Deployment of Armed Forces Begins on the Border as a Result of Critical Infrastructure Law: These Are the Powers That the Military Will Be Given. February 28. https://www.gob.cl/en/news/deployment-armed-forces-begins-border-result-critical-infrastructure-law-these-are-powers-military-will-be-given/.

Gomez-Cespedes, Alejandra. 1999. The Federal Law Enforcement Agencies. *Journal of Contemporary Criminal Justice* 15 (4): 352–369.

Grattan, Steven. 2024. "26 People Arrested in Crackdown on Illegal Deforestation along Paraguay, Brazil and Argentina Border." *Associated Press*. December 16. https://apnews.com/article/paraguay-brazil-argentina-border-deforestation-interpol-tree-trafficking-92599975a233802e62732a6a4de84a66.

Griswold del Castillo, Richard. 1990. *The Treaty of Guadalupe Hidalgo: A Legacy of Conflict*. Norman: University of Oklahoma Press.

Guerra, Santiago Ivan. 2022. Narcos and Narcs: Violence and the Transformation of Drug Trafficking at the Texas-Mexico Border. In *These Ragged Edges: Histories of Violence along the U.S.-Mexico Border*, eds. Andrew J. Torget and Gerardo Gurza-Lavalle, 297–319. Chapel Hill: University of North Carolina Press.

Guerrero de León, Carola. 2025. Guatemala Deploys Troops to Mexican Border as Cartel Violence in the Region Escalates. *Latin Times*. March 10. https://www.latintimes.com/guatemala-deploys-troops-mexican-border-cartel-violence-region-escalates-577878.

Guevara Moyano, Iñigo. 2020. Mexico's National Guard: When Police are Not Enough. Washington, DC: Wilson Center. https://www.wilsoncenter.org/sites/default/files/media/uploads/documents/MexicosNationalGuard.pdf.

Gundhus, Helene O. I., and Katja Franko. 2016. Global Policing and Mobility: Identity, Territory, Sovereignty. In *The Sage Handbook of Global Policing*, eds. Ben Bradford, Beatrice Jauregui, Ian Loader, and Jonny Steinberg, 497–514. London: Sage.

Hernández, Kelly Lytle. 2022. *Bad Mexicans: Race, Empire, and Revolution in the Borderlands*. New York: W. W. Norton.

Hochmüller, Markus, and Annette Idler. 2025. Porous Borders and the Emergence of Hybrid Sovereignties. *Territory, Politics, Governance* 13 (6): 847–866.

Human Rights Watch. 2023. Darién Gap: The Jungle Where Poor Migration Policies Meet. May 9. https://www.hrw.org/feature/2024/09/11/darien-gap/the-jungle-where-poor-migration-policies-meet.

Hunter, Wendy, and Francesca Reece. 2022. Denationalization in the Dominican Republic: Trapping Victims in the State's Administrative Maze. *Latin American Research Review* 57 (3): 590–607.

International Crisis Group. 2023. Bottleneck of the Americas: Crime and Migration in the Darién Gap. November 3. https://www.crisisgroup.org/latin-america-caribbean/andes/colombia-central-america/102-bottleneck-americas-crime-and-migration.

International Organization for Migration. 2018. Regional Action Plan – Venezuelan Migration. April 23. https://www.iom.int/sites/g/files/tmzbdl486/files/press_release/file/consolidated_action_plan_venezuela.pdf.

162   B. J. KYLE ET AL.

Interpol. 2024. Paraguay Leads Tri-border Clampdown on Illegal Deforestation. December 16. https://www.interpol.int/en/News-and-Events/News/2024/Paraguay-leads-tri-border-clampdown-on-illegal-deforestation.
Isacson, Adam. 2024. Migrants in Colombia: Between Government Absence and Criminal Control. Washington, D.C.: Washington Office on Latin America. https://www.wola.org/analysis/migrants-in-colombia-between-government-absence-and-criminal-control/.
Isacson, Adam, and Maureen Meyer. 2019. The 'Wall' Before the Wall: Mexico's Crackdown on Migration at its Southern Border. Washington Office on Latin America. December 17. https://www.wola.org/analysis/mexico-southern-border-report/#ftnt_ref34.
Jiménez, Beriah. 2025. ¿Quiénes son los Pakales? Conoce a la Fuerza de Reacción Inmediata de Chiapas. *Diario del Sur*. February 27. https://oem.com.mx/diariodelsur/policiaca/quienes-son-los-pakales-conoce-a-la-fuerza-de-reaccion-inmediata-de-chiapas-21892649.
Jones, Oakah L., Jr. 1996. *Los Paisanos: Spanish Settlers on the Northern Frontier of New Spain*. Norman: University of Oklahoma Press.
Justice in Mexico. 2021. Organized Crime and Violence in Mexico: 2021 Special Report. https://justiceinmexico.org/wp-content/uploads/2021/10/OCVM-21.pdf.
Kenyon, Gordon. 1961. Mexican Influence in Central America, 1821–1823. *Hispanic American Historical Review* 41 (2): 175–205.
Kenny, Paul, and Mónica. Serrano, eds. 2012. *Mexico's Security Failure: Collapse into Criminal Violence*. London: Routledge.
Kloppe-Santamaria, Gema. 2022. Mexico's Long War on Drugs: Past and Present Failures of a Punitive Approach to Drugs. *Journal of Illicit Economies and Development* 4 (2): 223–229.
Koulish, Robert, and Maartje van der Woude. 2020. Introduction: The 'Problem' of Migration. In *Crimmigrant Nations: Resurgent Nationalism and the Closing of Borders*, eds. Robert Koulish and Maartje van der Woude, 1–32. New York: Fordham University Press.
La Nación. 2024. En Asalto Tipo Comando, Destrozan Sucursal del BNF en Natalio. April 28. https://www.lanacion.com.py/pais/2024/04/28/en-asalto-tipo-comando-destrozan-sucursal-del-bnf-en-natalio/.
Latin American Security and Strategic Review. 2019. Chile Brings in the Army to Fight Drug Trafficking. September.
Latin American Security and Strategic Review. 2021. Chile's Tough Stance on Migration. March.
Latin American Security and Strategic Review. 2025. Argentine Government Bolsters Border Security. March.
Latin American Weekly Report. 2024a. Mexico: Army Involved in Migrant Killings. November 7.

Latin American Weekly Report. 2024b. Paraguay: Peña Moves to Crack Down on Arms Trafficking. February 15.

Latin American Weekly Report. 2024c. Panama's Mulino Moves on Darién Migration Pledge. July 18.

Latin American Weekly Report. 2025. Growing Tension with Haiti. April 3.

LatinNews Daily. 2021. Chile: Anti-migrant Violence Flares Up in Iquique. September 27.

LatinNews Daily. 2023a. Chile: Army to be Deployed for Migrant Checks. February 27.

LatinNews Daily. 2023b. Panama: Gov't Announces New Migration Measures. September 11.

LatinNews Daily. 2024. Paraguay: Armed Forces Deployed to Southern Border Region. May 30.

LatinNews Daily. 2025a. Guatemala: Gov't Downplays Mexico Incursion. June 10.

LatinNews Daily. 2025b. Argentina: Bolivian Border Fence Heightens Tensions. January 28.

LatinNews Daily. 2025c. Argentina: Milei Cracks Down on Migration. May 15.

LatinNews Daily. 2025d. Argentina: Bullrich Outlines Plans to Ramp Up Border Security. January 30.

LatinNews Daily. 2025e. Argentina: Bullrich Oversees Bolivian Border Fence Contract. February 11.

LatinNews Daily. 2025f. Dominican Republic: Gov't Cracks Down on Undocumented Haitians. April 23.

Loveman, Brian. 1999. *For la Patria: Politics and the Armed Forces in Latin America*. Wilmington, DE: Scholarly Resources.

Manning, Martin J. 2013. Cortina, Juan (1824–1894). In *Encyclopedia of U.S. Military Interventions in Latin America*, ed. Alan McPherson, 390–394. New York: ABC-CLIO.

Marcella, Gabriel, Orlando J. Pérez, and Brian Fonseca. 2022. Introduction. In *Democracy and Security in Latin America: State Capacity and Governance under Stress*, eds. Gabriel Marcella, Orlando J. Pérez, and Brian Fonseca, 1–5. New York: Routledge.

Mares, David. 2012. *Latin America and the Illusion of Peace*. London: International Institute for Strategic Studies.

Masterson, Daniel M., and Jorge Ortiz Sotelo. 2007. Peru: International Developments and Local Realities. In *Latin America During World War II*, eds. Thomas M. Leonard and John F. Bratzel, 126–143. Lanham, MD: Rowman and Littlefield.

Méndez, Alicia Liliana. 2023. FF.MM. de Colombia Lanzan Campaña Que Advierte a Migrantes Irregulares Sobre Peligros. *El Tiempo*. October 17.

MercoPress. 2025. Brazil Shoots Down Clandestine Aircraft Carrying Drugs. February 13.

Merrill, Tim L., and Ramón Miró. 1997. *Mexico: A Country Study*, 4th ed. Washington, DC: Library of Congress.

Meyer, Maureen. 2014. Mexico's Police: Many Reforms, Little Progress. Washington Office on Latin America. https://www.wola.org/sites/default/files/MexicosPolice.pdf.

Ministerio de Seguridad Nacional (Argentina). 2024. Fronteras Blindadas | Patricia Bullrich Lanzó el Plan Güemes en Salta. December 9.

Mirandé, Alfredo. 1987. *Gringo Justice*. Notre Dame, IN: University of Notre Dame Press.

Pappier, Juan, and Caitlyn Yates. 2023. How the Treacherous Darien Gap Became a Migration Crossroads of the Americas. Human Rights Watch. October 10. https://www.hrw.org/news/2023/10/10/how-treacherous-darien-gap-became-migration-crossroads-americas.

Passos, Anaís Medeiros. 2022. *Democracies at War Against Drugs: The Military Mystique in Brazil and Mexico*. London: Palgrave Macmillan.

Red de Documentación de las Organizaciones Defensoras de Migrantes (Redodam). 2019. *Procesos Migratorios en México: Nuevos Rostros, Mismas Dinámicas*. https://redodem.org/wp-content/uploads/2025/03/Informe_Redodem_2018_1_compressed_83744752bd.pdf.

RESDAL. 2024. *A Comparative Atlas of Defence in Latin America and the Caribbean*. Montevideo, Uruguay: RESDAL Internacional.

Rettie, John. 1985. Mexico's Southern Border. In *Politics in Mexico*, ed. George Philip, 194–205. London: Croom Helm.

Rochlin, James F. 1997. *Redefining Mexican "Security": Society, State, and Region under NAFTA*. Boulder: Lynne Rienner.

Rodríguez, Lincy. 2025. *Ejército de Guatemala Pone en Marcha la Operación Cinturón de Fuego Occidental*. March 4.

Rodríguez Mega, Emiliano, and James Wagner. 2024. Mexican Military Fatally Shoots Six Migrants. *New York Times*. October 2.

Sandos, James A. 1972. The Plan of San Diego: War & Diplomacy on the Texas Border 1915–1916. *Arizona and the West* 14 (1): 5–24.

Santoni, Pedro. 2008. The Civilian Experience in Mexico during the War with the United States, 1846–48. In *Daily Lives of Civilians in Wartime Latin America: From the Wars of Independence to the Central American Civil Wars*, ed. Pedro Santoni, 55–89. Westport, CT: Greenwood.

Schmitter, Philippe C., and Terry Lynn Karl. 1991. What Democracy Is…and Is Not. *Journal of Democracy* 2 (3): 75–88.

Seguridad Ciudadana: La Via Civil. 2018. Seguridad Pública Enfocada en el Uso de la Fuerza e Intervención Militar: La Evidencia en México

2006–2018. https://seguridadviacivil.ibero.mx/wp-content/uploads/2021/03/Informe_PSC_2019.pdf.

Seguridad Ciudadana: La Vía Civil. 2024. Enfrentamientos de la SEDENA, 2007 a 2023. https://seguridadviacivil.ibero.mx/interactivo/los-enfrentamientos-de-la-sedena/.

Slade, William F. 1917. The Federation of Central America. *The Journal of Race Development* 8 (1): 79–150.

Storr, Samuel. 2025. Guardia Nacional en la Frontera Norte: ¿Cambio en la Estrategia de Seguridad? Seguridad Ciudadana: La Vía Civil. February 22.

Stumpf, Juliet. 2006. The Crimmigration Crisis: Immigrants, Crime, and Sovereign Power. *American University Law Review* 56 (2): 367–419.

United States Department of State. 1999. Mexico: Country Reports on Human Rights Practices 1998.

United States Department of State. 2001. Mexico: Country Reports on Human Rights Practices 2000.

United States Department of State. 2002. Mexico: Country Reports on Human Rights Practices 2001.

United States Department of State. 2003. Mexico: Country Reports on Human Rights Practices 2002.

United States Department of State. 2004. Mexico: Country Reports on Human Rights Practices 2003.

United States Department of State. 2007. Mexico: Country Reports on Human Rights Practices 2006.

United States Department of State. 2008. Mexico: Country Reports on Human Rights Practices 2007.

United States Department of State. 2010. Mexico: Country Reports on Human Rights Practices 2009.

United States Department of State. 2011. Mexico: Country Reports on Human Rights Practices 2010.

United States Department of State. 2015. Mexico: Country Reports on Human Rights Practices 2014.

United States Department of State. 2019. Mexico: Country Reports on Human Rights Practices 2018.

United States Department of State. 2021. Mexico: Country Reports on Human Rights Practices 2020.

United States Southern Command. 2025. CENTAM Guardian Participants Demonstrate Increased Capacities in Culminating Event. May 23.

Vorobyeva, Yulia. 2015. Illegal Drugs as a National Security Threat: Securitization of Drugs in the U.S. Official Discourse. In *Drug Trafficking, Organized Crime, and Violence in the Americas Today*, eds. Bruce M. Bagley and Jonathan D. Rosen. Gainesville: University Press of Florida, 43–66.

Walker, David W. 1985. An American Dilemma: Undocumented Mexican Immigration to the United States. In *Politics in Mexico*, ed. George Philip, 171–193. London: Croom Helm.

Weber, Leanne. 2013. *Policing Non-citizens*. London: Routledge.

World Organization Against Torture. 2002. México: Un Soldado Mexicano Ha Sido Arrestado y Acusado del Asesinato de Dos Niños Centroamericanos y del Ataque a Dos Inmigrants Más. November 12.

CHAPTER 6

Violence for Profit in Peru: Repression and Economic Growth

INTRODUCTION

Though less commonly discussed in the state violence literature, this chapter documents how state actors engage in violence in the name of economic growth. The chapter begins by discussing the relationship, and related challenges, between economic development and democracy. We then explore the Peruvian context and outline three ways in which states perpetuate violence by providing protection and security, not to its citizens, but to private (or public) enterprise. These are: first, the criminalization of protest and the state's extreme response to protest; second, the use of force by state and private security actors on behalf of business, with a focus on the extractive industry, in particular; and third, direct participation in perpetuating violence as state-owned enterprises. The chapter takes each type of engagement in turn and offers illustrative examples from Peru. We conclude the chapter with reflections on these dynamics of violence across Latin America.

© The Author(s), under exclusive license to Springer Nature Switzerland AG 2025
B. J. Kyle et al., *State Violence and Democracy in Latin America*, Rethinking Political Violence,
https://doi.org/10.1007/978-3-032-06412-7_6

The Dilemma of Economic Development in Democracies

As Latin American countries transitioned to democracy, government leaders also sought to ensure strong economic growth. Though the relationship between democracy and economic growth was highlighted long ago (Lipset 1959), the nature and direction of the causal arrow have been debated in the political science literature (Boix 2011; Doucouliagos and Ulubasoglu 2008; Przeworski and Limongi 1993). A relatively recent consensus has emerged, however, that both democratization and democracy foster economic growth (Acemoglu et al. 2019). Democracies are more likely to experience GDP per capita growth over time, especially in those countries that invest in capital, education, and healthcare (Acemoglu et al. 2019, 48).

Even so, there are important nuances that also affect this relationship. In earlier work, for example, Daron Acemoglu and James A. Robinson (2006) and others (Karl 2000) find that democracies can become fragile when inequality is high. This rings true in Latin America, where the fruits of democracy and increased economic growth have not been evenly distributed. The Economic Commission for Latin America and the Caribbean (ECLAC) and Oxfam have documented the region's inequality. In a 2016 report, the authors note that "the fortunes of Latin America's billionaires grew by an average of 21%" between 2002 and 2015 and, as of 2014, "the richest 10% of people in Latin America had amassed 71% of the region's wealth" (Ibarra and Byanyima 2016). In 2024, the executive secretary of ECLAC stated that Latin America is in a "development crisis" that is driven, in part, by "high inequality and low social mobility and social cohesion...[as well as] weak institutional capacity and ineffective governance" (Economic Commission for Latin America and the Caribbean 2024).

Inequality is problematic not only for the well-being of those who remain poor, but also because it makes existing democracies more fragile. When inequality persists, pressure to address it through some type of redistributive policy increases, which prompts pushback from elites on such redistribution (Acemoglu and Robinson 2006). To protect their own gains, elites are incentivized to roll back democratic institutions, further weakening institutions that are often in their infancy or struggling to consolidate. In Brazil, for example, conservative elites' support for Jair Bolsonaro was, in part, a response to the major social and redistribution policies that the Workers' Party promoted under Presidents Luiz Inácio Lula da Silva and Dilma Rousseff. During his campaign Bolsonaro equated the policies of the left with those of Venezuela, which was experiencing severe economic and political crises that caused millions to flee (BBC 2018a). Despite his divisive, undemocratic rhetoric—including comments that condoned torture and lauded Brazil's former military dictatorship—he won the general election by more than 10 percentage points.

Another factor that shapes the relationship between political stability and economic growth affects a subset of countries that are particularly rich in natural resources. The "resource curse" (Ross 2015), or the "paradox of plenty" (Karl 1997), describes those countries that have a wealth of natural resources—usually oil or minerals—and which tend to develop weaker institutions, experience lower economic growth, and have greater conflict or violence, relative to those countries with fewer natural resources. The logic is that, due to the abundance of natural resources, the public and private sector become dependent on mineral or oil extraction. Political and economic leaders usually neglect the development of other industries (the Dutch disease), which makes them vulnerable to commodity price volatility and corruption.

As seen below, Peru has suffered from inequality and the resource curse. Together, these factors created an environment in which the government is willing to protect the resources considered essential by invoking violence in the name of economic development. Rather than promoting diverse sources of economic growth as a tool to improve the well-being of all citizens, the incentive is to weaken institutions and, as is the case in many Latin American countries, to use force to protect the wealth of a few citizens. The state, in short, does not work toward addressing the public interest, but rather becomes a tool of private, economic interests.

THE PERUVIAN ECONOMY AND ITS RESOURCE CURSE

Though rarely recognized today, "private" enterprise originated from the state. Organizations like the British East India Company and the Dutch East India Company were created by the state to incentivize others to explore the world, secure access to sought-after commodities, and importantly, to share the risk of doing so with private investors. To this day, states authorize corporations' existence (Ciepley 2013). The state can reserve ownership of specific sectors or enterprises for itself, whether to raise revenue for state operations or to assert national control over resources considered important for sovereignty, national security, and economic development. Many Latin American economies engaged in nationalizing private enterprise in the 1960s and 1970s for these reasons.

In Peru, state-owned enterprises reached their peak in the 1970s. General Juan Velasco Alvarado seized power in a bloodless military coup in 1968 and began to nationalize (or expropriate, at times) companies in the oil, telecommunications, and banking sectors. During military rule, the government created the first state-owned company in Peru, Empresa Minera del Perú, in 1970.[1] Just four years later, in 1975, the Peruvian government secured a monopoly of smelting and refining by acquiring the Cerro de Pasco smelting complex, which was built by a US company in La Oroya in 1922 (Lagos 2018, 4). By the end of the 1970s, the state controlled all iron production and a large percentage of the production of zinc (40%), lead (35%), and silver (25%) (Lagos 2018, 4–5).

General Velasco was ousted in 1975 by General Francisco Morales Bermúdez. Peru democratized in 1980, but this was also the year that the Shining Path, a Maoist guerrilla group, launched an armed insurgency to overthrow the Peruvian state. The 1980s and 1990s were dominated by the internal conflict, leading to the death of over 69,000 individuals, the majority of whom were Quechua-speaking civilians from rural areas (Truth and Reconciliation Commission Report 2003). The 1980s is commonly referred to as the "lost decade," as the Peruvian economy contracted because of internal conflict and several external shocks. Peru had also borrowed heavily in the 1970s and was overindebted; the country was eventually shut out of international credit markets and hyperinflation took hold under President Alan García's leadership between 1985 and 1990.

In 1990, Alberto Fujimori was elected president of Peru, but two years later he carried out a self-coup and dissolved Congress and the Supreme Court, arguing that Congress was slowing his progress and that he needed extraordinary powers to fight the Shining Path. He created a new Constitution in 1993, which expanded presidential powers and allowed him to run for reelection, which he did in 1995. The new constitution also fostered neoliberal economic reforms, in stark contrast to the policies of his predecessors. One feature was the promotion of free-market reforms and privatization, though Fujimori had already been encouraging foreign direct investment (FDI) through the Foreign Investment Promotion Law, the Framework Law for Private Investment Growth, the Private Investment in State-Owned Enterprises Promotion Law, and the Private Investment in Public Services Infrastructure Promotion Law.[2]

Because of this suite of regulatory changes, new mining operations were exempt from royalty payments and could defer the required 30% tax on their profits until their initial investments had been recovered (Arellano-Yanguas 2011, 620). Fujimori also signed a "fiscal stability agreement" with mining companies, which relinquished "the right of the government to change the mining tax regime without the companies' consent" (United States Department of State 2008). The World Bank (2025) reports that in 1992 FDI net outflows (in current USD) was -79 million (indicating foreign investment was fleeing the country) but increased to 3.47 billion in inflows by 1996.

Though Fujimori was eventually found guilty in 2009 of gross human rights violations (and received a presidential pardon in 2017), the economic policies he put into place were the catalyst for the economic growth, and resource dependence, that Peru has today. Like many Latin American countries, Peru's richness in resources has paradoxically contributed to political and economic crises, as noted above, the so-called "resource curse" (Arellano-Yanguas 2011; Ross 2015).

The Peruvian economy is heavily reliant on extractive industry. The mining industry accounts for nearly 9.5% of the country's GDP, while mineral exports account for 64% of the country's exports (García 2024). Peru is the world's second largest copper-producing country and has benefited from the increased global demand for copper and other minerals that are necessary for the "green" energy transition. The resource curse literature points to the ways in which corruption and poor governance are difficult to combat in such environments, as easy revenue reduces accessibility and encourages cronyism and power struggles among elites. Most of Peru's history has been marked by instability and recent decades have been no different. The last four presidents have failed to complete their terms, beginning with the attempted impeachment of Pedro Pablo Kuczynski (2016–2018), followed by his resignation in 2018 due to alleged corruption (Aquino 2022) and vote buying activities (BBC 2018b). Congress removed Martin Vizcarra (2018–2020) in 2020 for alleged corruption and Pedro Castillo (2021–2022) in 2022 amid political turmoil and allegations of corruption (Aquino 2022). Castillo's vice president, Dina Boluarte (2022–2025) became president of Peru, only to be ousted by Congress in late 2025 on the grounds of "permanent moral incapacity" (Rawnsley 2025). The previous three presidents also added to the disruption. Ollanta Humala (2011–2016) was found guilty of money laundering and sentenced to 15 years in prison (Buschschlüter 2025); Alejandro Toledo (2001–2006) was sentenced to 20 years in prison for corruption (Briceño and Garcia Cano 2024); and, finally, Alan Garcia, who served two terms (1985–1990 and 2006–2011), tragically shot himself when Peruvian police arrived at his home to arrest him due to bribery allegations (Aquino 2022).

In addition to political turmoil, the resource curse has contributed to high levels of state violence to protect state or private economic investments. State security forces help facilitate or protect state-owned companies, or once privatization is ushered in as a part of neoliberal policies, state actors help suppress opposition to assure foreign investors that their country is "open" for business. The Peruvian state engages in public order violence in the name of the economy. Elsewhere, scholars have referred to this as "economic complicity," whereby the state participates in human rights abuses on behalf of corporate actors (Olsen and Bernal Bermúdez 2024). As domestic and international firms expanded their operations (or, as noted below, as private firms took over state-owned companies during waves of privatization), the state responded to protests over economic activity with violence. Below, the chapter explores the variety of ways in which state actors—directly and indirectly—engage in violence on behalf of economic actors in Peru.

Violent Responses to Protests

Across Peru, protesters take to the streets to voice their grievances about environmental concerns, human rights abuses, land rights, the lack of public services, and other issues. This is particularly common in relation to the mining industry. It is also common for these protests to turn deadly. Mar Pérez of the Coordinadora Nacional de Derechos Humanos, a coalition of human rights groups, notes that: "Assassinations in protests are not a new event in Peru. Between 2003 and 2020 there were 167 deaths at the hands of the armed forces. The most serious situations have occurred when the Army intervenes. The impunity rate in these murders is close to 100%" (Infobae 2022). Unfortunately, years after Ms. Pérez made this statement, it is still true.

As of this writing, Peru is grappling with the state's violent response to protests that erupted across the country on December 7, 2022 when former President Pedro Castillo was ousted after he tried to dissolve Congress. Over the course of a few months, nearly 50 people were killed, as Castillo's supporters took to the streets. During this time, the Peruvian Armed Forces and the Peruvian National Police (PNP) used excessive force to suppress unarmed protestors. A *New York Times* investigation found that police in Ayacucho used "excessive, lethal force on civilians...[a] military register of weapons issued to soldiers deployed in Ayacucho...confirms that more than eighty soldiers were given Galil rifles that day" (McDonald and Tiefenthäler 2023). Ten individuals were killed, with another 60 injured (Infobae 2022). In early January 2023, 18 civilians, including three minors, were killed and an additional 70 people were injured, 31 of whom were wounded by gunfire (McDonald and Tiefenthäler 2023). Reporters, using forensics data, showed that the "police used deadly tactics, often in apparent violation of their own protocols, which call for a reasonable and proportionate amount of force when responding to civil unrest" (McDonald and Tiefenthäler 2023).

The state commonly uses violence to respond to citizens protesting about environmental concerns or human rights abuses committed by corporations. The Peruvian Ombudsman's Office began collecting data on social conflict in 2019. As of May 2025, there were 195 registered conflicts, 145 of which are active conflicts (the remaining 50 cases are latent). Over one in four (89 conflicts or 45%) are related to mining or natural gas and 127 cases (65%) involved at least one incident of violence since it began (Defensoría del Pueblo 2025). Given the ongoing protests, especially around mining, oil, and gas operations, or large development projects, the outsized police (and policy) response is often described as the "criminalization of social protest" (Arce 2014; Lindt 2023; MacLennan 2012). Rather than respecting an individual's right to peaceful assembly, state security forces respond with violence, increasingly through militarized tactics and tools, including tear gas, rubber bullets, and live rounds. Instead of seeing protest as a normal part of democratic participation, protest is seen as a threat; something to be suppressed.

Scholars have highlighted how states use the law to repress dissent (i.e., "lawfare"), by changing or reinterpreting laws around what civilian behavior might constitute "resisting authority" or generating "public disorder" (Vegh Weis 2023; Zaffaroni et al. 2023). Donatella della Porta and Olivier Fillieule (2004) illustrate the political determinants of police tolerance or repression of social protest. Peru's responses reflect what they refer to as a "tough" policing style, which "usually implies the repression of a large number of protest groups and a wide range of protest activities, via a massive use of force, and sometimes illegal tactics (such as the use of *agents provocateurs*), with low reliance on bargaining and a rigid, reactive implementation of the law" (218). These trends are seen consistently across Peru and, though the state engages in violent responses to peaceful protest generally, such conflicts emerge often in the context of extractive resources. In such instances, as illustrated below with discussion of Minero Horizonte, Newmont Mining, and Southern Copper, the state quells protests with excessive use of force on behalf of private enterprise.

Minero Horizonte

The mining company Consorcio Minero Horizonte operates in the Parcoy district of the La Libertad department in Peru. In 2016, nearby residents embarked on a series of dialogues with the company to address ongoing issues, concerning land concessions for artisanal or small-scale mining, as well as increased pollution of a nearby river.[3] Though two years earlier the company had set aside five plots of land for artisanal mining (Post 2016), according to the company, residents wanted access to more land. When the dialogue efforts failed, residents occupied a road—a common protest tactic in Peru and elsewhere in Latin America—in Alpamarca, which leads to a mining site. During this time a tailings dam—which is where the waste from mining and processing minerals is stored—broke, further worsening tensions between the community and the company.

In response, 130 armed police officers from the Special Services Division arrived to confront the protesters. Two people were killed and 23 were injured, many of whom were brought to a local hospital (Business & Human Rights Resource Centre 2016). The protesters were armed with guns and dynamite, and some of those injured were police officers (Post 2016). Ernesto Bendezú, the general counsel for the firm, explained it this way: "We, like any other citizen, communicate this to the Public Prosecutor's Office and the police, the only ones who are authorized to reinstate rule of law" (Mining Press 2016). On December 2, community members, representatives of the government, and representatives of Consorcio Minero Horizonte convened to discuss a non-violent path forward. They agreed to continued dialogue between the community and the mining company (Government of La Libertad 2016). Though the mining company is seeking an expansion of its operation to increase the life of the mine, protests continue. As of June 2024, community members were peacefully protesting the activities of the mine, while company executives were threatening to end talks, dissolve existing contracts, and "bring the PNP and 700 soldiers to expel [the protestors] from their own community" if leaders did not end the protests (MarcoNorte 2024).

Newmont Mining

In Northern Peru, the Yanacocha mine (owned by Newmont Mining, a US-based corporation) in Cajamarca has drawn the attention of scholars (Avant, Finn, and Olsen 2023; Taylor and Bonner 2017) and the media (Balch 2016; Perlez and Bergman 2010) due to the ongoing and contentious nature of the engagement between the company and nearby communities. Others have written about the company's missteps over a sizable mercury spill in 2000 that led to residents' illness and injury (Bury 2004, 2008; Li 2013). While still other scholars and journalists have documented the company's harassment and legal battle over land between Máxima Acuña and the company beginning in 2011 (Bazán 2024), in which the Peruvian Supreme Court ruled in favor of Ms. Acuña in 2017 (Reuters 2017). These events illustrate the deep tension between the company and the community that contributed to later incidents, which became violent.

One specific example occurred in 2012, when company personnel offered educational kits to schoolteachers in exchange for their signatures indicating support for an expansion of the mine, known as the "Conga project" (Ortiz 2012). Though reports differ about what happened next, community *rondas*, or autonomous peasant patrols, who have constitutional rights to determine who comes into their community, took seven Yanacocha employees into custody (Confederación Nacional de Comunidades del Perú Afectadas por la Minería 2012). The *Financial Times* reported that those who were held stated it was done so "without violence" (Mapstone 2012). Even so, when local schoolteachers refused to sign a document indicating their support for the Conga expansion, the police and company personnel arrived and sprayed tear gas at the school, according to reporting by a community organization (Confederación Nacional de Comunidades del Perú Afectadas por la Minería 2012). Héctor Medina, the mayor of Chugur, the town where this occurred, told a local radio station, "We do not want crumbs from Yanacocha...I don't think there will be aggression... Chugur and all its communities reject Conga and the presence of the Yanacocha mine because our river no longer has water. That is our concern" (Mapstone 2012).

In July 2012, three civilians were killed (including a 17-year-old) when "several thousand protesters tried to storm the municipal hall in Celendín, a town that is a stronghold of resistance to Conga even though its mayor had expressed support for the project" (Associated Press 2012). Two other individuals died later due to injuries (El Universo 2012). Ariel Taylor and Michelle D. Bonner's (2017) analysis shows how the post-conflict discourse by state actors sought to illustrate that protestors committed wrongdoing and provoked police, and that police action was necessary and legitimate (8–11). Newmont's operations in the region continue to face legal challenges (Personius 2025) and, as of February 2025, they indicated they would postpone additional investments in the project. In short, police violence has only heightened tensions between the community and the company, while the lack of transparency and accountability for the use of force further weakens citizens' sense of agency and trust in political institutions.

Southern Copper

Another example illustrates that state actors' involvement in violence often occurs over many years. Southern Copper, the world's second largest copper producer and a subsidiary of Grupo México, has been trying to open the $1.4 billion-dollar Tía María project in the province of Islay, Arequipa since 2008. In 2011, thousands of residents and farmers protested the mine by blockading roads due to concerns over water contamination (BBC 2011). Police arrived to suppress the protests in which over 50 protestors were injured and 3 killed (Federación Internacional de Derechos Humanos [FIDH] 2011). The President of FIDH, Souhayr Belhassen, stated: "We are very concerned by the Peruvian government's unwillingness to engage in dialogue with the protesters...We are even more concerned about the extrajudicial executions of three people who were very legitimately claiming the right to the environment and consultation. We have not forgotten the disastrous precedent that occurred in Bagua in 2009," referencing a previous massacre of 33 people, including 23 police officers and 10 civilians. Belhassen continued, "[t]he government must understand that it cannot implement its mining policy in total disrespect of the rights of the affected population" (FIDH 2011). During this period, national elections were also ongoing. The mine became an electoral issue and President Alan García's administration responded by ordering a cessation of the Tía María project in April 2011 (BBC 2011; Prado 2011).

In 2013, Southern Copper sought to address the environmental concerns that had prompted prior protests and presented a revised Environmental Impact Assessment to the Ministry of Energy and Mines; the project was reapproved in August 2014 (Dunlap 2019). The new approval of the mine, however, triggered another wave of protests involving hundreds of people living in the region. Opponents of the project started an indefinite strike in the Tambo Valley. In April 2015, police opened fire on the crowd and killed a local farmer and injured 12 others (Briceno 2015). In May, violent clashes led to the deaths of another local resident and a police officer; the Peruvian government deployed military troops for the first time to "help maintain law and order" in the region (BBC 2015). Agriculture Minister Juan Manuel Benites, the chief government negotiator in the dispute, told a local radio station that the Tía María conflict puts "at risk not just a single mining project but Peru's reputation as a country that can attract responsible investment" (Briceno 2015). By May 2015, the company extended its "voluntary 60-day pause," on account of the continued protests and related violence and, according to President Ollanta Humala, who supported the mine, to "allow for dialogue and address community concerns" (Post 2015). By this time, seven people had been killed since the protests began in 2011 (Post 2015).

Four years later, in 2019, the government approved the mine's development, contingent on improved social relations, which triggered another wave of protests (Aquino 2019). When President Pedro Castillo came into office in 2021 his administration signaled its lack of support for the project, stating the proposed mine was "socially and politically" unfeasible (Jamasmie 2021) and called the mine a "non-starter" (Attwood and Rochabrun 2024). Despite continued protests, the Boluarte administration announced the mine had all of the necessary permits (Attwood and Rochabrun 2024) and, as of this writing, construction of the mine is slated to begin in the third quarter of 2025, with operations beginning in 2027 (Delgado Tong 2025).

These illustrative cases show the broader trends that are pervasive in Peru: the state's response to public protest in the corporate context is excessive and violent. State actors continue to use police and military forces to quell protest; and, the state continues to ignore community members' environmental or economic concerns and, instead, justify public order violence in the name of economic growth. At the Asia–Pacific Economic Cooperation CEO summit, hosted by Peru, former President Boluarte reiterated the country's commitment to "economic reactivation," stating that "Peru opens its doors and gives the warmest welcome to investment funds and capital from all around the world by offering foreign investors legal stability, economic stability, and clear rules of the game that will guarantee sustainable growth" (Asia–Pacific Economic Cooperation 2024).

Public and Private Security for Hire

While the section above highlighted the ways in which state security forces—the PNP and Army—violently suppress protests in the name of economic activity, private security forces are another source of such violence. In Peru, there is significant crossover between public and private security.

Private security firms have proliferated across the region. A 2018 report notes that across Latin America and the Caribbean, there are over 16,000 private military and security companies that employ an estimated 2.4 million people (Kinosian and Bosworth 2018). In Peru, the government estimates that private security companies grew from 540 in 2011, to 780 in 2015, to 2,700 in 2021 (Ministerio de Justicia y Derechos Humanos 2021, 9). In 2007, a United Nations Working Group on the use of mercenaries made specific recommendations to the government, one of which was to adopt domestic legislation to better track and monitor private security companies. In 2012, the Peruvian government reorganized its oversight of private security and created the National Superintendency for the Control of Security Services, Arms, Ammunition and Explosives for Civilian Use, which oversees the control, supervision, and regulation of private security services. A government report highlights that some progress has been made in response to the UN Working Group's recommendations, but most of that progress is related to the registration and tracking of security companies, rather than direct monitoring (Ministerio de Justicia y Derechos Humanos 2021, 23).

Until 2016, when the government established a new legal framework for the PNP, police officers regularly worked second jobs directly with private security companies. The new decree prohibits this practice but allows companies to contract with the PNP directly.[4] In practice, this means that companies have their own security, contract out to private security companies, and employ the PNP for additional security. For example, the Cerro Verde mine in Arequipa (owned by US-based Freeport-McMoRan) reported that, at the end of 2021, they "employed 10 unarmed security employees and 312 private security contractors. Some private security contractors assigned to the protection of expatriate personnel are armed. In addition to these security personnel, the national government has assigned Peruvian National Police (PNP) to the site in teams on 7-day rotations...A total of 512 members of the PNP rotated through the site during 2021" (Freeport-McMoRan 2022). Concerns about the conflict of interest persist, as police are effectively employed—at varying times—to protect the public interest and private interests. Furthermore, this arrangement "implies that the use of force is not only part of Peruvian law but also the norm in its mining industry" (Oh, Shin, and Ho 2023, 645).

Newmont's engagement with the private security force Forza worked against them as they sought to smooth over an already strained relationship with the community (Cruz 2008). In 2005, the company sought to expand its footprint and mine on a sacred site called Cerro Quilish. In 2006, local agrarian communities, led by Father Marco Arana a co-founder of the NGO Grupo de Formación e Intervención para el Desarrollo Sostenible (GRUFIDES), feared that the mine's operations would contaminate water supplies in the region (Myplainview 2006). Citizens organized a blockade of the road between the local capital, Cajamarca, and the mine (Myplainview 2006). Protesters and Forza clashed, resulting in the death of one of the protesters, Isidro Llanos Echevarría (Salazar 2006).[5] According to Charis Kamphuis (2011), "Yanacocha deployed a team of nearly two hundred armed men: a mix of Forza agents and off-duty police officers paid by the company in accordance with the agreement signed with the police corps" (79).

In November 2006, Father Marco Arana was placed under video surveillance by an individual later identified by police as having connections to Forza. Forza and Yanacocha denied any involvement in the surveillance. During the same period, Arana and fellow GRUFIDES member Mirtha Vásquez received anonymous death threats. In response, Amnesty International issued an urgent action on November 22, 2006 warning that "their lives, and those of others associated with GRUFIDES, may be in danger" (Amnesty International 2006). That

same month, environmental activist Edmundo Becerra Corina was shot
and killed in Yanacanchilla, just north of Cajamarca. He had reportedly
received multiple death threats due to his opposition to the mine's expansion and was scheduled to meet with representatives from the Ministry of
Energy and Mines just days after his murder.

In August 2006, the Peruvian National Police and the Prosecutor
Alfredo Rebaza investigated the murder of Llanos Echevarría and
searched the Forza warehouse, which was located within the Yanacocha
mining site (Kamphuis 2011, 79). They seized weapons and ammunition
(Ivanou 2006) because the arsenal included military equipment, which
according to the Law on Private Security Services is illegal and constitutes
a violation of Peru's Constitution (Kamphuis 2011, 79).[6] Afterward, local
representatives of Combayo, which includes 18 small villages, agreed to
engage in dialogue with Yanacocha; the company agreed to pay for Llanos
Echevarría's funeral (Ivanou 2006). As noted above, however, additional
violence ensued and today tensions remain.

Forza has faced allegations of abuse elsewhere in Peru, as well. The
company provided security services to Minera Majaz, a subsidiary of the
U.K.-based Monterrico Metals. Forza employees, as well as members
of the PNP, are alleged to have tortured protesters in the facilities of
Minera Majaz (Coordinadora Nacional de Radio 2009).[7] Journalist Julio
César Vásquez Calle, who was also tortured, filed a complaint against the
company. He reported that "[t]he policemen had the order to torture
us, from the mining camp managers (…) we were all stripped of our
clothes. The women were subjected to undue touches, evidence of the
treatment and action of the DINOES police [an elite Peruvian police
unit trained for operations against subversive groups] who acted harshly
with the peasants… They beat us with a rod (…) we were hooded, tied
up, blindfolded. Inside these hoods there was tear gas, which makes it
difficult to breathe and burn the skin" (Coordinadora Nacional de Radio
2009). After reporting these abuses, Vásquez Calle began to receive death
threats demanding that he drop the complaint (Amnesty International
2009). One caller said, "Since when is your job to help terrorists? We are
going to make sure that you rot in prison if you don't withdraw your
complaint, if you don't drop your complaint you will go to prison in
pieces" (Amnesty International 2009).

The proliferation of private security, in addition to the contracts mining
companies can sign directly with the PNP, create a dangerous mix of
sources of violence, as well as serious conflicts of interest. A 2018 report

written by NGOs warns that such "contracts affect the Police's ability to be impartial and independent, as they favor the companies' interests, endangering indigenous communities that live in the areas where these projects take place" (EarthRights International et al. 2019). Such agreements bring into question for whom the police exist and who they are meant to serve. In this case, it is quite clearly private enterprise. The conflict of interest deepens, as the PNP generates revenue from the mining companies. The report referenced earlier estimates that private companies have paid the PNP over $14 million between 2010 and 2018 (EarthRights International et al. 2019, 15), though it should be noted this is a relatively small portion of the PNP's overall budget, which in 2024 was an estimated $1.36 billion. Even so, Weiss (2007) summarizes the problems with private security and the PNP's connection with private enterprise: "The social benefits, however, are meager. Any real security that they provide is generally limited to the narrow interests of their immediate employers, not that of the larger society" (9).

STATE-OWNED ENTERPRISES

Another source of public order violence, which is often overlooked, is the role that state-owned enterprises play in contributing to such violence in Peru and elsewhere. Most Latin American countries engaged in nationalizing private enterprise in the 1960s and 1970s in an effort to regain sovereignty and control over those industries deemed to be economically or politically important. In Peru (Lagos 2018), and elsewhere (Martin del Campo and Winkler 1991), state-owned enterprises reached their peak in the 1970s. The region has far fewer state-owned enterprises today than it did in then. As Peru, for example, adopted neoliberal economic policies, its revenues from privatization between 1990 and 2000 were estimated to be nearly 15% of its GDP (Lora 2001). Even so, state-owned enterprises are still a significant part of the economy. In 2024, the public sector accounted for 16% of market capitalization in Latin America (Organisation for Economic Co-operation and Development 2024, 12). Many of the state-owned enterprises are in the oil and gas industry, such as Petrobras in Brazil, Pemex in Mexico, YPF in Argentina, and Ecopetrol in Ecuador. State-owned mining companies also play a major role in the region, such as Chile's copper mining company, Codelco, which often ranks as one of the top copper producers in the world (Belder 2025).

Some Latin American countries also have state-owned financial institutions (e.g., Banco do Brasil or the Uruguay National Development Corporation) and airlines (e.g., Mexicana de Aviación).

In Peru, the military used a dispute between the government and the International Petroleum Company (IPC), a United States-based subsidiary of Standard Oil, to justify the 1968 coup (Klarén 2025, 72). The military government proceeded to nationalize the oil sector, creating Petróleos del Perú (better known as Petroperú) in 1969 (Klarén 2025, 82). This move garnered popular support for the military regime. It became a symbol of the restoration of national sovereignty, which the regime institutionalized in a national holiday, the "National Dignity Day," which was celebrated until the end of the dictatorship in 1980 (La República 2018a).

The nationalization of Petroperú held more significance than the nationalization of other companies. According to Rodley (1974), the government had been in a long dispute about the extent to which the previous owners explored oil fields beyond their allowed share (e.g., the "problem of la Brea y Pariñas"). The government believed the company owed taxes, dating back to the early 1900s. The Peruvian government set aside compensation for the nationalization of IPC, which was to be made available once the back taxes were paid by Standard Oil, but the amount allegedly owed by the company far exceeded the amount the government set aside (Rodley 1974, 118).

Despite its rather illustrious start, Petroperú's more recent history has been less celebrated domestically. EarthRights International reports that since 1996, the Peruvian government has documented 37 spills, while independent sources estimate there have been 190 spills along the Norperuano Pipeline, which Petroperú operates, that have contaminated the water and land used by nearby indigenous communities (EarthRights International 2025). In 2009, indigenous leaders in the Amazon protested new oil and mining laws that affected their ancestral land and Petroperú's pipeline. The PNP and military clashed with indigenous groups when 650 police officers were sent to clear the highway that had been blocked by unarmed protesters (Leon and Kraul 2009). Police reportedly shot into the crowd from helicopters; the Interior Minister accused the indigenous leaders of inciting the violence. Former President García described the event as "a subversive aggression against democracy and against the national police," while several human rights and environmental activist groups suggested the police provoked the violence

(Leon and Kraul 2009). Overall, nine indigenous protesters and 22 police officers were killed, nine of whom were first held hostage at a Petroperú pumping station (Leon and Kraul 2009). This event, known as the "Baguazo" protests, was Peru's deadliest conflict in a decade. In 2011, three senior police and army officers were given suspended prison sentences and small fines from a Peruvian military court for their role in the deaths of protesters. The laws in question have since been suspended, though efforts to further develop and expand oil extraction in the area continue.

Since 2015, ongoing legal battles from affected communities have challenged the government's failure to respond to spills which have destroyed local community's food and water sources. Continued spills alongside efforts to expand the company's operations have led to consistent opposition by various indigenous groups for the past decade. On November 27, 2018, for example, the Wampis Nation Autonomous Territorial Government (GTAW) reported an oil spill in the Mayuriaga indigenous community. GTAW said that the environmental damage posed a serious risk "to the health and life of citizens living in the Wampis territory, especially children, women and the elderly" (Servindi 2018). On December 6, 2018, the news outlet *La República* confirmed that Petroperú had been unable to stop the oil leak that occurred a month prior near the community of Mayuriaga nor had it stopped numerous other leaks which occurred in the area around the same time (La República 2018b). GTAW reiterated its demand for Petroperú and Peruvian authorities to clean up and stop the oil spill near the community (Servindi 2018).

Conclusion

Police or private security company violence toward protesters is not unique to Peru. Such patterns are seen across Latin America, raising concerns about the extent to which the state uses force in the name of economic growth and explicitly on behalf of corporate interests. Olsen and Bermúdez (2024), for example, find that state actors across Latin America are more likely to engage in human rights abuses on behalf of corporate actors when a country's economy relies heavily on mineral rents and when union representatives are present. More broadly, examples from Peru and elsewhere in Latin America illustrate the ways in which public order violence plays out on behalf of economic actors, further eroding the boundary of what might be considered legitimate or illegitimate use of force. The private sector is yet another way in which the cycle of public order violence simultaneously facilitates the proliferation of violence by the state, while also exacerbating legacy conditions: uneven state capacity, weak rule of law, and socioeconomic inequalities.

State violence has characterized Bolivia's relationship with natural resources and foreign corporations. In 1996, the government enacted the Hydrocarbon Industry Law no. 1689 that broke up and privatized most of the state-owned Yacimientos Petroliferos Fiscales de Bolivia oil company, which was founded in 1936.[8] Having discovered sizeable reserves of natural gas, a new consortium called Pacific LNG, comprised of Repsol YPF, British Gas, and PanAmerican Energy, planned to build a pipeline from the Margarita gas field through the Andean Mountains to Chile where it would be liquified and exported to Mexico and the United States. Much of the revenue from the project would go to foreign corporations, not the government. The export plan became public in August and by October widespread protests had swept across the country. The initial calls were for the government to export the gas through Peru rather than Chile, which had defeated Bolivia in the War of the Pacific (1879–83). They soon grew, however, into greater demands for the re-nationalization of natural gas and democratic reforms (Perreault 2012, 92–93).

The government responded to this opposition with violence. President Gonzalo Sánchez de Lozado, referencing Law 1405 of 1992 on the Armed Forces, declared an emergency with decree DS27209, deploying the military to break up the protests.[9] After several additional days of violent protests that resulted in at least 65 deaths, Sánchez de Lozado resigned. His successor, Carlos Mesa, faced continued protests demanding a new hydrocarbon law and he similarly responded by issuing decree DS28120, placing the military in charge of internal security. He too would resign shortly after (Wright 2015, 100).[10]

In Panama, the government violently attacked unionized workers in July 2020 who were peacefully protesting a proposed law that would eliminate union dues. Two workers were killed while more than 100 were detained (Sullivan 2012). This conflict continues. In May 2025, the government declared a state of emergency, which "restricts freedom of movement and allows the police to make arrests without a warrant," in the same province, Bocas del Toro (Rocha and Lukiv 2025). Protesters, largely led by Chiquita Brand employees, had taken to the streets to contest Law 462, which reformed workers' pension plans; the confrontation grew after the company fired thousands of employees who had been on strike (Rocha and Lukiv 2025).[11] Protesters committed property damage to one of Chiquita's facilities and the local airport, and looted local businesses (Rocha and Lukiv 2025). An estimated 2,500 police have been deployed to the region, resulting in one death (Al Jazerra 2025) and 304 arrests, including 18 minors (Newsroom Panama 2025).

States engage directly and indirectly in public order violence. As this chapter illustrates, they do so by challenging the legality of protest, by authorizing security forces to protect business assets and interests, and by participating in abuses directly, through state-owned enterprises that perpetuate violence toward citizens. Examining how public order violence has emerged in the context of economic growth illustrates yet another facet of this phenomenon. Through many avenues, state actors demonstrate that they are often inclined not to protect the public interest nor seek to resolve conflict in ways that might promote the overall well-being of citizens. Instead, as this chapter illustrates, state actors use violence to quell protest, to protect private interests, and to defend the state's economic objectives—all at the cost of citizens' security, well-being, and basic human rights.

NOTES

1. Decreto Ley N° 18225, de 14 de abril de 1970, "Independencia Económica e Industrialización del País son las Metas de la Nueva Ley de Mineria." Copies of all primary documents cited in the book are available at www.andyreiter.com.
2. Decreto Legislativo N° 662, de 2 de septiembre de 1991, "Otorgan un régimen de estabilidad jurídica a las inversiones extranjeras mediante el reconocimiento de ciertas garantías"; Decreto Legislativo N° 757, de 14 de noviembre de 1991, "Aprueba Ley Marco para el crecimiento de la inversión privada"; Decreto Legislativo N° 674, de 27 de setiembre de 1991, "Promulgan la Ley de Promoción de la Inversión Privada en las Empresas del Estado"; Decreto Legislativo N° 758, de 13 de noviembre de 1991, "Dictan normas para la promoción de las inversiones privadas en la infraestructura de servicios públicos."
3. Corporations and Human Rights Database, UniqueID 1704CMH0001 (Olsen 2023).

4. Decreto Supremo N° 1267, 28 de febrero de 2025, "Ley de creación de la Policía Nacional de Perú."
5. Corporations and Human Rights Database, UniqueID 1704MIY0051 (Olsen 2023).
6. Ley N° 28879, de 18 de agosto de 2006, "Ley de Servicios de Seguridad Privada"; Article 175, Peru's Constitution of 1993 with Amendments through 2021, https://www.constituteproject.org/constitution/Peru_2021.
7. Corporations and Human Rights Database, UniqueID 2115FOZ0004 (Olsen 2023).
8. Ley N° 1689, 30 de abril de 1996, "Ley de Hidrocarburos."
9. Ley N° 1405, 30 de deciembre de 1992, "Le Orgánica de las Fuerzas Armadas de la Nación"; Decreto Supremo N° 27,209, 11 de octubre de 2003.
10. Decreto Supremo N° 28,120, 16 de mayo de 2005.
11. Ley N° 462, 18 de marzo de 2025, "Que modifica, adiciona y deroga artículos de la Ley 51 de 2005, que reforma a la Ley Orgánica de la Caja de Seguro Social y dicta otras disponsiciones."

REFERENCES

Acemoglu, Daron, and James A. Robinson. 2006. *Economic Origins of Dictatorship and Democracy*. New York: Cambridge University Press.
Acemoglu, Daron, Suresh Naidu, Pascual Restrepo, and James A. Robinson. 2019. Democracy Does Cause Growth. *Journal of Political Economy* 127 (1): 47–100.
Al Jazeera. 2025. Panama Declares Emergency in Western Province After Deadly Pension Protests. June 21. https://www.aljazeera.com/news/2025/6/21/panama-declares-emergency-in-western-province-after-deadly-pension-protests.
Amnesty International. 2006. Fear for Safety. https://www.amnesty.org/es/documents/amr46/029/2006/en/.
Amnesty International. 2009. Peru: Death Threats. February 11. https://www.amnesty.org/en/documents/amr46/003/2009/en/.
Aquino, Marcos. 2019. Protest Begins Against Billion-Dollar Southern Copper Mining Project in Peru. *Reuters*. July 16. https://www.reuters.com/article/world/protest-begins-against-billion-dollar-southern-copper-mining-project-in-peru-idUSKCN1UA2GL/.

Aquino, Marco. 2022. Peru's Presidents and Years of Political Turmoil. *Reuters*. December 7. https://www.reuters.com/world/americas/perus-pre sidents-years-political-turmoil-2022-12-07/.

Arce, Moisés. 2014. *Resource Extraction and Protest in Peru*. Pittsburgh: Pittsburgh University Press.

Arellano-Yanguas, Javier. 2011. Aggravating the Resource Curse: Decentralisation, Mining and Conflict in Peru. *The Journal of Development Studies* 47 (4): 617–638.

Asia-Pacific Economic Cooperation. 2024. 8 Quotes from President Dina Boluarte of Peru at the APEC CEO Summit. November 14. https://www.apec.org/press/features/2024/8-quotes-from-president-dina-boluarte-of-peru-at-the-apec-ceo-summit.

Associated Press. 2012. Peru Anti-Mining Protests Escalate During State of Emergency. *The Guardian*. July 5. https://www.theguardian.com/world/2012/jul/05/peru-anti-mining-protests-escalate.

Attwood, James, and Marcelo Rochabrun. 2024. Southern Copper Eyes Start of Stalled Peru Mine Project as Soon as This Year. *Bloomberg News*. May 21. https://www.bloomberg.com/news/articles/2024-05-21/southern-cop per-eyes-start-of-stalled-peru-mine-project-as-soon-as-this-year.

Avant, Deborah, Devin Finn, and Tricia D. Olsen. 2023. Can CSR Strategy Mediate Conflict Over Extraction? Evidence from Two Mines in Peru. *World Development* 170: 106323.

Balch, Oliver. 2016. Peruvian Farmer wins David and Goliath Battle Against US Mining Giant. *The Guardian*. April 21. https://www.theguardian.com/sus tainable-business/2016/apr/21/peru-farmer-wins-battle-newmont-mining-corporation.

Bazán, Y. M. A. 2024. Máxima Acuña: Mujer Valiente por el Amor a su Región. *Revista Intercultural Manguaré* 3 (1): 63–68.

BBC. 2011. Peru Cancels Tia Maria Copper Mine Project After Protests. April 9. http://www.bbc.co.uk/news/world-latin-america-13025971.

BBC. 2015. Peru: Troops Deployed After Deaths in Tia Maria Mine Protests. May 9. https://www.bbc.com/news/world-latin-america-32677410.

BBC. 2018a. Jair Bolsonaro: Far-right Candidate Wins First Round of Brazil Election. October 8. https://www.bbc.com/news/world-latin-america-457 80176.

BBC. 2018b. Pedro Pablo Kuczynski: Under Fire Peru President Resigns. March 22. https://www.bbc.com/news/world-latin-america-43492421.

Belder, Dean. 2025. Top 10 Copper-Producing Companies. *Investing News Network*. June 24. https://investingnews.com/daily/resource-investing/base-metals-investing/copper-investing/top-copper-producing-companies/.

Boix, Carles. 2011. Democracy, Development, and the International System. *American Political Science Review* 105 (4): 809–828.

Briceno, Franklin. 2015. Month-Long Protest Over Peru Copper Mine Claims First Life. *Associated Press*. April 23. https://apnews.com/general-news-d9c 4f858750c42b6bf05b3221eee1046.

Briceño, Franklin, and Regina Garcia Cano. 2024. Peru's Ex-President Toledo Gets More Than 20 Years in Prison in Case Linked to Corruption Scandal. *Associated Press*. https://apnews.com/article/peru-toledo-prison-sen tence-odebrecht-5f23c3d8fd176dfc6ca8125e96b2e3ec.

Bury, Jeffery. 2004. Livelihoods in Transition: Transnational Gold Mining Operations and Local Change in Cajamarca, Peru. *Geographical Journal* 170 (1): 78–91.

Bury, Jeffery. 2008. Transnational Corporations and Livelihood Transformations in the Peruvian Andes: An Actor-Oriented Political Ecology. *Human Organization* 67 (3): 307–321.

Buschschlüter, Vanessa. 2025. Peru's Ex-President and First Lady Sentenced to 15 Years in Prison. *BBC News*. April 16. https://www.bbc.com/news/art icles/c33z6kn7xvyo.

Business & Human Rights Resource Centre. 2016. Peru: Two Community Members Killed and 23 Injured in Clashes with Police During Protests Over Mining Spill in Consorcio Minero Horizonte. November 9. https://www. business-humanrights.org/en/peru-two-community-members-killed-23-inj ured-in-clashes-with-police-during-protests-over-mining-spill-in-consorcio-minero-horizonte.

Ciepley, David. 2013. Beyond Public and Private: Toward a Political Theory of the Corporation. *American Political Science Review* 107 (1): 139–158.

Confederación Nactional de Comunidades del Perú Afectadas por la Minería. 2012. Milton Sánchez Rechazó Supuesto Secuestro a 7 Trabajadores de Yanacocha. March 16. http://www.conacami.pe/2012/03/milton-sanchez-rechazo-supuesto.html.

Coordinadora Nacional de Radio. 2009. Periodista que denunció torturas en Majaz es amenazado de Muerte. February 8. https://derechoshumanos.pe/ periodista-de-radio-cutivalu-es-amenazado-de-muerte-por-denunciar-torturas-en-majaz/.

Cruz, Edmundo. 2008. Crónica de un reglaje al 'Diablo.' *La República*. May 24. https://web.archive.org/web/20080524093400/http://www.lar epublica.com.pe/content/view/133634/.

Defensoría del Pueblo. 2025. Reporte de Conflictos Sociales N.° 255. May. https://www.defensoria.gob.pe/wp-content/uploads/2025/06/Reporte-de-conflictos-sociales-n.%C2%BA-255-%E2%80%93-mayo-2025.pdf.

Delgado Tong, Alejandro. 2025. Tía María, con una inversión elevada a USD 1.800 millones, comenzará su construcción en el tercer trimestre de 2025. *Infobae*. March 1. https://www.infobae.com/peru/2025/02/28/tia-maria-con-una-inversion-elevada-a-usd-1800-millones-comenzara-su-construccion-en-el-tercer-trimestre-de-2025/.
della Porta, Donnatella, and Olivier Fillieule. 2004. Policing Social Protest. In *The Blackwell Companion to Social Movements*, eds. David A. Snow, Sarah A. Soule, and Hanspeter Kriesi, 217–241. Malden, MA: Blackwell.
Doucouliagos, Hristos, and Mehmet Ali Ulubaşoğlu. 2008. Democracy and Economic Growth: A Meta-Analysis. *American Journal of Political Science* 52 (1): 61–83.
Dunlap, Alexander. 2019. Agro sí, mina NO! The Tía Maria Copper Mine, State Terrorism and Social War by Every Means in the Tambo Valley, Peru. *Political Geography* 71: 10–25.
EarthRights International. 2025. Norperuano Pipeline Contamination. https://earthrights.org/case/norperuano-pipeline-contamination/.
Earthrights International, Instituto de Defensa Legal, and Coordinadora Nacional de Derechos Humanos. 2019. Informe: Convenios entre la Policía Nacional y las empresas extractivas en el Perú. https://earthrights.org/wp-content/uploads/Informe-Convenios-entre-PNP-y-empresas-extractivas.pdf.
Economic Commission for Latin America and the Caribbean. 2024. ECLAC Calls for Comprehensive Policies to Address the Trap of High Inequality and Low Social Mobility in which Latin America and the Caribbean is Caught. June 25. https://www.cepal.org/en/pressreleases/eclac-calls-comprehensive-policies-address-trap-high-inequality-and-low-social.
El Universo. 2012. Obispo católico mediará en conflicto minero en Perú que dejó 5 muertos. July 6. https://www.ocmal.org/obispo-mediara-en-conflicto-minero-que-deja-5-muertos/.
Federación Internacional de Derechos Humanos. 2011. La FIDH condena represión y violencia para resolver conflicto minero en Islay. April 8. http://www.fidh.org/IMG/article_PDF/article_a9491.pdf.
Freeport-McMoRan. 2022. Voluntary Principles on Security and Human Rights: 2021 Annual Report to the Plenary. May. https://www.voluntaryprinciples.org/wp-content/uploads/2022/06/Freeport-McMoRan-2021-Voluntary-Principles-Report.pdf.
García, Marcial. 2024. Peru's Mining & Metals Investment Guide 2024/2025. Ernst and Young. October 9. https://www.ey.com/es_pe/insights/mining-metals/mining-metals-investment-guide-2024-2025.
Government of La Libertad. 2016. Minero Horizonte y comuneros de Alpamarca se reunirán el 2 de diciembre en Maltibamba. November 29. https://www.regionlalibertad.gob.pe/noticias/regionales/6581-minero-horizonte-y.

Ibarra, Alicia Bárcena, and Winnie Byanyima. 2016. Latin America is the World's Most Unequal Region: Here's How to Fix It. World Economic Forum. January 17. https://www.weforum.org/stories/2016/01/inequality-is-getting-worse-in-latin-america-here-s-how-to-fix-it/.

Infobae. 2022. Fuerzas Armadas Causaron 167 muertes durante protestas realizadas entre 2003 and 2020. December 26. https://www.infobae.com/america/peru/2022/12/26/crisis-en-peru-fuerzas-armadas-causaron-167-muertes-durante-protestas-realizadas-entre-2003-y-2020/.

Ivanou, Alex. 2006. Weapons Seized at Yanacocha Mine. International Metalworkers' Federation. August 10.

Jamasmie, Cecilia. 2021. Peru Minister Says $1.4bn Tia Maria Mine a 'No Go.' *Mining.com*. September 28. https://www.mining.com/peru-minister-says-1-4bn-tia-maria-mine-a-no-go/.

Kamphuis, Charis. 2011. La extracción de recursos mineros por empresas extranjeras y la privatización del poder coercitivo: un estudio de caso sobre la empresa de seguridad Forza. *Centro De Investigación De La Universidad Del Pacífico* 38 (68): 63–108.

Karl, Terry Lynn. 1997. *The Paradox of Plenty: Oil Booms and Petro-States*. Berkeley: University of California Press.

Karl, Terry Lynn. 2000. Economic Inequality and Democratic Instability. *Journal of Democracy* 11 (1): 149–156.

Klarén, Peter F. 2025. The Velasco Revolution in Peru, 1968–1975. In *Coups d'État in Cold War Latin America, 1964–1982*, eds. Sebastián Carassai and Kevin Coleman, 68–87. New York: Cambridge University Press.

Kinosian, Sarah, and James Bosworth. 2018. Security for Sale: Challenges and Good Practices in Regulating Private Military and Security Companies in Latin America. The Dialogue. Rule of Law Program Report. March. https://www.thedialogue.org/wp-content/uploads/2018/03/Security-for-Sale-FINAL-ENGLISH.pdf.

La República. 2018a. A 50 años de la nacionalización de la Brea y Pariñas, Talara sigue olvidada. October 18. https://larepublica.pe/economia/1334214-50-anos-nacionalizacion-brea-parinas-talara-sigue-olvidada.

La República. 2018b. Petroperú continúa sin poder detener fuga de petróleo en la Amazonía peruana. December 6. https://www.larepublica.ec/blog/economia/2018/12/06/petroperu-continua-sin-poder-detener-fuga-de-petroleo-en-la-amazonia-peruana/.

Lagos, Gustavo. 2018. Mining Nationalization and Privatization in Peru and in Chile. *Mineral Economics* 31 (1): 127–139.

Leon, Adriana, and Chris Kraul. 2009. Peru Clashes Leave 31 Dead. *Los Angeles Times*. June 7. https://www.latimes.com/archives/la-xpm-2009-jun-07-fg-peru-riots7-story.html.

Li, Fabiana. 2013. Relating Divergent Worlds: Mines, Aquifers and Sacred Mountains in Peru. *Anthropologica* 52 (2): 399–411.

Lindt, Angela. 2023. The Dark Side of Judicialization: Criminalizing Mining Protests in Peru. *Latin American Research Review* 58 (2): 368–382.

Lipset, Seymour Martin. 1959. Democracy and Working-Class Authoritarianism. *American Sociological Review* 24 (4): 482–501.

Lora, Eduardo. 2001. Structural Reforms in Latin America: What Has Been Reformed and How to Measure It. Working Paper W-466, Inter-American Development Bank, Research Department.

MacLennan, Gregor. 2012. Peru: 3 Years After the Tragedy of Bagua, NGO Says Little Has Changed - Criminalization of Social Protest Against Extractive Projects Continues. Business & Human Rights Resource Centre. June 6. https://business-humanrights.org/en/peru-3-years-after-the-tragedy-of-bagua-ngo-says-little-has-changed-criminalization-of-social-protest-against-extractive-projects-continues.

Mapstone, Naomi. 2012. Workers Kidnapped in Protest at Peru Mine. *Financial Times*. March 16. https://www.ft.com/content/f764b140-6f9b-11e1-b368-00144feab49a.

MacroNorte. 2024. Pataz: comunidad campesina La Soledad en conflicto con el Consorcio Minero Horizonte S.A. June 22. https://macronorte.pe/2024/06/15/pataz-comunidad-campesina-la-soledad-en-conflicto-con-el-consorcio-minero-horizonte-s-a/.

Martin del Campo, Antonio, and Donald A. Winkler. 1991. State-Owned Enterprise Reform in Latin America. LATPS Occasional Paper Series. World Bank. https://documents1.worldbank.org/curated/en/772001468914770301/txt/State-owned-enterprise-reform-in-Latin-America.txt.

McDonald, Brent, and Ainara Tiefenthäler. 2023. How Peru Used Lethal Force to Crack Down on Anti-Government Protests. *New York Times*. March 16. https://www.nytimes.com/2023/03/16/world/americas/peru-protests-police.html.

Mining Press. 2016. Sigue el conflict en Alpamarca. Qué dijo Minera Horizonte. August 11. https://miningpress.com/nota/302948/sigue-el-conflicto-en-alpamarca-que-dijo-minera-horizonte.

Ministerio de Justicia y Derechos Humanos. 2021. Plan Nacional de Acción sobre Empresas y Derechos Humanos: Seguridad Privada, Informe de Diagnóstico y Línea de Base. https://globalnaps.org/wp-content/uploads/2023/01/Peru_Seguridad-privada-Informe-de-DLB-del-PNA-2021-2025.pdf.

Myplainview. 2006. Peru: Minera Yanacocha y violencia en Cajamarca. Coordinadora de Derechos Humanos. August 9. https://www.business-humanrights.org/en/latest-news/doc-per%C3%BA-minera-yanacocha-y-violencia-en-cajamarca/.

Newsroom Panama. 2025. Bocas del Toro in Panama Reported More Than 300 Arrests in Violent Protests. June 26. https://newsroompanama.com/2025/06/26/bocas-del-toro-in-panama-reported-more-than-300-arrests-in-violent-protests/.

Oh, Chang Hoon, Jiyoung Shin, and Shuna Shu Ham. Ho. 2023. Conflicts Between Mining Companies and Communities: Institutional Environments and Conflict Resolution Approaches. *Business Ethics, the Environment & Responsibility* 32 (2): 638–656.

Olsen, Tricia D. 2023. *Seeking Justice: Access to Remedy for Corporate Human Rights Abuse.* New York: Cambridge University Press.

Olsen, Tricia D., and Laura Bernal-Bermúdez. 2024. Uncovering Economic Complicity: Explaining State-Led Human Rights Abuses in the Corporate Context. *Journal of Business Ethics* 189 (1): 35–54.

Organisation for Economic Co-operation and Development. 2024. Ownership and Governance of State-Owned Enterprises. October 28. https://www.oecd.org/en/publications/ownership-and-governance-of-state-owned-enterprises-2024_395c9956-en.html.

Ortiz, Jorge J. 2012. Celendin: Yanacocha y Policias Provocan a Pobladores. Celendin Libre. March 17. http://celendinlibre.wordpress.com/2012/03/17/celendin-yanacocha-y-policias-provocan-a-pobladores/.

Perlez, Jane, and Lowell Bergman. 2010. Tangled Strands in Fight Over Peru Gold Mine. *New York Times.* June 14. https://www.nytimes.com/2005/10/25/world/americas/tangled-strands-in-fight-over-peru-gold-mine.html.

Perreault, Thomas. 2012. Extracting Justice: Natural Gas, Indigenous Mobilization, and the Bolivian State. In *The Politics of Resource Extraction: Indigenous Peoples, Multinational Corporations and the State*, eds. Suzana Sawyer and Edmund Terence Gomez, 75–102. New York: Palgrave Macmillan.

Personius, Paula. 2025. Peruvian Communities Challenge Newmont Mining Operations as Investors Meet. Earthworks. May 12. https://earthworks.org/blog/peruvian-communities-challenge-newmont-mining-operations-as-investors-meet/.

Post, Colin. 2015. Southern Copper to Extend Tia Maria 'Pause.' *Peru Reports.* June 21. https://perureports.com/southern-copper-to-extend-tia-maria-pause/1545/.

Post, Colin. 2016. Protest Against Gold Mine Leaves One Dead in Northern Peru. *Peru Reports.* November 8. https://perureports.com/protest-gold-mine-leaves-one-dead-northern-peru/4906/.

Prado, Elizabeth. 2011. Declaran nulo el proyecto Tía María. *La República.* April 9. http://www.larepublica.pe/532010-declaran-nulo-el-proyecto-tia-maria-0.

Przeworski, Adam, and Fernando Limongi. 1993. Political Regimes and Economic Growth. *Journal of Economic Perspectives* 7 (3): 51–69.

Rawnsley, Jessica. 2025. Peru's President Removed from Office Amid Soaring Crime. *BBC News*. October 10. https://www.bbc.com/news/articles/c1e dw3x6vl2o.

Reuters. 2017. Peru Supreme Court Rules Against Newmont in Dispute Over Gold Mine. May 3. https://www.reuters.com/article/peru-mining-new mont/peru-supremecourt-rules-against-newmont-in-dispute-over-gold-mine-idINL1N1I51GN.

Rocha, Leonardo, and Jaroslav Lukiv. 2025. Panama Declares Emergency Over Banana Region Unrest. *BBC News*. June 20. https://www.bbc.com/news/articles/cql0r430qglo.

Rodley, Nigel S. 1974. The Nationalization by Peru of the Holdings of the International Petroleum Company. In *International Law in the Western Hemisphere*, eds. Nigel S. Rodley and C. Neal Ronning, 112–125. The Hague: Martinus Nijhoff.

Ross, Michael L. 2015. What Have We Learned About the Resource Curse? *Annual Review of Political Science* 18 (1): 239–259.

Salazar, Milagros. 2006. Peru: Leaching Out the Water with the Gold. *Inter Press Service*. September 20. http://www.ipsnews.net/2006/09/peru-leaching-out-the-water-with-the-gold/.

Servindi. 2018. Gobierno Wampis Pide Limpiar Derrame Y Desmiente Acusaciones. *Servindi*. December 18. https://www.servindi.org/17/12/2018/pro nunciamiento-wmpis.

Sullivan, Mark P. 2012. Panama: Political and Economic Conditions and U.S. Relations. Congressional Research Service. November 27. https://sgp.fas. org/crs/row/RL30981.pdf.

Taylor, Ariel, and Michelle D. Bonner. 2017. Policing Economic Growth: Mining, Protest, and State Discourse in Peru and Argentina. *Latin American Research Review* 52 (1): 3–17.

Truth and Reconciliation Commission. 2003. General Conclusions of the Final Report of the Comisión de la Verdad y Reconciliación. https://www.cverdad. org.pe/ifinal/conclusiones.php.

United States Department of State. 2008. 2008 Investment Climate Statement – Peru: Openness to Foreign Investment. https://2009-2017.state.gov/e/eb/ ifd/2008/100999.htm.

Vegh Weis, Valeria. 2023. What Does Lawfare Mean in Latin America? A New Framework for Understanding the Criminalization of Progressive Political Leaders. *Punishment & Society* 25 (4): 909–933.

Weiss, Robert P. 2007. From Cowboy Detectives to Soldiers of Fortune: Private Security Contracting and its Contradictions on the New Frontiers of Capitalist Expansion. *Social Justice* 34 (3/4): 1–19.

World Bank. 2025. Foreign Direct Investment, Net Inflows, Balance of Payments Database. https://data.worldbank.org/indicator/BX.KLT.DINV. CD.WD?locations=PE.

Wright, Claire. 2015. *Emergency Politics in the Third Wave of Democracy: A Study of the Regimes of Exception in Bolivia, Ecuador, and Peru*. Lanham, MD: Lexington.

Zaffaroni, Eugenio Raúl, Cristina Caamaño, and Valeria Vegh Weis. 2023. *Lawfare: The Criminalization of Democratic Politics in the Global South*. Leiden: Brill.

CHAPTER 7

The Legal Foundations of State Violence and Avenues for Change

INTRODUCTION

In this book we explain the evolution and architecture of state violence in Latin America, the underlying legacy conditions—uneven state capacity, weak rule of law, and socioeconomic inequalities—driving its recent expansion across the region, and the ways in which this violence is deployed. In our final chapter, we explore how state actors are seeking to make state-sponsored violence legal. We then end the chapter by highlighting some possible avenues for reform and argue that, despite the prevalence and pervasiveness of violence across the region, there are still facets of democratic institutions that can be strengthened. If done so quickly, we believe there is still an opportunity to challenge the legal framework that underpins the political application of state violence today and reduce public order violence.

Leaders throughout the region who carry out state violence go to great lengths to make it legal. This occurs through three distinct, though complementary, processes. First, executives use constitutional states of exception to temporarily restrict civil liberties and increase the government's power to use force. Second, legislatures enact new laws, in the name of protecting national security, that grant state security forces expanded roles and reduce the restrictions on their actions. Third, governments and security forces cooperate to formally and informally create

B. J. Kyle et al., *State Violence and Democracy in Latin America*, Rethinking Political Violence, https://doi.org/10.1007/978-3-032-06412-7_7

a system of impunity for those who commit human rights violations during operations. The lack of any systematic deterrent for such behavior contributes to its perpetuation. We discuss each in turn below. In the final section, we demonstrate how government dependence on this legal structure to carry out violence also represents an avenue for combatting it. We highlight three avenues—democratic electoral politics, civic action, and judicial rulings—by which these legal actions can be checked and rolled back, making it much more difficult for governments to continue to commit widespread public order violence.

STATES OF EXCEPTION

Nearly all democratic constitutions acknowledge the "inevitability of crises and the need for expansive powers to cope with them" (Finn 1991, 14). They thus contain provisions that allow the government to enact temporary states of exception to deal with regional or national emergencies. There is variation across countries, but states of exception contain some mixture of the following elements. First, they often alter the processes by which the government creates policy. Typically, this involves allowing the executive to govern through decrees, providing a more expedient process for combatting the alleged security threat than more democratic, slower, legislative processes. These decrees often have minimal legislative or judicial oversight and it is difficult to overturn them, at least in the short term.

Second, states of exception often limit civil liberties that are constitutionally protected during normal periods. This frequently involves enacting curfews, banning protests or public gatherings of certain sizes, and restricting other forms of free speech. They also lower the requirements needed by state security forces to search persons and dwellings. In addition, they can reduce the requirements around surveillance, allowing intelligence units to collect more information than they otherwise could. State security forces may also be able to temporarily detain civilians without charging them with a crime or bringing them before a judge. In rare cases, civilians may be subject to military rather than civilian courts when accused of committing certain crimes against the state.

Third, during states of exception, governments often attempt to increase the lethality of state security forces. This can affect behavior, such as allowing state agents to fire live ammunition into crowds of protesters where they may have been limited previously to tear gas and rubber bullets. It can also affect who is deployed, such as when regular military units, often constitutionally restricted to external defense in normal times, are used for domestic security. Such units are more heavily armed and often under the jurisdiction of military justice systems that show more leniency for abuses committed in the line of duty.

Combined, these three elements create a system in which more security forces use higher levels of violence against a greater percentage of the population with less accountability. This is an environment highly likely to lead to human rights violations. Many scholars argue that times of emergency may necessitate such a relaxation of constitutional protections to safeguard the democratic system (e.g., Posner 2003, 292–308). Others, however, caution that such provisions can easily lead to democratic backsliding and even the collapse of the democratic system, often citing Article 48 of Weimar Germany's constitution that enabled the Nazi Party to seize control of the country (Rossiter 1948, 29–73). Latin America represents another cautionary tale. Since independence, the region's constitutions have almost always included provisions for states of exception that governments have used frequently, leading to nearly two centuries of "constitutional dictatorships" (Loveman 1993).

During the Cold War, in particular, states of exception facilitated the high levels of repression that characterized the region. The military regimes of South America were in an almost constant state of exception. Argentina was under a state of siege nearly half of the time from 1930 to 1970 and the military junta that ruled from 1976 to 1983 maintained a state of siege for its entirety, using it as the legal foundation to carry out the "dirty war" (Loveman 1993, 290). Chile was under a state of emergency or state of siege for almost all of Augusto Pinochet's 17-year rule (New York Times 1987). President Juan Bordaberry of Uruguay declared a state of internal war shortly after taking office in 1972 (Handelman 1981, 384–385). This precipitated the end of democracy and rise of a brutal military regime that would follow.[1] Paraguay's Alfredo Stroessner renewed the state of siege every 90 days from when he took power in 1954 until 1987 (Folch 2013, 45).

Those countries embroiled in civil war also employed states of exception. Colombia, for example, spent the majority of three decades under a state of siege (Ríos-Figueroa 2016, 51–56). The Sandinistas placed Nicaragua under a state of emergency from 1982 to 1988 (Close 1990, 14). In El Salvador, the government declared a state of siege numerous times during the 1980s, instituting martial law and placing civilians under the jurisdiction of military courts (Gomez 2001). Throughout the 1980s the Peruvian government relied on the state of emergency in its fight against the Shining Path rebel group (Wright 2015, 58–60) and by 1991 there were 87 provinces, representing half of the population, under direct military rule (Vásquez 1994, 107).

As we demonstrated in Chapter 1, the new democracies in the post-Cold War period went to great lengths to significantly revise existing constitutions or, in most cases, draft and enact entirely new ones. These expanded protections of civil liberties and put increased restrictions on governments' use of violence. Yet, as shown in Table 7.1, all of the region's constitutions still contain provisions for states of exception that allow the government to limit those civil liberties and reduce the restrictions on its use of violence.

The use of states of exception was rare across the region in the first two decades following the end of the Cold War. Their recent resurgence is alarming. Governments now regularly resort to states of exception to deal with security threats. Colombia and Peru continue to grapple with the legacies of their civil wars. In its fight against the National Liberation Army, the Colombian government declared a state of internal disturbance in January 2025 and deployed new military and police units to the region of Catatumbo (Pannell 2025). In Peru, former President Dina Boluarte declared multiple states of emergency during her time in office (2022–2025), and especially when protestors took to the street to show their support for the recently ousted President Pedro Castillo. The government suggested the protestors are remnants of the Shining Path guerrilla group and/or criminal gangs (Coronel 2023). On March 18, 2025, President Boluarte declared a state of emergency in the provinces of Lima and Callao in response to the murder of Paul Flores, the popular 39-year-old lead singer of the Peruvian band Armonia 10. The declaration allowed her to deploy the military to assist with policing operations and gave them the power to detain people without a judicial order (Associated Press 2025).

Other countries have relied on states of exception as a key part of their playbook to confront the rising violence from organized crime, gangs, and drug traffickers. In 2021, Ecuadorian President Guillermo Lasso declared a state of emergency to confront drug trafficking, deploying the military to police the country (New York Times 2021). He did so again in several provinces and cities in 2023 after the mayor of Manta was murdered (Reuters 2023b). His successor, Daniel Noboa has pursued "iron fist" policies to combat rising crime and declared several states of emergency.

Table 7.1 Constitutional states of exception in Latin America

Country	Constitutional Provisions	States of Exception
Argentina	Article 23	State of Siege
Bolivia	Articles 137-40	State of Emergency
Brazil	Articles 136-41	State of Defense, State of Siege
Chile	Articles 39-45	State of Assembly, State of Siege, State of Catastrophe, State of Exception
Colombia	Articles 212-15	State of Foreign War, State of Internal Disturbance, State of Emergency
Costa Rica	Article 121 (7)	Public Necessity
Dominican Republic	Articles 262-66	State of Defense, State of Interior Commotion, State of Emergency
Ecuador	Articles 164-66	State of Exception
El Salvador	Articles 129-31	State of Exception
Guatemala	Articles 138-39	State of Prevention, State of Alarm, State of Public Calamity, State of Siege, State of War
Honduras	Articles 187-88	State of Exception
Mexico	Article 29	Emergency Powers
Nicaragua	Articles 185-86	State of Emergency
Panama	Article 55	State of Emergency
Paraguay	Article 288	State of Exception
Peru	Article 137	State of Emergency, State of Siege
Uruguay	Article 168	Prompt Measures of Security
Venezuela	Articles 337-39	State of Alarm, State of Economic Emergency, State of Internal or External Commotion

In 2024, he went further and declared a state of internal armed conflict, deploying military forces to combat 20 drug gangs and cartels (CBS News 2025). In 2019, Guatemala's Congress approved a state of siege, which imposed martial law, in six northeastern provinces, in response to the killing of three soldiers by suspected drug traffickers (Reuters 2019). In November 2022, Honduran President Xiomara Castro declared a state of emergency to combat organized crime. The government has renewed and expanded it repeatedly and over 90% of the population now lives in areas affected (Woolston 2024). The legislative assembly in El Salvador passed a state of exception in March 2022 at the request of President Nayib Bukele in response to rising gang violence. It has been renewed every month since. The state of exception grants security forces, including the military, which participates in domestic policing, broad powers to detain and arrest citizens. Security forces have detained over 85,000 people since the state of exception came into force (Méndez Dardón 2025). As described in Chapter 4, "iron fist" responses often enjoy popular support; Ecuadorian voters, for example, overwhelmingly approved the expansion of the military's role in policing through a popular referendum in April 2024 (National Public Radio 2024).

Governments have also used states of exception to combat social protests. The Chilean government declared a state of exception and deployed the military to break up protests over social policies in 2019 (Torres-Salinas 2023), and the Mapuche communities, which have a long-standing land dispute with the government, have been under a near-constant state of emergency since 2021 (MercoPress 2025). Guatemala similarly declared a state of siege in 2021 to combat protests in a land dispute with indigenous communities (Hodel 2022) and Peru has done so, as well, to combat indigenous protests over mining developments (Reuters 2023c). In May 2025, the Panamanian government declared a state of emergency in Bocas del Toro after US banana giant Chiquita Brands laid off approximately 5,000 workers following a strike that had ground its production to a halt (Tico Times 2025). The government claimed the use of the state of emergency was merely to remove bureaucratic hurdles to address economic and social issues more quickly, but there were soon reports of increased securitization of the region and abuses by security forces (Latin News Daily 2025).

Even Costa Rica, which has a distinguished track record of aiding migrants, has taken this approach. Faced with a dramatic increase in the flow of migrants from Panama, the government declared a state of emergency in September 2023. While this facilitated increased coordination and supply of humanitarian aid, President Rodrigo Chaves also pointed to recent riots by migrants and instructed "the security ministry to take a firm stance with anyone who takes Costa Rica's kindness for weakness" (Reuters 2023a).

In Argentina, presidents have relied on decrees of necessity and urgency (DNUs) to respond to security threats. Such decrees are notoriously difficult to overturn. There is congressional oversight of DNUs but it requires the creation of a special Bicameral Commission which then makes a non-binding recommendation to both houses of congress, both of which must vote to reject the decree. There is no specified time in which this has to happen and so the result is "many DNUs languishing in limbo, effectively in force indefinitely, as they sit unaddressed, sometimes for years, due to the lack of an explicit rejection" (Fernández Blanco and Kristan 2024).[2] From the democratic transition in 1983 until Javier Milei assumed the presidency in 2023 there were 1,380 DNUs in Argentina (Leiras 2024). Within days of taking power, Milei issued a sweeping DNU (referred to as the "Megadecreto") with 366 articles that dramatically reshaped the economic and political life of the country.[3] While the Senate rejected it several months later, the Chamber of Deputies as of June 2025 had yet to take up a vote. Milei went on to issue over 50 DNUs during his first year in office (Directorio Legislativo 2024).

Today, states of exception are not at all exceptional in Latin America. The dramatic increase in their use across the region is a dangerous development. They have facilitated a corresponding rise in state violence. More lethal forces are actively policing the streets of Latin America with greater authority and fewer restrictions than at any time since the Cold War.

National Security Legislation and Regulatory Reform

Beyond states of exception, governments across the region have used normal bureaucratic and legislative processes to address national security threats. Such legal initiatives often redirect financial resources to security forces, create new specialized units within them, and remove oversight of their activities. They also redefine what level of force state agents are allowed to use and change the conditions under which such force can be used. New legislation and regulations can revise existing rules on when police or military can intervene in social protests, for example, and what actions constitute "disturbing the peace" or "resisting authority," giving security forces more discretion and leeway in how they choose to engage. In recent years, sweeping national security laws and regulatory overhauls have dramatically reshaped the landscape of state violence throughout the region. Legislatures have endorsed many political leaders' "tough-on-crime" positions by approving their desired bills to address national security threats.

There are many examples of governments restricting the rights of civilians to make policing and controlling them easier. In Argentina, for example, a resolution, known as the "Anti-Picket Protocol" (Resolution 943/2023) criminalizes those protests that obstruct traffic, opening up the possibility of stronger repression by security forces. In 2025, Peru passed a similar law (number 32183) which redefines acts of protest—such as roadblocks or public space occupations—as extortion. As argued by Dejusticia, a well-known Colombian-based human rights organization, "[t]his approach not only stigmatizes social protest, but also builds a wall between the state and its citizens, treating legitimate demands that are collectively claimed in the public space as threats to order" (Alba and Amaya 2025).

Other legislation seeks to militarize security forces. Honduras, for example, passed two laws in 2013 that created the Special Response Team and Intelligence Troop and the Military Police of Public Order.[4] The former is a specialized military police unit while the latter force is made up of members of the armed forces and reservists and acts as a parallel force to the national police (Washington Office on Latin America 2020). Mexico's legislature passed a major constitutional amendment in September 2024 that places the National Guard, a force of over 100,000, under military control and grants it the power to investigate common crimes (De Vicente Encarnación 2024; Rodríguez Mega 2024). This is just the latest in a long list of efforts to militarize security in the country. Between 2006 and 2023, the executive branch transferred civilian functions to the armed forces through various decrees and regulatory reforms on nearly 300 occasions, and the legislature introduced 87 different bills expanding the military's power during the same period (México Unido Contra la Delincuencia 2024). In recent months, the trend of militarizing security has continued across the region. In April 2025, Brazilian President Luiz Inácio Lula da Silva submitted a proposal to congress for a constitutional amendment to create a unified public security system, shifting power from states to the federal forces.[5] In May, Ecuadorian President Daniel Noboa began his new four-year term by proposing a new national security bill that would permit arrests without warrants and would give greater authority to the police and military to coordinate domestic policing, effectively allowing for the creation of special security zones.[6]

While governments frequently resort to states of exception to increase their ability to use violence, these changes are temporary. Democratic leaders today are unable to maintain permanent states of exception like their Cold War predecessors. They thus seek to make more permanent changes to laws and regulations. In particular, across the region the structure and mission scope of state security forces are being redefined, with a trend toward greater militarization.

A System of Impunity

The third component of the legal apparatus enabling continued state violence is a system that ensures impunity for excessive violence committed by state security forces during operations. It is common for governments to do so by ensuring the jurisdiction of such cases is in the military justice system rather than the civilian justice system, and by enacting new legislation that is designed to shield security forces from accountability.

With regard to jurisdiction, military justice systems themselves are not a problem. Militaries have their own codes of justice, police, courts, and prisons due to their unique nature where conduct such insubordination or being absent without leave (AWOL) are crimes. When military courts overstep and extend their jurisdiction over their personnel for non-military crimes such as human rights violations, however, this contributes to a culture of impunity and increases state violence. At times, superior officers may be directly responsible for deciding whether to pursue charges against subordinates. Military trials are often closed to the public and records sealed on the grounds of national security. Where military investigators are in charge of cases involving human rights violations, evidence can go missing, witnesses intimidated, and perpetrators remain protected on bases.

Military courts have had extensive power in Latin America since the time of independence when the *fuero militar*, or military privilege, established by Spain and Portugal in the 1500-1600s was incorporated into the region's first constitutions (Castro and Lara 2008). This "privilege" granted soldiers the right to be judged separately from civilian authorities. Military courts became a key tool of the repression of the Cold War-era authoritarian regimes, trying civilians labeled as enemies of the state and protecting state security forces from any accountability for their actions (Pereira 2005). Through concerted efforts by democratic activists and high courts, the power of military courts was gradually rolled back in many countries during the wave of democratization that swept across the region (Kyle and Reiter 2021).

Yet in many countries, military courts continue to shield members of the armed forces from accountability. In Uruguay, while common crimes are required to be tried in civilian courts, military courts retain jurisdiction over members of the military for many crimes committed in the line of duty. Moreover, while the civilian Supreme Court of Uruguay serves as the final appeal for all military court cases, when doing so, two military judges are added to the bench.[7] Military courts still have broad jurisdiction over members of the military in Chile and as of June 2025, the Chilean legislature is debating a bill that would potentially extend the military justice system's jurisdiction to cover the Carabineros, the main police force in the country (Inter-American Commission on Human Rights 2024).[8] In 2015, Colombia's Congress passed a law that gives military courts jurisdiction over most crimes committed by members of the military in the line of duty, including human rights violations (Rosser 2015).[9] Contestation between the civilian and military justice systems over cases continues in concerning ways (Human Rights Watch 2023). Contestation also characterizes Peru, where the military has openly resisted attempts to reform its legal prerogatives, primarily by refusing to comply with civilian court rulings (Ríos-Figueroa 2016, 110).

Besides shifting the jurisdiction of cases against state agents to military courts, governments have also enacted laws and created new regulations that directly protect security forces from accountability. President Lasso in Ecuador announced in 2021 that he would create "a legal defense unit to defend uniformed officers who, he said, had been sued for fulfilling their duty" (New York Times 2021). The proposed national security bill put forth by his successor, Noboa, would permit the president to grant pardons preemptively to members of the state security forces who are being prosecuted for acts committed in the line of duty (Latin American Weekly Report 2025). The Brazilian government increasingly deployed the military to police the favelas of major cities in the lead up to the 2014 World Cup and 2016 Olympics. The federal government has also used "Guarantee of Law and Order" operations extensively to deploy the regular army in policing (Zaverucha 2008). Once fully embroiled in domestic policing, high-ranking officers in the military insisted on increased legal protections, and in 2017 the congress enacted a new law that protects military personnel from legal consequences for crimes committed in the line of duty (Valente 2017).[10] In El Salvador, President Bukele authorized security forces to use lethal force even when it is not a last resort and stated that "the government will see to the legal defense of those who may be unjustly charged for defending the lives of honorable people" (Human Rights Watch 2021). Peru's congress passed the Police Protection Act in 2020, which exempted state security forces from any legal responsibility for conduct in their duties (Human Rights Watch 2020). Likewise, shortly after taking office in Bolivia in 2019, President Jeanine Áñez issued Decree 4078, which provided impunity for members of the military and police for their actions in restoring order.[11]

The combination of targeted laws and regulations designed to prevent accountability and the use of parallel justice systems in which accountability for human rights violations is rare has created a system in which state security forces in many countries have little fear of repercussions for their behavior. This has the effect of increasing the lethality and reducing the threshold for when violence is used, violating the widely accepted global norm of the principal of proportionality.[12] In short, human rights violations during domestic policing are increasingly common throughout the region, with few perpetrators punished.

AVENUES FOR CHANGE

As we have demonstrated above, the rise in state violence has been undergirded by a complex legal apparatus, which includes aspects of the executive, legislative, and judicial branches. These efforts restrict civil liberties, including the ability to gather, protest, and be free from arbitrary arrest. They increase the lethality of those state security forces deployed, often placing military units in prominent policing roles. They also remove restrictions placed on the use of force by state agents. Finally, they make accountability for abuses by state agents much less likely, increasing the likelihood of the recurrence of such abuses.

The reliance on this legal framework, however, also opens up possible avenues for reform. If the right to protest (e.g., the right to peaceful assembly as stated in Article 20 of the Universal Declaration of Human Rights) is preserved, civil society is more likely to be able to bring about policy changes. When the military is kept off of the streets, the lethality of state security forces is reduced. Where cases of abuses by state security forces are kept in civilian courts, accountability is more likely, leading to greater deterrence. We argue that aiming to combat the legal apparatus undergirding state violence is the most feasible way to affect real change in the short term. We identify three key ways in which citizens can check or rollback the resurgence of state violence.

First, democratic politics still matters. In the 2024 presidential elections in Uruguay, Guido Manini Ríos, a former army chief, ran on a platform of increasing security, promising to declare a public security national emergency if elected. Yet he garnered just three percent of the vote in the first round of elections. At the same time, in a referendum, the population rejected a proposed constitutional amendment that would have removed the ban on nighttime raids by security forces. There are many reasons for this, including the memory of the military regime's abuses and a general "pragmatic political culture" (Gedan 2024). Yet, Uruguayans rejected the proposal because the main political parties have had success in reducing crime by addressing the underlying legacy conditions, like strengthening rule of law and reducing inequality, and have avoided being dragged into the *mano dura* approaches that have characterized the region.

Likewise, despite facing rising crime and homicide rates like its Central American neighbors, Costa Rica has avoided overly securitizing the issue. President Laura Chinchilla (2010–14) ran on a moderate campaign of "Punish with a strong hand, prevent with an intelligent hand," and focused on a holistic response to crime. Security was not a major issue in subsequent presidential campaigns and the administrations since have largely focused on economic and social policies intended to address the root causes of crime (Malone et al. 2023, 105–107). In Panama, President Martín Torrijos (2004–09) backed a *mano amiga* (friendly hand) approach to preventive policing. His successor, Ricardo Martinelli took a *mano dura* approach, but after it failed to curb violence, subsequent presidents returned to a focus on prevention (Malone et al. 2023, 144–151).

In other cases, where security is a major concern, citizens have rejected the "tough-on-crime" candidate at the ballot box. In the 2022 Colombian presidential election, for example, Gustavo Petro defeated Rodolfo Hernández, the latter of whom praised figures like Bukele and promoted heavy-handed governance. In 2022, the authoritarian-style populist Jair Bolsonaro became the first president in Brazilian history to lose a reelection bid, with the country electing Luiz Inácio Lula da Silva, a left-wing politician who had previously served as president from 2003 to 2011.

Second, civic action is effective.[13] In Bolivia in 2000, for example, President Hugo Banzer declared a state of siege to battle protesters rallying against the privatization of the municipal water supply in Cochabamba in what is known as the Water War. The military cut power to part of the city to take down the local radio and TV stations and attempted to violently suppress the protests (Assies 2003). These efforts backfired, however, leading to increased protests, and the government canceled the state of siege and eventually conceded to many of the demands of the protestors. A representative of the Defensoría del Pueblo was quoted: "It is not so easy to dictate a state of siege when the social movements are protagonists and contestatory and mobilize over any problem or irregularity" (Wright 2015, 99). In subsequent years, Presidents Gonzalo Sánchez de Lozado and Carlos Mesa enacted emergency decrees to deploy the military to break up protests over the government's role in managing hydrocarbons. Resistance intensified and forced both from power (Wright 2015, 100–102).

Presidents in Ecuador have frequently used states of exception to attempt to quell protests, but rather than being effective means to consolidate their rule, many were last ditch efforts to cling to power that ultimately failed in the face of increased opposition. Facing protests over his efforts to dollarize the economy, President Jamil Mahuad Witt issued decree DE1674 in 2000, which placed the army in control of internal order, suspended some civil liberties, and expanded the military justice system to cover civilians. Yet protests led by the Confederation of Indigenous Nationalities of Ecuador continued in defiance and Witt was forced to resign. In 2005, President Lucio Gutiérrez experienced a similar fate. He issued decree DE2752 to combat the protests, known as the Rebelión de los Forajidos, against his rule. The protests intensified and the military soon withdrew its support for Gutiérrez and congress voted to remove him from office (Wright 2015, 132–134). In 2019, President Añez's Supreme Decree 4078, discussed above, provided immunity for state security forces, but was repealed two weeks later due to widespread domestic and international condemnation (Página Siete 2020).

Though still unfolding, activism in Mexico by the families of victims who have disappeared has led to important legislative changes. Groups such as Centro Prodh, SERAPAZ, and Movimiento por Nuestros Desaparecidos en México helped uncover clandestine graves and engaged in activism to increase international pressure on Mexico to improve its human rights record. As a result, the government enacted the General Law on Enforced Disappearances in 2017, which recognized command responsibility (e.g., officials that do not commit the abuse can still be held responsible) and created the National Search System and a National Search Commission, which coordinate efforts to find missing people across Mexico. Though this law came into effect after the disappearances of 43 students in Ayotzinapa, Guerrero in 2014, its passage and the arrests of numerous high-ranking officials involved in the crime—including former General José Rodríguez Pérez; Gualberto Ramírez, the former head of the Attorney General's anti-trafficking unit (Associated Press 2023), and most recently, Lambertina Galeana Marín, the former head of the Guerrero's Superior Tribunal of Justice (Buschschlüter 2025)—are important indicators of the role activism can play, even in unlikely circumstances.

Third, courts can serve as powerful checks on state violence. The Constitutional Court in Colombia, created with the country's new constitution in 1991, became increasingly assertive over time, eventually striking down and limiting many of the national security laws and executive decrees made in the subsequent decades (Kyle and Reiter 2021, 109–115). The court "is widely regarded by experts as one of the best-known and activist courts worldwide" (González 2020, 189). This is, in large part, due to its willingness to hear cases associated with individual rights, as well as social and economic rights; the court's willingness to introduce international human rights and humanitarian law into domestic law and to "scrutinize executive orders enacted by the President at exercising extraordinary powers" (González 2020, 190). The court, for example, has ruled in favor of general well-being by supporting full citizenship of the country's most vulnerable populations, whether those decisions are based on access to water, access to health, housing, forced displacement, or the fundamental rights of inmates (Agudelo 2021, 25).

Examples from elsewhere in Latin America illustrate the possible power of courts. The Peruvian Constitutional Tribunal, for example, eventually struck down most of President Alberto Fujimori's anti-terrorism legislation (González-Ocantos 2016, 159; Ríos-Figueroa 2016, 105–115). The Supreme Court in the Dominican Republic was crucial in shifting cases of human rights violations committed by state security forces from military to civilian courts (United States Department of State 2001). In Brazil, the Supreme Court sought to intervene to challenge Bolsonaro's anti-democratic claims, including suspending appointments of a close acquaintance as the head of the Federal Police, and ultimately disqualified, Bolsonaro from running for office again. In addition, the Inter-American Court of Human Rights has also been an important judicial check on state violence. Rulings against Chile, Peru, and Mexico, and a friendly settlement with Argentina, led to positive and meaningful reforms of the scope of military justice systems (Kyle and Reiter 2021, 72–74).

CONCLUSION

The resurgence of state violence in Latin America is alarming. As we show in this book, police forces are heavily militarized and the military is often deployed alongside them. There has been a proliferation of specialized counternarcotics, intelligence, and tactical forces using high levels of violence against citizens in urban and rural areas. Politicians go to great lengths to ensure that these forces have a freer hand in conducting their operations and experience little accountability if abuses occur. Today's era of public order violence is a result of a vicious cycle of violence driven by legacy conditions—uneven state capacity, weak rule of law, and socioeconomic inequalities. Yet as we have shown above, there is hope. In many places, citizens, politicians, and judges have stood up against this trend. They have prevented or reversed attempts by the government to limit civil liberties and further empower state security forces. These legacy conditions do not condemn countries to high levels of state violence. If there is enough resistance, public security can align with the principles of democracy and human rights.

NOTES

1. The Uruguayan military also enacted eight Institutional Acts that provided it with a legal framework to govern in place of the constitution (Barahona de Brito 1997, 41–42). The Brazilian military took a similar approach and governed through extralegal Institutional Acts, the most notorious of which was Number 5, which ushered in a period of extreme repression (Alves 1985, 80–100). Copies of all primary documents cited in the book are available at www.andyreiter.com.
2. For the first two decades after the transition, congress did not even review DNUs in Argentina. It was only after a 2006 law that this process was implemented, see: Ley 26.122 de 2006 (julio 28), "Regimen legal de los decretos de necesidad y urgencia, de delegacion legislativa y de promulgacion parcial de leyes."
3. Decreto DNU 70 de 2023 (diciembre 20), "Bases para la reconstrucción de la economía Argentina."

4. Ley Estrategia Interinstitucional en Seguridad y Toma Integral Gubernamental de Respuesta Especial de Seguridad (TIGRES), Decreto N° 103-2013 (27 de junio del 2013); Ley de la Policía Militar del Orden Público, Decreto N° 168-2013l (22 de agosto de 2013).

5. Ministério da Justiça e Segurança Pública, "Presidente Lula entrega a PEC da Segurança Pública ao Congresso Nacional," 23 de abril de 2025.

6. Secretaría General de Comunicación de la Presidencia, Boletín N° 603, 17 de mayo de 2025, "Nuevo proyecto de Ley económica urgente para desarticular la economía criminal. Ecuador no se detiene en la lucha contra la inseguridad."

7. Article 508, Decreto Ley N° 10.326 de 28 de enero de 1943, Codigo Penal Militar, Codigo De Procedimiento Penal Militar, Codigo De Organizacion De Los Tribunales Militares.

8. Proyecto de ley para la regulación del uso de la fuerza (Boletín 15805-07), lunes 10 de abril de 2023.

9. Ley 1765 de 2015 (julio 23), "Por la cual se reestructura la Justicia Penal Militar y Policial, se establecen requisitos para el desempeño de sus cargos, se implementa su Fiscalía General Penal Militar y Policial, se organiza su cuerpo técnico de investigación, se señalan disposiciones sobre competencia para el tránsito al sistema penal acusatorio y para garantizar su plena operatividad en la Jurisdicción Especializada y se dictan otras disposiciones."

10. Lei N° 13.491, de 13 de Outubro de 2017, "Altera o Decreto-Lei n° 1.001, de 21 de outubro de 1969 - Código Penal Militar."

11. Decreto Supremo N° 4078, de 14 de noviembre de 2019.

12. United Nations General Assembly Resolution 34/169, "Code of Conduct for Law Enforcement Officials," December 17, 1979, https://www.ohchr.org/en/instruments-mechanisms/ins truments/code-conduct-law-enforcement-officials.

13. In the Latin American context, civic action is mostly visible as mass protests, but the term incapsulates many means by which citizens can influence social policy (Moro 2010).

REFERENCES

Agudelo, Agudelo, and Carlos Alberto. 2021. The Colombian Constitutional Court from a Prodemocratic Reading. *Revista Jurídicas* 18 (1): 17–35.

Associated Press. 2023. Mexico Arrests Former Official in Disappearance of 43 Students in 2014, Charges 8 Soldiers. June 26. https://apnews.com/article/mexico-43-missing-students-human-rights-9e92f3b1b9fcf184b87ba1479e3 8f77f.

Alba, Sofia Forero, and Betsy Zavaleta Amaya. 2025. The Right to Protest Under Threat: The Situation in Peru. Dejusticia. March 6. https://www.dejusticia. org/en/the-right-to-protest-under-threat-the-situation-in-peru.

Alves, Maria Helena Moreira. 1985. *State and Opposition in Military Brazil.* Austin: University of Texas Press.

Assies, Willem. 2003. David versus Goliath in Cochabamba: Water Rights, Neoliberalism, and the Revival of Social Protest in Bolivia. *Latin American Perspectives* 30 (3): 14–36.

Associated Press. 2025. Peru Declares an Emergency and Deploys the Army as Violence Surges in the Capital. March 18. https://apnews.com/article/peru-state-of-emergency-violence-singer-death-f2a2addd25f983dec817fda0 a25062cf.

Barahona de Brito, Alexandra. 1997. *Human Rights and Democratization in Latin America: Uruguay and Chile.* Oxford: Oxford University Press.

Buschschlüter, Vanessa. 2025. Mexican Judge Arrested Over 2014 Disappearance of 43 Students. *BBC News.* May 15. https://www.bbc.com/news/articles/c74qeepk39eo.

Coronel, Omar. 2023. Understanding the Protests in Peru. *Al Jazeera.* February 15. https://www.aljazeera.com/opinions/2023/2/15/understanding-the-crisis in peru.

Castro, Gustavo Fabián, and Dolores Bermeo Lara. 2008. *Justicia Militar, Códigos Disciplinarios y Reglamentos Generales Internos.* Buenos Aires: Red de Seguridad y Defensa de América Latina.

CBS News. 2025. Ecuador Imposes State of Emergency Before Razor-Close Election. April 12. https://www.cbsnews.com/news/ecuador-imposes-state-of-emergency-election/.

Close, David. 1990. Responding to Low-Intensity Conflict: Counterinsurgency in Sandinista Nicaragua. *New Political Science* 9 (1–2): 5–19.

De Vicente Encarnación, Jonathan. 2024. Reform of Mexico's National Guard: Towards Total Militarization. Wilson Center. October 2. https://www.wilsoncenter.org/article/reform-mexicos-national-guard-towards-total-militarization.

Directorio Legislativo. 2024. Balance Legislativo: El primer año de Javier Milei. https://directoriolegislativo.org/es/balance-legislativo-2024-como-fue-el-primer-ano-de-javier-milei/.

Fernández Blanco, Carolina, and M. Victoria Kristan. 2024. The Year of the Defense of Life, Liberty and Property: Javier Milei's Omnibus Executive Order. *Verfassungsblog*. February 12. https://verfassungsblog.de/the-year-of-the-defense-of-life-liberty-and-property/.

Finn, John E. 1991. *Constitutions in Crisis: Political Violence and the Rule of Law*. New York: Oxford University Press.

Folch, Christine. 2013. Surveillance and State Violence in Stroessner's Paraguay: Itaipú Hydroelectric Dam, Archive of Terror. *American Anthropologist* 115 (1): 44–57.

Gedan, Benjamin N. 2024. Uruguay's Crime-Fighting Lessons for the World. *Foreign Policy*. November 18. https://foreignpolicy.com/2024/11/18/uruguays-crime-frente-amplio-yamandu-orsi/.

Gomez, Mayra. 2001. The Role of International Intervention in Facilitating Violence and Peace in El Salvador, 1977–1998. *Human Rights Review* 2 (3): 76–91.

González, Diego. 2020. Explaining the Institutional Role of the Colombian Constitutional Court. In *From Parchment to Practice: Implementing New Constitutions*, eds. Tom Ginsburg and Aziz Z. Huq, 189–207. Cambridge: Cambridge University Press.

González-Ocantos, Ezequiel A. 2016. *Shifting Legal Visions: Judicial Change and Human Rights Trials in Latin America*. New York: Cambridge University Press.

Handelman, Howard. 1981. Labor-Industrial Conflict and the Collapse of Uruguayan Democracy. *Journal of Interamerican Studies and World Affairs* 23 (4): 371–394.

Hodel, Steven. 2022. Guatemala State of Siege Extended for Feuding Communities. *Tico Times*. January 20. https://ticotimes.net/2022/01/20/guatemala-state-of-siege-extended-for-feuding-communities.

Human Rights Watch. 2020. Peru: Law Protects Abusive Policing. May 12. https://www.hrw.org/news/2020/05/12/peru-law-protects-abusive-policing.

Human Rights Watch. 2021. El Salvador: Events of 2020. https://www.hrw.org/world-report/2021/country-chapters/el-salvador.

Human Rights Watch. 2023. Colombia: Ensure Justice for Army Killings: Human Rights Watch Submits Brief to High Court. September 18. https://www.hrw.org/news/2023/09/18/colombia-ensure-justice-army-killings.

Inter-American Commission on Human Rights. 2024. IACHR and OHCHR Ask Chilean Legislators to Respect Human Rights Standards Concerning Security. June 3. https://www.oas.org/en/iachr/jsForm/?File=/en/iachr/media_center/preleases/2024/124.asp.

Kyle, Brett J., and Andrew G. Reiter. 2021. *Military Courts, Civil-Military Relations, and the Legal Battle for Democracy: The Politics of Military Justice.* New York: Routledge.

Latin American Weekly Report. 2025. Ecuador: Noboa Begins New Term with Bold Energy and Security Plans. May 29.

LatinNews Daily. 2025. Panama: Police under Further Pressure Over Protest Response. June 11.

Leiras, Santiago. 2024. Javier Milei, Between Necessity and Urgency. *Latinoamérica 21.* January 9. https://latinoamerica21.com/en/javier-milei-between-necessity-and-urgency/.

Loveman, Brian. 1993. *The Constitution of Tyranny: Regimes of Exception in Spanish America.* Pittsburgh: University of Pittsburgh Press.

Malone, Mary Fran T., Lucía Dammert, and Orlando J. Pérez. 2023. *Making Police Reform Matter in Latin America.* Boulder: Lynne Rienner.

Méndez Dardón, Ana María. 2025. Mass Incarceration and Democratic Deterioration: Three Years of the State of Exception in El Salvador. Washington Office on Latin America. March 27. https://www.wola.org/analysis/mass-incarceration-and-democratic-deterioration-three-years-of-the-state-of-exception-in-el-salvador/.

MercoPress. 2025. Chile's Senate Okays State of Emergency Extension to Tackle Mapuche Crisis. May 16. https://en.mercopress.com/2025/05/16/chile-s-senate-okays-state-of-emergency-extension-to-tackle-mapuche-crisis.

México Unido Contra la Delincuencia. 2024. *Inventario Nacional de lo Militarizado: Una radiografí de los proceso de militarización en Mexico.* https://www.mucd.org.mx/wp-content/uploads/2024/04/INM-2024.pdf.

Moro, Giovanni. 2010. Civic Action. In *International Encyclopedia of Civil Society*, eds. Helmut K. Anheier and Stefan Toepler, 145-150. New York: Springer.

National Public Radio. 2024. Ecuadorians Vote in Referendum to Approve Toughening Fight Against Gangs. April 22. https://www.npr.org/2024/04/22/1246269509/ecuadorians-vote-in-referendum-to-approve-toughening-fight-against-gangs.

New York Times. 1987. Chile Will End State of Siege. January 1. https://www.nytimes.com/1987/01/01/world/chile-will-end-state-of-siege.html.

New York Times. 2021. Ecuador's President Declares State of Emergency to Battle Crime. October 19. https://www.nytimes.com/2021/10/19/world/americas/ecuador-state-of-emergency.html.

Página Siete. 2020. Periodistas, políticos y organismos aplauden derogación del decreto que penaliza la desinformación. May 15. https://web.archive.org/web/20200801225704/https://www.paginasiete.bo/nacional/2020/5/15/periodistas-politicos-organismos-aplauden-derogacion-del-decreto-que-penaliza-la-desinformacion-255624.html.

Pannell, Alfie. 2025. Colombia's President Petro Declares State of Emergency in Northeastern Catatumbo Region. *The Bogota Post*. January 22. https://thebogotapost.com/colombias-president-petro-declares-state-of-emergency-in-northeastern-catatumbo-region/53350/.

Pereira, Anthony W. 2005. *Political (In)Justice: Authoritarianism and the Rule of Law in Brazil, Chile, and Argentina*. Pittsburgh: University of Pittsburgh Press.

Posner, Richard A. 2003. *Law, Pragmatism, and Democracy*. Cambridge: Harvard University Press.

Reuters. 2019. Guatemala Congress Approves Controversial State of Siege Legislation. September 8. https://www.reuters.com/article/world/guatemalan-congress-approves-controversial-state-of-siege-declaration-idUSKCN1VS0RJ/.

Reuters. 2023a. Costa Rica to Declare State of Emergency Amid Migrant Surge. September 26. https://www.reuters.com/world/americas/costa-rica-declare-state-emergency-amid-migrant-surge-2023-09-26/.

Reuters. 2023b. Ecuador Declares State of Emergency Amid Violent Clashes. July 24. https://www.reuters.com/world/americas/ecuador-declares-state-emergency-amid-violent-clashes-2023-07-24/.

Reuters. 2023c. Peru Extends State of Emergency in Key Mining Region Ahead of Fresh Protests. July 12. https://www.reuters.com/world/americas/peru-extends-state-emergency-including-mining-corridor-fresh-protests-expected-2023-07-12/.

Ríos-Figueroa, Julio. 2016. *Constitutional Courts as Mediators: Armed Conflict, Civil-Military Relations, and the Rule of Law in Latin America*. New York: Cambridge University Press.

Rosser, Emma. 2015. Colombia's Congress Approves 3rd Attempt to Transfer Military Crimes to Military Courts. *Colombia Reports*. June 12. https://colombiareports.com/colombias-congress-approves-3rd-attempt-to-transfer-military-crimes-to-military-courts/.

Rodríguez Mega, Emiliano. 2024. Mexican Senate Votes to Give Military Control of Civilian National Guard. *New York Times*. September 25. https://www.nytimes.com/2024/09/25/world/americas/mexico-national-guard-military-control.html.

Rossiter, Clinton L. 1948. *Constitutional Dictatorship: Crisis Government in Modern Democracies*. Princeton: Princeton University Press.

Tico Times. 2025. Panama President Demands End to Road Blockades in Chiquita Banana Strike. May 30. https://ticotimes.net/2025/05/30/panama-president-demands-end-to-road-blockades-in-chiquita-banana-strike.

Torres-Salina, Robinson. 2023. Resistance in Chile's 'State of Exception.' *Majority Post*. January 24. https://majoritypost.com/resistance-in-chiles-state-of-exception/.

United States Department of State. 2001. Dominican Republic: Country Reports on Human Rights Practices 2000. https://2009-2017.state.gov/j/drl/rls/hrrpt/2001/wha/8345.htm.

Valente, Rubens. 2017. Military Courts Given Jurisdiction Over Crimes Against Civilians During Armed Forces Operations. *Folha de S. Paulo*. October 17. https://www1.folha.uol.com.br/internacional/en/brazil/2017/10/1927693-military-courts-given-jurisdiction-over-crimes-against-civilians-during-armed-forces-operations.shtml.

Vásquez, George L. 1994. The Peruvian Army in War and Peace: 1980–1992. *Journal of Third World Studies* 11 (2): 100–116.

Woolston, Sam. 2024. Honduras Doubles Down on Flawed Mano Dura Strategy. InSight Crime. June 25. https://insightcrime.org/news/honduras-doubles-down-on-flawed-mano-dura-strategy/.

Wright, Claire. 2015. *Emergency Politics in the Third Wave of Democracy: A Study of the Regimes of Exception in Bolivia, Ecuador, and Peru*. Lanham, MD: Lexington.

Zaverucha, Jorge. 2008. The 'Guaranteeing Law and Order Doctrine' and the Increased Role of the Brazilian Army in Activities of Public Security. *Nueva Sociedad* 213: 70–86.

INDEX

Fiscal Police (Mexico), 143
Flores, Paul, 198
Forza security company (Peru),
179–180
Fox, Vicente, 72, 143
Francia, José Gaspar Rodríguez de, 61
French military trainers, 49, 63
Fuero militar, 203
Fujimori, Alberto, 11, 88, 170–171,
208

G
Gadsden Purchase (1854), 140
Galeana Marín, Lambertina, 208
García Meza, Luis, 11
García, Alan, 170, 172, 177, 182
Gendarmes (Argentina), 116
General Directorate of Citizen
Security and Public Order
(Ecuador), 81
General Directorate of Investigation
(Ecuador), 81
General Directorate of Police
Intelligence (Ecuador), 81
General Law on Enforced
Disappearances (Mexico), 207
General Treaty of Peace and Amity
(1923), 52
German military trainers, 49
Gran Colombia, 46, 137
Great Britain, 51, 61–62, 120. See
also United Kingdom
Group of Fourteen (Honduras), 65
Group of Ten (Honduras), 65
Guarantee of Law and Order
operations (Brazil), 114, 204
Guatemala Constitution of 1985,
13–14, 27
Guatemala, 11–16, 18, 26, 47–48,
50, 52, 54–55, 58–60, 62–64,
73, 75–76, 79, 83, 85–86, 88,

135, 140, 142, 146, 149–150,
199–200
Guatemalan Army, 142, 149–150
Guatemalan military regime, 142
Guatemalan National Police, 55, 75,
150
Gutiérrez, Lucio, 207

H
Haina Military Academy (Dominican
Republic), 52
Haiti, 47, 52, 62, 153
Hernández, Rodolfo, 206
Herzog, Vladimir, 104
Heureaux, Ulises, 49
Honduran National Police, 202
Honduras Constitution of 1982, 13,
14, 26
Honduras, 13–15, 18–19, 26, 46–47,
50, 52, 54–56, 58, 60–61, 63,
73–74, 76, 79, 82–84, 88, 147,
150, 199, 202
Humala, Ollanta, 171, 177

I
Institutional Act No. 3 (Brazil), 105
Institutional Act No. 5 (Brazil), 102,
105, 209
Institutional Acts (Brazil), 102, 105,
209
Institutional Acts (Uruguay), 12, 209
Institutional Revolutionary Party
(Mexico), 63, 73, 143
Intelligence Troop and Special
Security Response Groups
(Honduras), 84
Inter-American Air Force Academy
(US), 78
Inter-American Commission on
Human Rights, 3, 18

The manufacturer's authorised representative in the EU is Springer
Nature Customer Service Centre GmbH, Europaplatz 3, 69115 Heidelberg,
Germany. If you have any concerns regarding our products, please
contact ProductSafety@springernature.com

Printed and bound by CPI Group (UK) Ltd, Croydon, CR0 4YY

19/01/2026

02037407-0005